Perennials and biennials combined to make a colorful flower border.

ALL ABOUT THE PERENNIAL GARDEN

Books by Montague Free

ALL ABOUT THE PERENNIAL GARDEN

GARDENING

ALL ABOUT HOUSE PLANTS

ALL ABOUT AFRICAN VIOLETS

ALL ABOUT THE

PERENNIAL

GARDEN THE AMATEUR

GARDENER'S HANDBOOK OF HARDY FLOWERS:

HERBACEOUS AND WOODY PERENNIALS, INCLUDING

BULBS AND SHRUBS, BIENNIALS AND ANNUALS

WITH 153 PHOTOGRAPHS, 5 FULL-COLOR ILLUSTRATIONS,

AND 22 LINE DRAWINGS

by *Montague Free*

SENIOR EDITOR, *Flower Grower, The Home Garden Magazine*
FORMERLY HORTICULTURIST, BROOKLYN BOTANIC GARDEN
GRADUATE OF THE ROYAL BOTANIC GARDENS, KEW, ENGLAND

The American Garden Guild and
Doubleday & Company, Inc., Garden City, N.Y.

FOR TOM CANDLER

Who was a source of inspiration during my years as a journeyman gardener in England.

Library of Congress Catalog Card Number 55–6493 ·

DESIGNER: JOSEPH P. ASCHERL

Preface

For more than fifty years I have been more or less concerned with hardy herbaceous perennials—in England, at the Cambridge University Botanic Gardens, on the estate of the late Ellen Willmott, and at Royal Botanic Gardens, Kew, England; in this country, in the Department of Agriculture at Cornell University, the Pennsylvania School of Horticulture for Women, and for thirty years at the Brooklyn Botanic Garden. In spite of this long association herbaceous perennials have not lost their charm and interest and it was with enthusiasm that I started to grow them four years ago in a perennial garden designed to provide illustrative material for this book and to serve as sort of refresher course for me.

While a flower garden can be made of none but herbaceous perennials, better results are possible, as in the case of a turkey dinner, when some trimmings are used. So, although the book is mainly about herbaceous perennials, some attention has been given to annuals, biennials, and shrubs—woody perennials.

More than 500 perennials are described or mentioned. For the benefit of those to whom botanical names are frightening, a list of common names with their scientific equivalents is given on pages 328–337. It should be pointed out, though, that not all plants have English names and that scientific names are necessary when precision is required.

Although this book is written largely from the viewpoint of a gardener in the Northeast, the principles of culture are valid throughout the United States and Canada. I would guess, too, that most of the plants mentioned could be grown anywhere in these countries, except, perhaps, in Southern Florida and in the hot desert regions. Those who live in difficult climatic regions would do well before ordering any plants to submit their lists for approval to a local authority, a county agricultural agent, or to the state agricultural experiment station unless they have an urge to experiment and are willing to take a chance.

My thanks go to my former colleague, Ralph Bailey, for his help and encouragement in the preparation of this book; and, as always, to my good wife.

Hyde Park, New York.   MONTAGUE FREE
May, 1954

Contents

LIST OF ILLUSTRATIONS

ALL ABOUT THE PERENNIAL GARDEN

CHAPTER ONE

What Kind of a Garden?

You are the one to decide what kind of a garden to plant and here are some considerations that will help you to make a decision. There is a wide-spread belief that because hardy perennials *are* perennial there's little or no work required once they are planted. This is only partially true, for while there are some that can endure neglect and persist presentably for many years, there are others which, to do their best, need to be divided and reset annually (Chrysanthemums and hardy Asters), and some, notably Iris, need this attention every three or four years. Others, especially Physostegia, Mist-flower, and perennial Sunflowers, are so rambunctious that they must be restrained by digging them up every two years, replanting part of the clump, and throwing the major portion away; or you can give the surplus to a friend and so stick him with a job of work.

As this book is mainly about perennials, we had better define the term before going any further. Technically it is applied to plants which live for more than two full years—it does not include annuals or biennials. A woody perennial is a plant (tree, shrub, or vine), with woody, persistent trunk or stems, which usually lives much longer than two years. A herbaceous perennial is a plant which lacks a permanent or woody stem. The stems of most herbaceous perennials die to the ground annually, but the plant itself persists indefinitely by means of the underground parts which may be roots, rootstocks, rhizomes, tubers, corms, or bulbs. Although, in general, bulbs are true herbaceous perennials (an exception is the garden Onion, which is a biennial) most gardeners do not think of them as such and, as there is some advantage in considering bulbs and trees and shrubs in separate groups, when the term perennial is used without qualification in this book, it refers to non-bulbous herbaceous perennials. Perennials can be winter-hardy or tender to frost. We are chiefly concerned with those that can survive at least 12 degrees F.

USES OF PERENNIALS

There are many ways in which perennials can be used. Many of the strong-growing, vigorous kinds can be naturalized either in a meadow, for those which grow best in full sun (Butterfly-weed, New York Asters, Baptisia, Tall Bearded Iris, etc.); in wet spots or alongside a stream (Goats-beard, Rose-mallow, Siberian Iris, Purple Loosestrife); or in partial shade of thin woodland (Columbine, Bugbane, Dames-rocket, Daylily, Bee-balm, Meadow-rue, Plantain-lily).

Perennials are valuable as fillers in newly planted shrubbery where they can be looked on as expendables to be removed when the shrubs begin to crowd them, or they can serve as a reserve for later planting in a flower garden. Hollyhocks can serve the useful function of a screen and are beautiful when seen against a garage wall. Plume-poppy and various perennial Sunflowers are strong growing kinds which are effective as screens during summer and fall. These must be used with care because they are so invasive that they may become a nuisance.

Many are excellent for use as cut flowers (see list on page 308) and these are best grown in a reserve garden by themselves so that the display garden need not be depleted of blooms by "arrangers."

But perennials perform their most important function in the flower garden where they give a feeling of stability and permanence and collectively provide a longer flowering season, especially in spring, blooming before most of the annuals have even germinated. In the fall Chrysanthemums continue to be colorful after frosts have put the quietus on the annuals. They can be displayed among shrubs, in beds, or, and this is usually the most satisfactory, in long borders with a background of some kind. In general perennials are not adapted to severely formal planting—they do not fit properly in geometric beds. For these we must rely on spring bulbs, principally Tulips and Hyacinths, followed by "bedding plants" such as Begonias and Pelargoniums.

Chrysanthemums, Daylilies, Peonies, and Phlox are among the most beautiful and showy of all garden flowers. But many perennials have a comparatively short blooming season and this is a factor that has to be recognized. Britain has long been famous for its perennial gardens and it is there that the perennial border has reached the greatest height of perfection. It must be remembered, though, that the cool summer climate permits perennials to remain in bloom longer than they do here. But even in Britain it is recognized that a garden of perennials alone cannot present an over-all blaze of color throughout the entire growing season.

If you are a purist it is possible to have a garden exclusively of hardy herbaceous perennials which will have something of one kind or another in bloom seven months of the year. If early-flowering hardy spring bulbs such as Crocus, Chionodoxa, and Narcissus are included, the blooming period can be extended by about one month, but unless you are content with a garden that has considerable areas of nothing but foliage, plus at times a few bare patches, it will not be good enough. However, there are ways of partially overcoming this drawback. The obvious one, applicable only where there is plenty of space, is to have spring, summer and fall gardens as separate entities which would be at their best in May–June, July–August, and September–October respectively. By selecting the right plant material it is possible to have these seasonal gardens almost entirely full of bloom during their season.

If you have room for only one flower border, it is still possible to make it presentable by grouping together, in balanced array, the spring, summer, and fall-blooming plants with stretches of green in between. This helps to avoid the spotty, skimpy effect which might accrue if all were scattered indiscriminately throughout the border. If you have a small plot anywhere on the place that can be used as a nursery-*cum*-reserve garden, the situation can be greatly improved. For example: English and Polyanthus Primroses make a wonderful display in the spring, but when their flowering period is over, their foliage becomes unattractive, and sometimes when it is marred by slugs and partially browned by attacks of spider mites, it is positively repulsive. Fortunately these Primroses are easily transplanted and can be moved to the reserve garden and their place taken by Sweet William or Canterbury Bells, which in turn will give way to Chrysanthemums. This will provide blooms almost continuously from April until October.

The best way to secure plenty of color is to make full use of long-blooming perennials, getting early effects with the hardy spring bulbs and such plants as Leopards-bane, English Daisies, Pansies,

Doronicum, Bleeding-heart, Polyanthus, Primrose, and English Daisy.
MALCOLM R. KINNEY

Primroses, which can either be discarded or transplanted to the reserve garden after they have ceased blooming; and to fill any vacant places during May and June with summer-flowering bulbs (Gladioli, Dahlias, etc.); bedding plants (Pelargonium, Begonia, etc.) and annuals; and, for the fall, transplant Chrysanthemums from the reserve garden when they are about to bloom.

Usually it is more convenient to buy bedding plants and annuals from the local florist or garden center. After Memorial Day by shopping around it is possible to find bargains in these kinds of plants. But much depends on the time and facilities at your disposal. With a greenhouse or even a cold frame most of this material can be home-grown. Among the advantages of home-grown plants are that: you can raise the kinds in the colors that appeal especially to you and do not have to take what the dealer happens to have on hand; and you can be sure that the plants are not so hardened by partial starvation that they will be slow to start into growth.

BULB PROBLEMS

Although the hardy bulbs are welcome harbingers of spring, their use in the perennial garden does present some problems which, however, are not impossible to solve. Chief among the objections to their use are: their unsightly ripening foliage, which must be left to mature if the bulbs are to stay in place to bloom the following spring; the gaps they may leave when the foliage finally dies down; the difficulty of working in the soil without injury to the bulbs when filling in gaps late in the season with plants having root systems such as those of Chrysanthemums. These troubles can be overcome in part by:

1. Looking on the bulbs as expendable and digging them up as soon as their flowers have faded and replacing them with annuals, summer-flowering bulbs, or Chrysanthemums. (These bulbs thus removed are not necessarily a complete loss. They can be dug up without too much root disturbance and planted in the reserve gar-

Curved perennial border, showing Foxglove, Verbascum, and Iris in foreground. GOTTSCHO-SCHLEISNER

den where next year they will produce blooms which, while not of first-class quality, will be acceptable for cutting.)

2. Planting them toward the rear of the border so that their ripening foliage is obscured by the growth of the perennials. (Narcissi are the real problem children among the bulbs, because in some varieties the bedraggled but still functioning foliage persists into August. When the border has a background of shrubs, Narcissi might well be left out of the flower border proper and instead planted in the foreground of the shrubs.)

3. Planting Narcissi and Tulips with at least 6 inches of soil over their bulbs so that they are out of danger when bedding plants or annuals are set out among them. If this is done, you will have to close your eyes to the ripening foliage of the bulbs until the plants set in the soil above them grow up to hide it.

4. Small bulbs—Chionodoxa and Crocus—which should not be planted more than 3 inches deep, can be set in six or eight groups of about five bulbs each with 6 inches between the groups. This will make a sizable patch with sufficient space to plant summer-flowering plants in between each group.

And finally, the kind of garden will be determined largely by whether your interest is in plants as plants or as material with which to make a garden picture. If you are primarily a plantsman, you will want to grow a great variety of them: there are hundreds of different kinds of perennials available (see lists pages 191 and 268), but this will make it difficult to carry out color schemes and broad artistic effects in the garden.

SUMMING UP

The garden may consist of nothing but true perennials; of spring-flowering bulbs and perennials; or spring-flowering bulbs, perennials, summer-flowering bulbs, annuals, biennials, tender bedding plants, and shrubs.

It can consist of several separate entities, or you can do your best to make a single, colorful, all-season border or garden which will need forethought and care and the use of all available material. In the belief that the all-season garden is the most satisfactory in beauty, interest, and adaptation to the needs of the average gardener with limited space at his disposal, it is the kind of garden that will be given the most attention in this book.

Combination perennial-biennial garden featuring Foxglove, Canterbury Bells, and Astilbe. GOTTSCHO-SCHLEISNER

CHAPTER TWO

Site and Soil Preparation

ORIENTATION

Many plants, because of a tendency of their flowers to face south or east, are most effective when viewed from these directions, and this needs to be considered when planting them. It is with some trepidation that I write on this subject, because there are some tricky little factors connected with it. For example, apparently the degree of latitude in which they are grown has much to do with the behavior of the sun followers; the way the flowers of Narcissi face when growing singly may differ from those growing in crowded clumps; the presence of shade may cause flowers to face in a direction opposite to that assumed when growing in the full sun.

The flower heads of the common garden Sunflower (*Helianthus annuus*) are popularly supposed to always turn their heads to face the sun. During the years I have grown Sunflowers here, I have kept rather close watch on them and find that 95 per cent of the flower heads face east and stay that way; the remainder may point to almost any point of the compass including even north! And yet there is good authority, mostly, however, from northern observers, for the belief that Sunflowers really are sun followers. So one might suspect that heliotropism—turning toward the light—is more apparent in those regions and situations where the sun is not so high in the heavens and light is less intense. The Silverleaf Sunflower, *Helianthus argophyllus*, also an annual, is a bushy plant with side branches pointing in every direction. The top photograph on page 22, taken with the camera pointing northwest when the plant was just coming into bloom, shows most of the flowers facing toward southeast. Later in the season, when more and more flowers developed on the

Silverleaf Sunflower, flowers facing southeast.
STEENSON & BAKER

laterals, their tendency to face the southeast was less obvious, but up until frost this was the best side of the plant.

The flowers of Leopards-bane (Doronicum) are true sun followers facing east in early morning, upwards about 10:30 *A.M.*, and west in the afternoon. This impartiality simplifies their placement. Furthermore the reverse of the flowers is just about as effective as

Daisy-like flowers of Doronicum face east in early morning (see text). Dicentra Bountiful in foreground. MALCOLM R. KINNEY

Author's perennial garden—looking southwest in April. Notice Daffodil blooms back to camera. MALCOLM R. KINNEY

the obverse, because the calyces (more correctly the involucres) are not conspicuous, so they are showy even when seen from the rear.

When they are grown in full sun, flowers of most Narcissus varieties face south, southeast, or east. This is particularly noticeable in freshly planted clumps when each bulb has ample room; but when the clump becomes crowded, the flowers, especially those of the short-cup varieties, can be found facing every point of the compass.

The location with respect to the points of the compass is only part of the story—it is the source of the greatest amount of light that is

Author's perennial garden—same as above looking northwest.
MALCOLM R. KINNEY

the determining factor, and flowers which normally face south or east may find themselves turning to the opposite direction if planted where they are shaded by a wall or hedge. It seems that sometimes shade falling on the base of the stems is effective in determining the position of the flowers. For example: a clump of Gladiolus planted on the west side of some perennials faced to the west, while the same variety planted in the open faced south.

Then there is the leaning toward the light of the entire inflorescence. Flowers of Hemerocallis are so arranged at the top of the leafless scapes that they may face north one day and succeeding blooms are just as likely as not to face in the opposite direction. But when they are shaded on one side, the scapes themselves lean toward the lighted side. This is also true of Phlox.

Thus the tendency of some flowers to face toward the source of light should be kept in mind when orienting the garden and when planting flower beds and borders. My own perennial garden was placed on the south side of the house for two reasons: (1) the most used rooms are on the south; (2) it was the only practicable place to locate it! But it would have been much more effective when seen from the house had it been placed on the north side. This is especially noticeable in the spring because the Daffodils, Violas, Chionodoxas, and so on, in the main, face away from the house. It is especially important to be careful in the placement of Violas, otherwise you may be in the position of a writer in a garden magazine who told of the unsatisfactory result of edging both sides of a walk running east and west with a Viola. One can readily imagine that the planting looked like a hog with one ear.

In general, those which need to be planted with care to secure proper orientation include: single-stemmed flowers such as Viola, Pansy, and Daffodils; some Lilies and various members of the Sunflower family such as the Shasta Daisy and *Aster Frikarti;* those which produce their flowers in spikes or racemes with a tendency toward one-sidedness—Foxglove, Gladiolus, Penstemon (Veronica, Tritoma and Lavender, when growing in full sun, produce their flowers all around the main stalk); a few with panicled or laxly racemose inflorescences (though it is less important with these) whose flowers especially, when partly shaded, have a tendency to face toward the greatest source of illumination—Canterbury Bells and Coral-bells. The condition is likely to be accentuated when

Newly planted clump of Narcissus, flowers facing east and south.
MALCOLM R. KINNEY

there is overhanging shade on the north side. Then there are those plants which produce their flowers singly or in clusters—Tulips, some Lilies, Phlox, Sweet William, Hemerocallis—which, when shaded, bow their entire stems toward the source of light.

Faulty orientation will not necessarily ruin everything, but placing the flowers so that they "face towards London" is a refinement which improves the appearance of the garden. So study light factors as they affect plants in your garden and act on them. It will add to your interest.

CHOOSING THE SITE

The nature of the terrain must also be considered to provide a suitable depth of good soil and to avoid as far as possible the need for extensive earth moving to ensure acceptable grades. Often it is

Chinking stone retaining wall. STEENSON & BAKER

possible to reduce the amount of grading needed and at the same time add to the interest of the garden by making it on two or more levels with steps and low retaining walls of stone (see picture on facing page), or of brick, or grassy banks may be used to hold up the terraces.

A garden, or beds, or borders for the cultivation of perennials should for the most part be located in the open. Some shade is not objectionable over part of the layout provided there is not too much competition from tree or shrub roots.

The area should be related to its surroundings. Sometimes it may be an informal affair, roughly paralleling the outlines of a shrub border with a curving front edge, the lawn in the foreground, and the border providing a desirable background. This is perhaps the simplest way of installing a perennial border. But it has some troublesome features. There is competition with tree and shrub roots to be dealt with and ultimately the growth of the shrubs will gradually eliminate the rear rank of perennials. This will necessitate replanting the border, moving it forward, and stealing another 2 or 3 feet from the lawn area. One way of handling the situation is to maintain a walk between the shrubbery and the perennials to eliminate root competition. Then by restricting the shrubs by annual pruning, it is possible to maintain the status quo for many years. Another, but expensive, way is to sink a barrier of metal or concrete 2 feet deep in the soil to hold back invading shrub roots. In such case the annual pruning must be more severe than is necessary when a walk separates the two features.

A formal clipped hedge makes an excellent background for perennials. Here again there should be a space of at least 3 feet between it

Informal border
with background
of shrubs.
JESSIE TARBOX BEALS

and the flowers, not only to avoid root competition, but to prevent mutual injury and permit shearing the hedge without interfering with the flowers.

Often in the case of small properties a strip 2 or more feet wide along the boundary fence or alongside a wall may be the most satisfactory location. A fence or wall can be embellished with vines or espaliered shrubs to enhance the background. When the border is much in excess of 3 feet and room permits, it is desirable to allow a vacant space 2 feet wide between flowers and fence to facilitate the care of the vines on the fence or wall and the flowers in the border.

Plan of
perennial garden
installed at
the author's home
to provide
illustrative material
for this book.

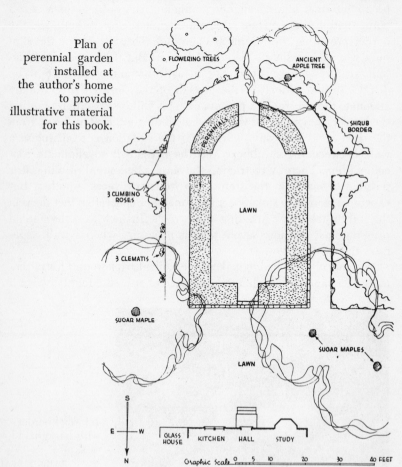

Site of author's perennial garden. Owing to the slope in original site, it was necessary to remove soil from some areas and fill in others (see diagram below). STEENSON & BAKER

Preparing the basic site for the author's perennial garden: Arrow 1 above shows how topsoil was taken from nearby knoll by tractor to fill lowest part. Arrow 2 shows where soil was removed from one corner. After rough leveling 3 inches of half-rotted leaves (3) was spread over entire area. Manure was spread 3 inches deep over cutaway portion (4) near tree and 1 inch over remaining flower beds (5)

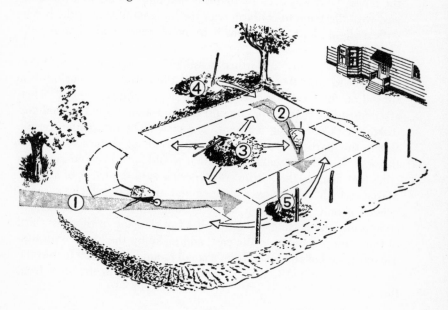

On larger properties the flower garden can be a deliberately con-
trived affair enclosed by a screen of shrubs or a formal clipped
hedge with the perennials displayed in beds and borders which may
be informal or partly formal in character. Such was the garden
planned and planted chiefly to obtain illustrative material for this
book. This garden had to be situated at the rear of the house (the
long axis of which runs east and west), because the terrain in front
consists of poor soil and steeply sloping grades which are entirely
unsuitable. The site selected for the garden proper occupies an area
34 by 51 feet. This is bounded by grass walks 7 feet wide, then an
enclosing shrubbery border of indeterminate width—it can be ex-
panded on three sides for 20 feet or more to accommodate additional
shrubs if needed. The lay of the land was high to the west with a
drop of 3 feet to the east in a stretch of about 40 feet and it had a
slight slope toward the south. The layout of the garden would have
been relatively simple if the steep slope had been in a north-south
direction. Then it would have been possible to make the garden on
two levels, separated by a wall or bank that would look right. But
with the slope running the other way there would have been a feeling of lopsidedness and instability owing to conflict with the lines of
the house. So it was decided that the area must be made level in the
east-west direction to conform with the horizontal lines of the house,
with a slight slope away from it to avoid unnecessary grading expense.

The simplest way to do this, possible in most cases, would have
been first to strip the surface soil from the entire area, cut into the
subsoil on the west, use this to fill the depression to the east. Then
after spreading manure or compost on the rough-graded subsoil and
disking it in or mixing it in with a rotary tiller, return the topsoil.
But in this particular case there were serious objections to doing it
this way. In order to make the grade it would have been necessary to
cut 3 feet deep in the northwest corner close to the trunk of a Sugar
Maple, which would have endangered the tree, which is really
needed if only to shade my study in summer. So it was decided to
compromise by cutting about 9 inches from the top of the west third
of the garden, move it to the east, and make up the grade with topsoil composed of sod taken from a small mound about 100 feet to the
south. This resulted in an all-round improvement in the view from
the house.

Author's
perennial garden,
tractor with scoop
moving soil
from nearby knoll.
STEENSON & BAKER

GRADING

On a job of this size, considering the scarcity and cost of manual labor, some kind of power-driven mechanical device for earth moving is a necessity. A bulldozer was considered, but the weight of this implement has a destructive effect on soil structure. Finally the work was done by a small tractor with a scoop attachment which did a fair job. (See illustrations.) But the machine is not capable of leveling the surface as well as a bulldozer, so the work of three men with shovels and rakes for four hours was necessary to put on the final touches preparatory to the next step.

The soil was packed quite hard even by the comparatively light tractor used, therefore a rotary hoe tiller was hired to loosen the surface to a depth of 9 inches and at the same time chop up sods and

Dumping soil
on low areas
of garden site.
STEENSON & BAKER

Rough grading has been completed, leaving the future perennial borders comparatively level. Piles of decayed leaves are ready to be spread over entire area and worked into soil. Poles at right will support climbing Roses and Clematis vines. STEENSON & BAKER

Rotary hoe tiller is being run over garden beds to loosen soil surface to a depth of 9 inches (even the light tractor compressed the soil to some extent) to chop up the sods present in soil and mix in organic matter (half-rotted leaves). STEENSON & BAKER

Rotary hoe tiller has churned leaves, odd bits of sod, and soil leaving comparatively level area ready for next phase: laying out the beds. STEENSON & BAKER

mix in organic matter (see photographs page 30). The churning effect of the rapidly revolving hoe pulverized the sods, and so mixed throughout the soil a 3-inch layer of partly rotted leaves, plus a 1-inch layer of cow manure on the sites of the future perennial beds that little of the organic matter was visible when the job was completed. The entire area was sprinkled with commercial fertilizer, 5-10-5, at the rate of 5 pounds per 100 square feet, before tilling it, to provide nutrients to take care of any depletion as a result of their withdrawal from the soil by "breakdown" organisms working on the organic matter.

The bed in the area to the west where a cut was made exposing the subsoil was treated to a special application of a 3-inch layer of cow manure. It is proposed to double-dig this bed two or three years from now to work in more manure and deepen the soil. The soil in the eastern filled area, 18 to 36 inches deep, consisting as it does of sods containing plenty of humus-forming material, should stay in good condition for many years.

Fortunately most of you will not be faced with a situation such as that described, and all you will have to do is to mark out the edges of the beds and prepare them for planting. Preferably they should be dug a month or so ahead of actual planting time to allow the earth to settle. The best time in the year to do this is in September, which will permit most of the planting to be done in October; and the remainder in the spring. Of course, from the standpoint of the comfort of the operator, the digging should be done in October or November, but, if it is left too late, freezing weather might prevent any planting until the spring, and you would have to forgo the pleasure of spring-flowering bulbs for the season. A perennial garden can be made and planted in the spring, but by the time the ground has dried up sufficiently and has been prepared for planting, it might be too late to get best results from the summer-blooming plants. (See Chapter Six for planting seasons.)

SOIL PREPARATION

Some plants—Gas-plant and Peony, for example—improve with age if left undisturbed for a number of years; therefore, it is desirable to provide a good depth of rich topsoil at the start. Even those plants which may need to be transplanted every three or four years respond by richer growth and larger flowers to careful initial preparation of the soil. Furthermore plants are less bothered by dry spells because the improved soil holds more moisture and the roots are able to penetrate more deeply to get it. An adaptation of the procedure just outlined might be followed by some; if not, double-digging, whereby the ground is loosened and organic matter is mixed in to a depth of about 18 inches, should be done if it is possible.

Old-time gardeners are convinced of the value of deeply preparing the soil, and modern experiments substantiate their belief. Deep preparation provides a greater bulk of soil in which the plant roots can ramify. It enables them to penetrate to a greater depth so that they are able to obtain moisture during periods of minor drought and it offers an opportunity to mix, deeply, humus and humus-forming materials, which increase the moisture-holding capacity of the soil.

Investigations carried on at Cornell University showed that the roots of Radiance Rose on multiflora understock two and a half years after planting had penetrated the soil to a depth of more than 50 inches and that 43 per cent of their roots were below the 18-inch level. Experiments carried out at Pennsylvania State College with eight different soil mixtures, each prepared to depths of 8, 16, and 24 inches, invariably showed greater flower production per bush in the more deeply prepared plots. The New York State Institute of Agriculture at Farmingdale, Long Island, prepared soil for Delphiniums 6, 12, and 18 inches deep; the growth of the plants corresponded to the depth of soil preparation—those in the 18-inch soil being twice the size of those in the 6-inch depth.

I have been told that in Holland soil mixtures are sometimes prepared to a depth of 6 feet! This I take with a grain of salt, but old-timers thought nothing of trenching the soil to a depth of 3 feet. Today, with the labor situation what it is, and with the almost universal endeavor to escape the curse of Cain, such deep preparation is outside the realm of practical politics So I, for one, am prepared to settle for double-digging. This is how it's done:

First, mark out the boundaries of the bed or border with mason's cord. At one end measure off 2 feet and stretch a string across the width of the plot. Dig out the topsoil to spade depth in this area, which, if your spade is the same size as mine, will leave a trench that is 11 inches deep. The topsoil should be wheeled to the opposite end

PICTURE 1. First, sods and soil are removed from far end of bed (extreme rear). These will be dug in last.
MALCOLM R. KINNEY

PICTURE 2. Second level of first-opened strip is turned over and enriched with rotted manure, compost, or leaf mold.
MALCOLM R. KINNEY

PICTURE 3. Second-strip sods are inverted on first-strip sublayer.
MALCOLM R. KINNEY

PICTURE 4. Topsoil covers inverted sods and humus is dug into the subsoil.
MALCOLM R. KINNEY

of the plot to be used to fill in the last trench. If the new bed is being made on ground covered with grass, the sod should be put in a separate pile (picture 1 page 33).

In the bottom of the trench spread a layer of rotted manure, compost, or leafmold, and mix it in as deeply as possible with a spading fork (picture 2).

Move the transverse string 2 feet along the bed, skin off the sods from this area and put them upside down in the first trench. Sprinkle them lightly with 5-10-5 fertilizer (¼ pound to a square yard), chop it into the sods with a spade, then proceed to dig out the second trench to spade depth and throw the soil into the first trench (picture 3). If you have rotted manure or compost to spare, it can be mixed in as the work proceeds. This process is repeated in 2-foot stretches until the final trench is reached and made, when the sods and soil which were removed from the initial trench are used to fill it (picture 4). If this method is followed, the ground will be loosened and humus mixed in it about 18 inches deep.

It is possible to get by with ordinary digging if a 2- to 3-inch layer of rotted manure or compost is put on the surface and dug into the full depth of the spade, but double-digging or some other procedure whereby the ground is prepared at least 18 inches deep is far preferable.

CHAPTER THREE

Laying Out the Beds

Now to discuss the principles and actual process of laying out the flower garden beds. The plan on page 26 will serve to illustrate most of the problems encountered. It is a simple one consisting of two L-shaped beds and two smaller curved beds surrounding a panel of lawn. The beds are 6 feet wide and, combined, provide space of about 750 square feet in which to grow perennials. This is as much as one person can conveniently manage as a spare-time project. If a greater area for perennials were desired, it could be gained by widening the beds to 7 or 8 feet, but it would result in a garden of less pleasing proportions.

This garden is enclosed by an informal border of miscellaneous shrubs on the west, south, and part of the east boundaries, possible in this case because of the abundant room. When there are spatial limitations, or when a more formal effect is desired, a clipped hedge could be substituted. The shrubs (or hedge) serve a double purpose: they provide a background against which the perennials can be viewed to their advantage; and they enclose the garden so it can be seen as a unit. A grass walk 7 feet wide, separating the perennials and the shrubs, eliminates competition among their roots.

In this garden the axis is a continuation of that of the hallway of the house; in other cases it might be centered on a picture window, a terrace, or some other distinctive feature.

TRANSPLANTING THE PLAN

Tools needed as an aid in laying out the beds and marking their outlines include a 50-foot measuring tape (steel preferred, though a cheap cloth one will serve in a pinch); a carpenter's rule 6 feet or longer, a garden line 100 feet long (a clothesline will do); 40 feet of non-stretching cord or clothesline for striking arcs and scribing the curved edges of the beds; a ball of mason's cord to outline the rectangular beds; 24 stakes about 1 foot by 1 inch, sharpened at one end; one 2-foot, round stake for a pivot when scribing the curved beds; and a hammer or mallet.

The first step is to establish the axis of the garden, from which all lateral measurements will be made. By assuming it is to be at a right angle to the house, this can be done by driving a stake in the ground (or making a mark on the wall) at the point on which the axis is centered. Then on either side measure off equal distances (say, about 15 feet) parallel with the house, and drive in stakes. From these stakes, strike arcs, using a line about 30 feet long, and place a stake at their intersection. A line stretched from the central point and projected through the stake will be at a right angle to the house, and serve as the garden axis. This is line AA on the diagram on the following page.

The next item is line BB. There are two possible ways of locating this: (1) measure equal distances from the house foundations opposite the BB, and put in stakes; or (2) put in a stake at a, and others equidistant on either side of it along the line AA; and from these strike arcs as described in the preceding paragraph.

If an obstruction along the line prevents the use of this means, the 3-4-5 method may be used, as also shown on the diagram. From stake a measure 3 yards along line AA and mark with a stake. Strike an arc 4 yards from a as nearly as possible at a right angle to the line AA. Intersect this with an arc 5 yards from the "3-yard" stake and put in a stake at the intersection. Now you have your rough right angle. Accurate measurements are essential, so, having secured the stakes in the approximate positions, repeat the work and drive nails into the stakes to obtain an exact right angle. A line projected through a and the intersection of the arcs will form right angles with AA, which may then be projected to BB.

From now on everything is relatively simple. From a measure 37 feet along the line AA and put in a stake (aa); from it at a right angle strike an arc to the west with a 17-foot radius (half the width of the garden); then from B strike an arc with a 37-foot radius (the length of the main beds) to intersect it, and drive a stake. A line stretched from this through the 37-foot stake on line Aa will enable you, by measuring with the 6-foot rule, to establish stakes dddd. By

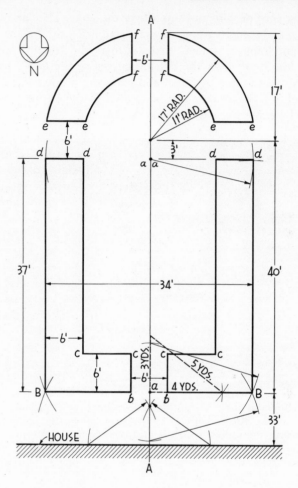

Working diagram of author's perennial garden showing method of laying out beds.

measuring 6 feet from the north along lines *Bd* and proceeding similarly, you will be enabled to locate *cccc*. The 6-foot rule centered on *AA* parallel with *BB* will let you locate *bb*.

Now for the curved beds at the south end of the garden. Measure 3 feet southward from the 37-foot stake (*aa*) on line *AA* and firmly drive in the round 2-foot stake. Make a loose loop in a piece of non-stretching cord or wire and slip it over the stake. Then at a distance of 17 feet make another loop, insert a scriber (a short stake, harrow tooth or anything convenient that will mark the ground) and, keeping the line taut, mark the outside curves of the two south beds. Then shorten the line by 6 feet and mark the inside curves (photograph below). Stakes *eeee* can be located by measuring from *dddd;* and *ffff* by centering a 6-foot rule on *AA.*

In the photograph above the author is describing the arc which marks the inner side of the curved corner bed at upper left in the diagram. A taut string governs the radius, which is measured from a stake on the center line of the garden. A stake at the string's end is the "pencil." STEENSON & BAKER

Careful measurements at all stages are essential for good results. You can, if you wish, check your accuracy by measuring the diagonals B*d*B*d,* which should be exactly the same. I would not advise doing this, however, if the layout looks right—you might find an inch or two out of the way and spend hours backtracking to find the error!

With the corners of all the beds located the rectangular ones can be outlined by connecting the stakes with mason's cord; and the curved ones marked by scratching their outlines on the ground as already described. We are now in a position to put the final touches on the grading preparatory to sowing the seeds in the grassy areas. The desired levels can be established by driving in pegs to the required height. It was not done in this particular case because workmen were available with a good eye for leveling, and it was felt that a line properly leveled across the top end of the plot would be a sufficient guide. This was established by means of a "line level" hung on a tightly stretched length of mason's cord.

Line level
used to determine
correct grade.
STEENSON & BAKER

Line along north edge of garden provides guide for workmen leveling plot. STEENSON & BAKER

Final touches: preparing to sow grass seed; wrapped plants from nursery laid out in beds for planting. STEENSON & BAKER

Does this sound complicated? Well, it is, but if you study the diagrams, it will be readily understood. And when you get working on the ground, you should have no difficulty.

When curved beds which do not permit the use of geometry are to be laid out, a garden hose can be laid on the ground and kicked and pulled around until a pleasing curve or set of curves is obtained. It will be noticed that the lawn comes right up to the edge of the beds. This poses a maintenance problem which can be solved by putting in an inanimate edge of stone or concrete which could serve as an all-weather walk. This is fully discussed in the chapter on garden edgings, which you should consult before making any decisions.

CHAPTER FOUR

Choosing the Plants

As previously mentioned the mainstays of the outdoor flower garden
are the hardy herbaceous perennials. The hardy spring-flowering
bulbs are essential for an early, highly colorful display, but they are
transitory, and when their flowers are faded their foliage is distressing. Annuals and biennials, hardy and tender summer-flowering
bulbs and perennials are available as fillers to carry on after the
early bulbs have performed their function of brightening the early
spring garden. Shrubs (woody perennials) play their part in making
a successful flower garden by giving shade and shelter. Also they are
sometimes used as accents in the border and often to provide a desirable background. It is, however, the hardy herbaceous plants that
are pre-eminent in the mind of the gardener and are his chief reli-
ance for the long pull.

By making the right selection of species and varieties it is possible
to have bloom from May to October inclusive. They should be carefully chosen, however, including chiefly those kinds which have few
enemies and are reasonably easy to grow. Select those with a long
blooming season—Chrysanthemum, Heliopsis, Gaillardia, Phlox, etc.;
those which have good foliage when they are not in bloom—Dianthus, Siberian Iris, Peony; or, so spectacular in bloom, even though it
covers only a short period, that it cannot be omitted—Oriental
Poppy, for example. The hybrid Delphiniums, despite the fact that
they are temperamental and pest-ridden, are so beautiful that their
culture must at least be attempted when there is any chance at all of
success. In gardens throughout those regions where the summer
climate is terrifically hot they can be treated as biennials with a fair
chance of success.

There are hundreds of genera of hardy herbaceous perennials suitable for garden use; catalogues of firms specializing in this group list upwards of a hundred with numerous species and garden varieties. From these selection (below) has been made on the basis of merit, and, in general, on their adaptability of growth over most of the United States. Very few of them, however, will survive in Florida and similar subtropic regions. Some will not succeed in really dry areas without copious irrigation. Flowers of Japanese Anemone and late Chrysanthemums are subject to frost injury in northern and mountainous areas where the onset of winter is early. In order to get the longest blooming period, it is desirable to do some pruning by cutting off faded flowers. Some kinds in particular respond to this treatment—Helenium, Gypsophila, Gaillardia, and Phlox.

This list, in this man's opinion, contains the cream of the perennials. Personal predilections or their ability to thrive in your garden may lead you to choose some of them in preference to others. (For fuller descriptions, see Chapter Sixteen.)

Thirty basic perennials for the well-planned border, height and blooming season.

Anemone japonica alba, Japanese Anemone, 3–5 feet, September–October

Aquilegia, Columbine, 1–3 feet, May–August

Arabis albida, Wall Rock-cress, 9–12 inches, April–May

Aster Frikarti, Wonder of Staffa, 2 feet, July–November

Aster novi-belgi, Michaelmas Daisy, 3–5 feet, September–October

Campanula carpatica, Carpathian Harebell, 9–15 inches, July–September

Chrysanthemum morifolium, Garden Chrysanthemum, 1–4 feet, July–November

Coreopsis verticillata, Thread-leaved Tickseed, 2 feet, all summer

Delphinium elatum, Candle Larkspur, 5–8 feet, June–July and in fall

Dianthus plumarius, Cottage Pink, 10–15 inches, June–September

Dictamnus albus, Dittany, Gas-plant, 2–3 feet, May–June

Gaillardia aristata, Blanket-flower, 2–2½ feet, June–October

Gypsophila paniculata, Babys-breath, 2½–3 feet, June–July
Helenium autumnale, Sneezeweed, 3–5 feet, August–September
Heliopsis scabra incomparabilis, Golden Sunflower, 3–4 feet, July–September
Hemerocallis, Daylily, 1½–3½ feet, May–September
Heuchera sanguinea, Coral-bells, 1½–2 feet, June–July
Iberis sempervirens, Perennial Candytuft, 1 foot, May–June
Iris, Tall Bearded, 2–4 feet, May–June
Iris sibirica, Siberian Iris, 2½–3½ feet, May–June
Lilium regale, Regal Lily, 4–7 feet, June–July
Monarda didyma, Bee-balm, 3 feet, July–August
Nepeta Mussini, Border Catmint, 1 foot, June–August
Paeonia albiflora, Peony, 2–3 feet, May–June
Papaver nudicaule, Iceland Poppy, 1–2 feet, May–July
Papaver orientale, Oriental Poppy, 2–4 feet, June
Phlox paniculata, Summer Phlox, 2–4 feet, July–September
Platycodon grandiflorum, Balloon Flower, 2–3 feet, June–August
Veronica maritima subsessilis, Speedwell, 2½ feet, July–September
Viola cornuta, Tufted Pansy, Horned Violet, 6–9 inches, May–September

And here are thirty more perennials which are almost as good as those in the preceding list:

Aconitum Fischeri, Monkshood, 4–5 feet, August–September
Althaea rosea, Hollyhock, 4–10 feet, July–August
Alyssum saxatile, Golden-tuft, 1 foot, April–May
Anthemis tinctoria Kelwayi, Golden Marguerite, 1½ feet, May–September
Aruncus sylvester, Goats-beard, 5–7 feet, June–July
Aster novae-angliae, New England Aster, 4–5 feet, September–October
Astilbe Fanal, 1½–2 feet, June–July
Brunnera macrophylla (Anchusa myosotidiflora), under 1½ feet, April–May
Campanula persicifolia, Peach-leaved Bellflower, 2½–3 feet, June–July

Ceratostigma plumbaginoides (*Plumbago Larpentae*), 1 feet, August–October

Chrysanthemum maximum, Shasta Daisy, 2–3 feet, June–July

Coreopsis grandiflora, 2½ feet, June–October

Delphinium grandiflorum, Chinese Larkspur, 2–3 feet, June–September

Dicentra eximia, Fringed Bleeding-heart, 1½–2 feet, April–October

Dicentra spectabilis, Bleeding-heart, 2½–3 feet, May–June

Doronicum caucasicum, Leopards-bane, 2 feet, April–May

Echinacea (*Rudbeckia*) *purpurea,* Coneflower, 3–4 feet, July–August

Eupatorium coelestinum, Mist-flower, 2–3 feet, September–October

Geum chiloense, Chilean Avens, 2 feet, June–August

Linum perenne, Perennial Flax, 1½–2 feet, May–July

Lupinus polyphyllus, Lupine, 3–5 feet, May–June

Lythrum salicaria, Purple Loosestrife, 3–4 feet, July–September

Oenothera fruticosa Youngi, Sundrop, 2–2½ feet, June–July

Phlox nivalis, Trailing Phlox, 8 inches, May–June

Phlox suffruticosa vars., 1½ feet, June–September

Physostegia virginiana, False Dragonhead, 3–4 feet, August–September

Primula polyantha, Polyanthus, 9–12 inches, April–May

Primula vulgaris, English Primrose, 4–6 inches, April–May

Rudbeckia Sullivanti, 2½ feet, July–August

Veronica incana, Hoary Speedwell, 1–1¼ feet, June–July

If these two lists do not provide enough variety for you, please turn to the "Descriptive List of Perennials" beginning on page 191 which contains many other perennials.

Some suggestions—companionable plants to keep the border in bloom:

Golden Columbine (*Aquilegia chrysantha*), 3 feet, May–July. Aster Wonder of Staffa (*Aster Frikarti*), 1½–2 feet, July–November. May-flowering Tulips in between. Glory-of-the-snow (*Chionodoxa Luciliae*) and Viola Chantryland interplanted in foreground. Flowers April–October; best display, May–June.

Japanese Anemone (*Anemone japonica alba*), 3–5 feet, September–October. Monkshood (*Aconitum Fischeri*), 4–5 feet, August–September. Peony, 2 feet, June. Leopards-bane (*Doronicum caucasicum*), 1½–2 feet, April–May. Tussock or Carpathian Harebell (*Campanula carpatica*), 1 foot, July–September. Flowers May–June, August–October; best display, September.

Aster Gay Border Blue, 5 feet, September–November. Golden Sunflower Summer Gold (*Heliopsis scabra incomparabilis*), 3–4 feet, July–September. Chinese Larkspur (*Delphinium grandiflorum*), 2–3 feet, June–August. Coral-bells (*Heuchera sanguinea*), 1½–2 feet, June–July. Dianthus Silvermine, 9 inches, June–September. Flowers June–November; best display, June and September.

Balloon Flower (*Platycodon grandiflorum*), 3 feet, June–August. Chrysanthemum King Midas, 2 feet, September–November. Gasplant (Dittany, Burning-bush) (*Dictamnus albus rubra*), 2–3 feet, May–June. May-flowering Tulips. Golden-tuft (*Alyssum saxatile*), 1 foot, April–May. Flowers May–June; August–October.

Hybrid Delphinium, 5 feet, June–July. Madonna Lily (*Lilium candidum*), 3–5 feet, June–July. Phlox Daily Sketch, 3½ feet, July–November. Phlox Miss Lingard, 2½ feet, June–November. Hardy Plumbago, Blue Leadwort (*Ceratostigma plumbaginoides*), 1 foot, August–October. Coral-bells (*Heuchera sanguinea*). Flowers June–October; best display, June.

Helenium Riverton Gem, 4–5 feet, August–September. Tall Bearded Iris, 3 feet, June. Regal Lily (*Lilium regale*), 4–7 feet, June–July, or Showy Japanese Lily (*L. speciosum*), 3–5 feet, August–September. Blanket-flower (*Gaillardia aristata*), 2–2½ feet, June–October. Border Catmint (*Nepeta Mussini*), 1–1½ feet, June–August. Candytuft (*Iberis sempervirens*), 1 foot, May. Flowers May to October.

Oriental Poppy (*Papaver orientale*), 2–4 feet, June. Babys-breath Bristol Fairy (*Gypsophila paniculata*), 3 feet, July–September. Lemon Daylily (*Hemerocallis flava*), 2½ feet, May–June. Wall Rockcress (*Arabis albida florepleno*), 6–10 inches, April–May. Hardy Plumbago, August–October; main display, May and June.

Monarda Cambridge Scarlet, 3 feet, July–August. Siberian Iris, 3 feet, May–June. Lemon Daylily (*Hemerocallis flava*), 2½–3 feet, May–June. Peony Festiva Maxima, 2½ feet, June. Blanket-flower. Carpathian Harebell. For June mainly; good foliage through season.

Hollyhock, 6 feet, July–August. Bugloss (*Anchusa azurea*), 3–5 feet, May–June. Daylily Patricia, 3 feet, July. Veronica Blue Champion, 2 feet, July. Peony Walter Faxon, 2½ feet, June. Candytuft Snowflake. Viola Royal Purple, 9 inches, June–August. Flowers May–August.

CHAPTER FIVE

Making the Planting Plan

The time has now come to write about one of the most enjoyable indoor sports of the gardener—that of making actual planting plans. Of course it is possible to plant perennials without any previous planning—I have on occasion been guilty of it myself—but it is a hit-or-miss proposition at the best and one may expect far better results if considerable thought is given to the subject and our conclusions are set down on paper before putting out any plants.

A plan can also serve as a record of what has been planted, both of kinds and varieties, so that labeling can be eliminated; also it can be pasted on a stout cardboard of large size and the margins can serve as a notebook for reminders of desirable changes. Before starting, however, there are a few factors to be considered which are fundamental in making any good garden plan whatever its size, type, or design.

1. *Season of Bloom.* If the owners are habitually away during part of the growing season, there is no point in setting out plants which are at their height of bloom at that time. Choose only those plants which are at their best when you are there to enjoy them.

2. *Character of Plant Material.* Without doubt the most colorful border is the one which makes use of annuals and tender perennials to fill gaps caused by the passing of early-blooming perennials. A greater sense of satisfaction comes, however, when the effect is achieved by using mostly hardy perennials, including, of course, the hardy spring- and summer-flowering bulbs.

3. *Accent.* What is an accent plant? Ralph Bailey defines it as follows: "An accent plant is one which attracts attention to itself

by exceptional beauty; by its contrast to its fellows in size, form, or color; by its placement in a position where its dominance over other plants around it adds to the effectiveness of the whole." Accepting this definition, we may inquire further: "What is their purpose?" One can say that primarily they are used to liven up the garden by providing highlights; to contrast with their neighbors; and to avoid a monotonous appearance. When entire components of the border are harmoniously massed in groups of approximately equal size, the result, while not necessarily monotonous—the change of emphasis owing to seasonal bloom will take care of that—is likely to be placid or bread-and-butterish and wholesome, but not exciting. So we distribute a little cake or pie here and there to promote eye-catching interest. In the sample plans you will, in most cases, notice circles indicating accent plants. For example, in the curved beds on pages 50–51, Nos. 7, 8, 11, 13, 26 are placed primarily as accents.

4. *Size of Groups.* Two factors enter here: the size of the garden, and the predilections of the owner. It is generally advised, in order to avoid spottiness, to use several plants of a kind in each group. But, if the garden is small, this severely limits the number of kinds that can be grown, and results in noticeably large areas devoid of color when the plants are not in bloom. The size of the groups should be determined by the size of the garden so that they are in proportion. If the owner's predominant interest is plants rather than the appearance of the garden as a whole, he will, in most cases, plant only one of a kind in order to secure the greatest variety in the space available.

In general, a middle-of-the-road policy is best for the average garden. Single plants of large-growing kinds and those used for accents are permissible in the garden of medium size (Peony, the larger Asters, Helenium, Gas-plant, Bleeding-heart, etc.). Plants of moderate size (Chrysanthemum, Phlox, Heliopsis, Iris, etc.) can be used in groups of two to seven. Plant low-growing, front-line plants in groups of three to nine; while six to twenty-four bulbs of Tulips and Narcissus and twelve to thirty-six Crocus and Chionodoxa are desirable.

After deciding on a general policy the next step is to select a number of plants that appeal to you, with special emphasis on long-blooming kinds. (See the lists on page 326.) List those chosen in

three categories: one, 3 feet and over; two, 1½–3 feet; three, below
1½ feet. Indicate approximate time of blooming and color of each
kind. Then obtain some graph paper (¼-inch squares—¼ inch to a
foot is a convenient scale with which to work), and outline the beds
or borders to scale. You are now ready to start actual planning.

With a pencil lightly outline the space to be assigned to each
variety. In general, those in Category 1 will be placed in the rear
ranks; those in 3 in the front; and 2 in between. But don't be too
rigid in this respect; vary the sky line from front to back, also along
the length of the border, and let each category to some extent encroach upon its neighbors. For example, Nos. 16 and 27 are tall in
comparison with their neighbors and serve as accents as well as
variations in height from front to back; similarly in the rear row of
plants the height is varied partly according to season—in June the
Delphinium will tower over its neighbors on either side; when it is
cut back after flowering, the Phlox and Heliopsis will be dominant.

On pages 50 and 51 are Plans 1, 1A, devised for the two curved
beds which are part of ·the larger plan, page 26. As is shown by
other variations on pages 50 and 51, their shape and proportions may be easily modified to fit varying conditions. If required
as a terminal feature with no dividing walk (Plan 2), the two beds
could be pulled together. In such case I would suggest additional
plants for plots 6 and 19 (or either one), and increasing the plants
of 12 to three. The two beds could be straightened out and put
together to form one long border. This would greatly increase the
area available for front-rank plants; and slightly that of those in the
middle. Or Plan 1 alone would be straightened out, as shown on
page 50, Plan 3, to make a smaller and much less elaborate bed.
Adjustments could be made by increasing the length of the groups
in the middle; and by inserting a couple of additional groups in the
front. These could be long-blooming varieties of garden Pinks, such
as Old Spice, Rock Raven Red, and Silvermine; Coral-bells, and
Basket-of-Gold (Alyssum). Another "freehand" version, suitable for
setting off a corner shrub grouping, is suggested in Plan 4, page 51.

While the material in the two beds of Plans 1 and 1-A is balanced,
one bed is not an exact replica of the other. Variation in the content
was deliberate to add interest and to accommodate a few additional
varieties. If your tastes lie along the lines of exact duplication, there
is no reason why you should not indulge them.

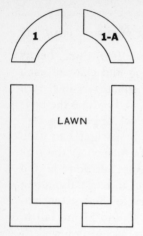

Diagram above locates areas detailed in Plans 1 and 1A

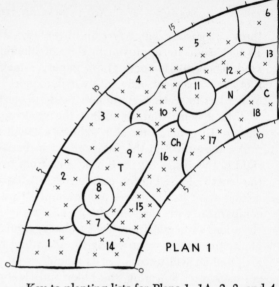

PLAN 1

Key to planting lists for Plans 1, 1A, 2, 3, and 4. Number of plants indicated by figures in parentheses.

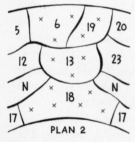

PLAN 2

Plan 2 will link Plans 1 and 1A to make a semicircular bed. This plan calls for extra plants: two plants in 6, one in 19, one in 13.

1. Perennial Candytuft Purity (6)
2. Phlox Marie Louise (10)
3. *Heliopsis incomparabilis* (3)
4. Anchusa Dropmore (3)
5. Phlox Cheerfulness (5)
6. Helenium Riverton Gem (1 or 3)
7. Babys-breath Bristol Fairy (2)
8. Oriental Poppy Dorothy Rowe (1)
9. Chrysanthemum Canary (6)
10. Bearded Iris Tiffany (7)
11. Peony Festiva Maxima (2)
12. Daylily Patricia (5)

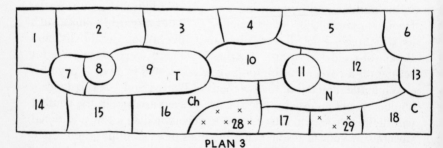

PLAN 3

The basic plan (Plans 1, 1A) is adaptable to many shapes. In Plan 3, above, the substance of Plans 1 and 1A is fitted to a rectangular outline. In straightening the border the front line is lengthened and two more species, 28 and 29, have been added to the basic list.

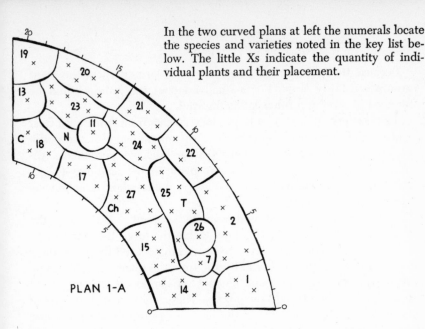

In the two curved plans at left the numerals locate the species and varieties noted in the key list below. The little Xs indicate the quantity of individual plants and their placement.

PLAN 1-A

13. Coreopsis Golden Shower (2 or 3)
14. *Campanula carpatica* (9)
15. Viola Chantryland (12)
16. Aster Wonder of Staffa (6)
17. *Nepeta Mussini* (6)
18. *Ceratostigma plumbaginoides* (6)
19. Helenium Riverton Beauty (1 or 2)
20. Phlox B. Comte (5)
21. Aster Blue Gown (3)
22. Anchusa Opal (3)
23. Bearded Iris Elsa Sass (6)
24. Daylily Dauntless (5)

25. Chrysanthemum Eugene A. Wander (5)
26. Oriental Poppy Spring Morn (1)
27. *Oenothera Youngi* (6)
28. Dianthus Silvermine (5)
29. *Alyssum saxatile* (3)
30. *Heuchera sanguinea* (13)

Bulbs
T Tulips (24–36)
N Narcissus (12–24)
C Crocus (36–48)
Ch Chionodoxa (36–48)

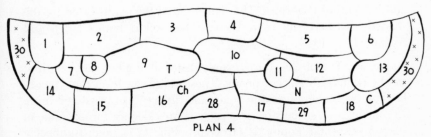

PLAN 4

Plan 4. Here again Plans 1 and 1A are the basis, with added foreground varieties from Plan 3, and another low edging plant (30) to swing the ends. This is the sort of free-hand border, best outlined on the ground with a length of hose. As in the other plans spring-flowering bulbs precede the main bloom parade. Adjoining plants that develop later will cover up the fading bulb foliage.

Because they are part of a comparatively large garden, the plant groups are fairly large. For a smaller layout the groups could be reduced in size, and other kinds inserted.

The borders are designed to produce flowers from April until frost and are "all-perennial" borders. The ripening foliage of the early-blooming bulbs will be hidden by other adjacent perennials. Another way of achieving this end is to plant annual seedlings (Nicotiana, Marigold, Zinnia, etc.) among the bulbs when their flowers are beginning to fade.

Having made a trial run with a limited amount of material in the two small curved beds, let us now tackle the large L-shaped beds.

With twice as many varieties to be accommodated the situation is a little more complicated, and by the time the plants are pleasingly arranged, one feels the same kind of satisfaction that comes from solving an elaborate jig-saw puzzle. These plants can be adapted to other garden shapes along the lines suggested in the preceding pages. The fundamental factors outlined and the technique required are the same for these plans as for the preceding, but additional information and discussion will be helpful.

Shade. The short, transverse elements of the two L-shaped beds shown on pages 53 and 55 are shaded by adjacent Maples for about half the day, so the plants used in them are shade-loving, or shade-enduring, kinds. It is not likely that your shaded areas (if any) are situated in the same relation to the rest of the flower beds, but adaptations to any local situation could be accomplished by transferring the plan of the two shaded areas (as a whole or in part) to the shaded portion of yours, and replacing it with a corresponding section of sun lovers. If the entire garden is in sun, you could substitute sun-enduring plants of similar size for the Epimedium, Helleborus, and Polyanthus Primroses. The remainder of the plants listed for the shaded area can endure full sun if the soil is humus-laden and reasonably moist.

Accents. The circles, fairly evenly distributed along the length of the beds, indicate accent plants. These stand out from their neighbors by reason of contrast in color, and differences in size and form. In some cases a succession of accents is provided as, for example, in Plan 5: Oriental Poppy (24), Gypsophila (25), and Rudbeckia (26), located in proximity, take over the accenting in turn from late

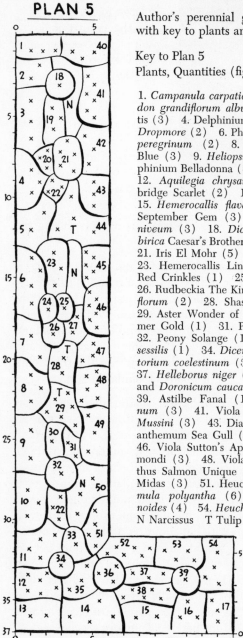

PLAN 5

Author's perennial garden—east border, Plan 5, with key to plants and quantities.

Key to Plan 5

Plants, Quantities (figures in parentheses)

1. *Campanula carpatica* Blue Carpet (3)   2. *Platycodon grandiflorum album* (2)   3. Phlox Charles Curtis (3)   4. Delphinium, Tall Hybrid (3)   5. Anchusa *Dropmore* (2)   6. Phlox Columbia (4)   7. *Helenium peregrinum* (2)   8. Aster Blue Gown or New Blue (3)   9. *Heliopsis incomparabilis* (2)   10. Delphinium Belladonna (3)   11. Phlox Marie Louise (4)   12. *Aquilegia chrysantha* (6)   13. Monarda Cambridge Scarlet (2)   14. *Anemone japonica alba* (4)   15. *Hemerocallis flava* (2)   16. *Anemone japonica* September Gem (3)   17. *Epimedium grandiflorum niveum* (3)   18. *Dictamnus albus* (1)   19. *Iris sibirica* Caesar's Brother (3)   20. *Lilium speciosum* (3)   21. Iris El Mohr (5)   22. *Lilium candidum* (6)   23. Hemerocallis Linda (3)   24. *Papaver orientale* Red Crinkles (1)   25. Gypsophila Bristol Fairy (1)   26. Rudbeckia The King (1)   27. *Delphinium grandiflorum* (2)   28. Shasta Daisy Wirral Supreme (2)   29. Aster Wonder of Staffa (6)   30. Heliopsis Summer Gold (1)   31. Phlox Miss Lingard (2)   32. Peony Solange (1)   33. *Veronica maritima subsessilis* (1)   34. *Dicentra spectabilis* (1)   35. *Eupatorium coelestinum* (3)   36. Dicentra Bountiful (3)   37. *Helleborus niger* (3)   38. *Brunnera macrophylla* and *Doronicum caucasicum* intermixed (6)   39. Astilbe Fanal (1)   40. *Alyssum saxatile citrinum* (3)   41. Viola Jersey Gem (6)   42. *Nepeta Mussini* (3)   43. Dianthus Beatrice (3)   44. Chrysanthemum Sea Gull (4)   45. *Papaver nudicaule* (5)   46. Viola Sutton's Apricot (6)   47. Heuchera Rosamondi (3)   48. Viola Royal Purple (6)   49. Dianthus Salmon Unique (3)   50. Chrysanthemum King Midas (3)   51. Heuchera Matin Bells (4)   52. *Primula polyantha* (6)   53. *Ceratostigma plumbaginoides* (4)   54. *Heuchera sanguinea* Perry's White (4)
N Narcissus   T Tulip

Accent Plants—*Gypsophila paniculata*, Bristol Fairy, as accent plant, obscuring faded Oriental Poppy.
MALCOLM R. KINNEY

May until the fall. Heuchera (47, 51) serve as accents during the time they are in bloom.

Variety in Sky Line. Variation in silhouette and height add interest to the sky line. For example, Phlox (3) has a rounded silhouette; Delphinium (4) is spirelike; and Anchusa (5) is more or less pyramidal. Height will be varied throughout the season by different rates of growth, and by cutting off fading flower spikes (Delphinium). Notice that fairly tall plants, Chrysanthemums (44 and 50) and Heuchera (47), occasionally are brought down into the front rank to avoid the monotony of a row of plants of similar height.

Character of Plant Material. I have leaned rather heavily on Violas. The reason for this is that they do well in my own garden and bloom all season. They are not a success in every garden, though, and if they do not thrive for you, or if you are uncertain of their behavior, it would be well to eliminate them or cut down on the quantity used, and substitute easily grown plants such as Ajuga, Dwarf Hardy Asters, Dianthus, Moss-Phlox and double-flowered variety of Tunica. *Papaver nudicaule* (Iceland Poppy) likewise cannot be relied on in regions with hot summers. I like it very much, but, not knowing how well it would thrive for me (it does not, so far!), I limited the planting to two small patches; Tritomas have so far proved to be winter-hardy in my garden (we have subzero temperatures rather frequently), but in a really severe climate in heavy soil they might succumb. The rest of the plants are easily grown and hardy if given care normal for perennials in any specific region.

Author's perennial garden—west border, Plan 6, with key to plants and quantities.

PLAN 6

Key to Plan 6

Plants, Quantities (figures in parentheses)

1. *Campanula carpatica* Blue Carpet (3) 2. *Platycodon grandiflorum* (2) 3. Aster Survivor (2) 4. Delphinium Belladonna (3) 5. Helenium Chippinsfield Orange (3) 6. Aster Blue Gown (2) 7. Anchusa Dropmore (2) 8. Heliopsis Gold Greenheart (2) 9. Delphinium Bellamosa (3) 10. Phlox White Admiral (6) 11. Monarda Cambridge Scarlet (2) 12. *Anemone japonica* Marie Blanchard (3) 13. *Hemerocallis flava* (2) 14. *Anemone vitifolia robustissima* (3) 15. *Epimedium grandiflorum niveum* (3) 16. Phlox Mies Copyn (3) 17. *Dictamnus caucasicus* (1) 18. Shasta Daisy Mark Riegel (2) 19. *Lilium candidum* (3) 20. Hemerocallis Tasmania (3) 21. Gypsophila Bristol Fairy (1) 22. *Papaver orientale* Glowing Rose (1) 23. Tritoma Summer Sunshine (2) 24. *Lilium speciosum* (1) 25. Iris Gudrun (6) 26. Pyrethrum Helen (2) 27. *Campanula persicifolia* (3) 28. Liatris, White (1) 29. Aster Wonder of Staffa (4) 30. Peony Solange (1) 31. *Aquilegia chrysantha* (6) 32. *Dicentra spectabilis* (1) 33. *Lobelia siphilitica* (3) 34. *Dicentra eximia* Bountiful (1) 35. *Helleborus niger* (3) 36. *Brunnera macrophylla* and *Doronicum caucasicum* intermixed (6) 37. Astilbe Fanal (1) 38. *Alyssum saxatile citrinum* (3) 39. Viola Jersey Gem (6) 40. *Nepeta Mussini* (3) 41. *Veronica incana* (6) 42. Dianthus Rock Raven Red (6) 43. Chrysanthemum Summertime (5) 44. *Papaver nudicaule* (5) 45. Phlox Miss Lingard (3) 46. Geum Fire Opal (3) 47. Chrysanthemum Canary (3) 48. Rudbeckia Goldsturm (1) 49. *Heuchera sanguinea* (3) 50. *Primula polyantha* (6) 51. *Ceratostigma plumbaginoides* (4) 52. *Heuchera sanguinea* Perry's White (3) N Narcissus T Tulip

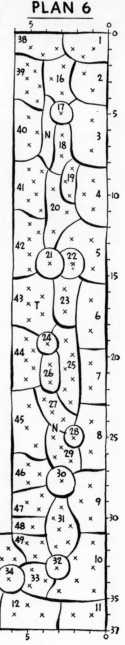

Differences in the Plans. As in the case of the curved beds, Plan No. 6 is not an exact replica of No. 5. Sometimes the variation is accomplished by using a different variety of a given species, and occasionally by introducing an entirely new genus or species as, for example, Geum, Lobelia, Peach-leaved Bellflower, Pyrethrum, and Tritoma. The use of a few "uncertain" plants in limited numbers is, I think, a good thing because it adds variety to the planting, and it might happen that they will grow surprisingly well and indicate a freer use of them as your garden develops in succeeding years.

Number of Plants. To furnish the entire garden, approximately 320 plants; plus 6 dozen Narcissus bulbs; 6 dozen Tulips; and 200 each of Crocus and Chionodoxa (the latter to be interspersed with other plants in the foreground to lengthen the blooming season) are indicated in the planting lists. Even though this is just about half the number that the average nurseryman would recommend for a comparable area, the plants will soon be crowding each other if all of them grow. There were two major reasons for using plants in fairly liberal quantities: (1) the desire to make a good showing the first year; and (2) I have never forgotten a remark passed by Ellen Willmott, a former employer (in my opinion the foremost woman horticulturist of the early part of the century), who said: "It is wise to plant perennials thickly; one might as well fill the beds with flowers—there will be less room for the weeds."

Anyone whose budget does not permit the purchase of plants in the quantities indicated could, except where single plants are concerned, cut down the number of each kind by half, or even two thirds, omit the bulbs entirely, and rely on annuals for temporarily filling the gaps. By the end of the year it will be possible, in most cases, to increase the perennials by division to make up the number that will ultimately be required.

Your Plan or Mine? Naturally I believe that these planting plans are good, but I realize that personal predilections entered into their making. You probably have your own preferences in plant materials, and in ways of arranging them; and I would advise you not to suppress them if they conflict with mine. While you can, if you wish, slavishly follow these plans (or adaptations of them previously suggested), I submit that you will get more satisfaction from the garden if you yourself have had a major part in planning it. Therefore, in using these plans only as a rough guide, I urge you to go ahead and make a plan that is truly personal. Local growing conditions, as previously mentioned, must also be considered.

Now for some planting plans made by others. First, a basic plan with four variations presented by courtesy of my former colleague, Ralph Bailey. These are undoubtedly first-class plans. The only criti-

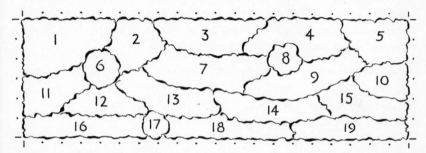

Plan 7. HERE IS A SIMPLE, EFFECTIVE BORDER PLAN OF PERENNIALS Dots around edge represent 1-foot intervals (key to varieties, quantity, color and bloom time, below). For alternate ways in which to use Plan 7, see Plans 8, 9, 10, and 11.

Key: Variety, Quantity (figure in parentheses), Color and Bloom Time for Plan 7

1. Aster Survivor (5)
2. Salvia Pitcheri (5)
3. Delphinium, tall hybrids (5)
4. Helenium Riverton Beauty (5)
5. Liatris September Glory (5)
6. ACCENT: Peony Walter Faxon (1)
7. Phlox Daily Sketch (10)
8. ACCENT: *Lilium speciosum album* (3)
9. Iris, set alternately
     Tall Bearded, Missouri (5 or 6)
     Kaempferi, Gold Bound (5 or 6)
10. *Platycodon grandiflorum* (5) Blue, Summer
11. *Delphinium chinense* (as listed) (6)
12. *Anemone japonica* (6)
13. Shasta Daisy (*Chrysanthemum maximum*) Mt. Shasta (9)
14. *Dicentra eximia* (Plumy Bleeding-heart) (6)
15. Chrysanthemum Allegro (6)
16. Heuchera Rosamondi (12)
17. ACCENT: Astilbe Fanal (1 or 3)
18. *Iberis sempervirens* (12)
19. *Campanula carpatica* (9)

cisms I have are minor: 1. The planting is rather crowded if it is to be placed in a lawn setting, because plants in the first row will lop over, be in the way of the lawn mower, and spoil the neat edge. Of course, if the border is bounded by a concrete, flagstone, or brick walk, this criticism does not apply. 2. I am not sure that the mingling of varieties of Tall Bearded and Japanese Iris in one area is culturally good. 3. I dislike *Salvia Pitcheri,* the flowering stalks of which, for me, flop uncontrollably. I would prefer to use *Salvia farinacea* even though it is not reliably hardy and is best when treated as an annual in northern gardens.

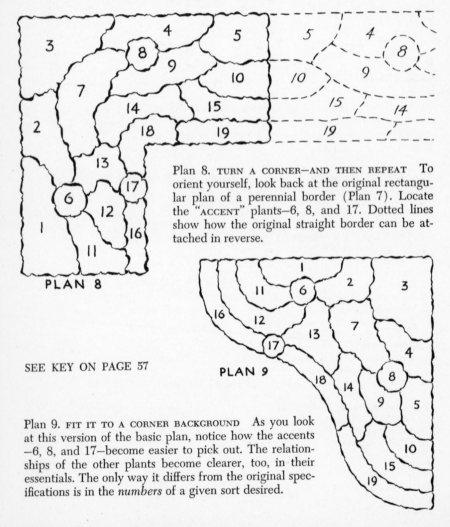

Plan 8. TURN A CORNER—AND THEN REPEAT To orient yourself, look back at the original rectangular plan of a perennial border (Plan 7). Locate the "ACCENT" plants—6, 8, and 17. Dotted lines show how the original straight border can be attached in reverse.

PLAN 8

SEE KEY ON PAGE 57

PLAN 9

Plan 9. FIT IT TO A CORNER BACKGROUND As you look at this version of the basic plan, notice how the accents —6, 8, and 17—become easier to pick out. The relationships of the other plants become clearer, too, in their essentials. The only way it differs from the original specifications is in the *numbers* of a given sort desired.

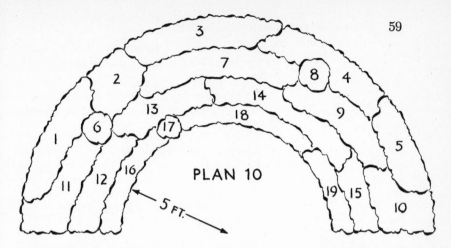

Plan 10. TERMINAL BORDER FOR A GARDEN PANEL   It's as easy to swing a circle as to turn, or fill, a corner. Here a central turf panel is implied, with a crosspath between curved bed and straight side borders. The original plan (Plan 7), turned to fit, might form side beds. A good plan, with color changes, will bear repetition.

SEE KEY ON PAGE 57

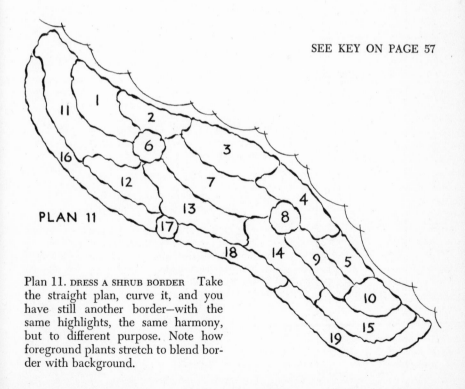

Plan 11. DRESS A SHRUB BORDER   Take the straight plan, curve it, and you have still another border—with the same highlights, the same harmony, but to different purpose. Note how foreground plants stretch to blend border with background.

A series of four plans each with a key to plants, by the late Philip L. Robinson, landscape architect.

Plan 12. KEY TO THE STRAIGHT BORDER EDGING 1 foot wide, any small, restrained plant, such as Viola or Alyssum:
A—Annuals P—Perennials F—Floribunda Roses
M—Medium-height Hybrid Teas   T—Tall Hybrid Teas

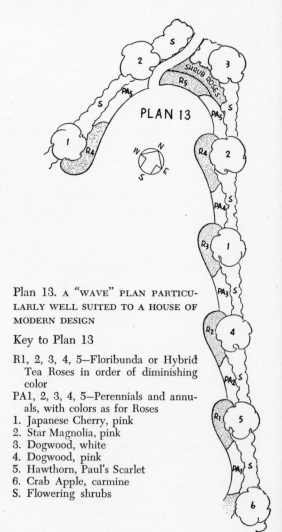

PLAN 12

EDGING

PLAN 13

Plan 13. A "WAVE" PLAN PARTICU-LARLY WELL SUITED TO A HOUSE OF MODERN DESIGN

Key to Plan 13

R1, 2, 3, 4, 5—Floribunda or Hybrid Tea Roses in order of diminishing color
PA1, 2, 3, 4, 5—Perennials and annuals, with colors as for Roses
1. Japanese Cherry, pink
2. Star Magnolia, pink
3. Dogwood, white
4. Dogwood, pink
5. Hawthorn, Paul's Scarlet
6. Crab Apple, carmine
S. Flowering shrubs

And here are four plans by the late Philip L. Robinson, landscape architect. These feature Roses rather than herbaceous perennials, but the latter (and also annuals and biennials) play an important though subordinate part. Some such scheme as those presented here might well be a challenge to the somewhat advanced gardener, both in working out a detailed plan for planting perennials and in solving cultural problems presented by the proximity of Roses and herbaceous plants.

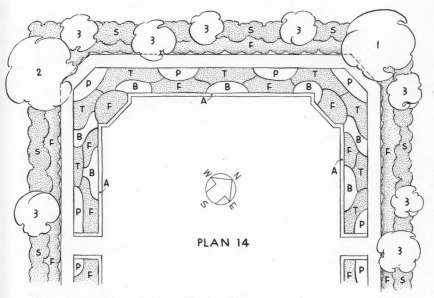

Plan 14. A U-SHAPED GARDEN THAT MIGHT FILL A BACK YARD

Key to Complete Border—Plan 14

F—Floribunda Roses   T—Hybrid Teas   S—Shrub Roses   A—Edging annuals
B—Biennials, then annuals   P—Perennials   1—Flowering Crab Apple   2—Dogwood   3—Lilacs

The Future. Fortunately most misplaced perennials can be moved whenever it seems necessary, in some cases even when in full bloom (see pages 79 to 81), so don't worry too much about your planning. Do not expect to make a garden that will never require any

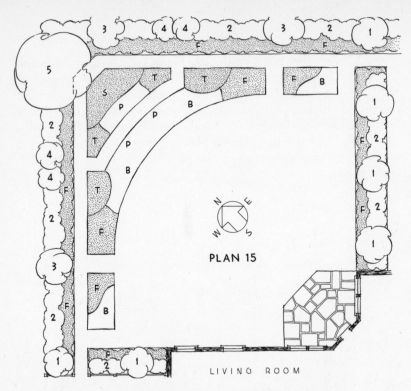

Plan 15. FOR THE RIGHT LOCATION—A REAL DOORYARD GARDEN

Key to dooryard plan

F—Floribunda Roses   T—Hybrid Teas   S—Shrub Roses   B—Biennials, then annuals   P—Perennials   1—Kousa Dogwood   2—Spirea Vanhoutte   3—Star Magnolia   4—Gordonia   5—Flowering Cherry

adjustment. No one can predict the behavior of all the varieties of plants in any one garden. Some will grow too vigorously, perhaps, and have to be curbed or liquidated; some will sulk; and a few will die. Do not be in too great a hurry in deciding that a variety is not man enough for the job—some may double their height the second season. Almost inevitably unpleasing color combinations will develop that will need rectification. But don't be deterred: you will have lots of fun in its planning. You will enjoy the result in the garden even if it is not perfect; and the planting, the care of the plants, and their rearrangement will add to your store of gardening know-how.

CHAPTER SIX

Planting the Garden

SEASONS FOR PLANTING

As we shall see later, most perennials can be planted at any time except when the ground is hard-frozen. But there are preferred seasons for the job when they can be planted without much fuss and bother and with the least injury to the plants.

Although practically all perennials can be planted either in the spring or the fall, the general rule is: early-blooming *hardy* perennials are best moved in the fall with the objective of allowing as long a period as possible between planting and blooming to enable new roots to form; and late bloomers are best moved in the spring. Then there is a group which becomes more or less dormant about midsummer and can be planted more effectively in August. Some are indifferent to season and may be planted in either fall or spring when they are dormant.

Among the early bloomers (April–June) for which fall planting is preferred are: Peony, Phlox, Heuchera, Japanese and Siberian Irises, most Lilies, and the hardy spring-flowering bulbs. Exceptions are: Primroses, English Daisies, Rock-cress, and Viola, which, having compact root systems, permit spring planting without detriment to flowering; and Alyssum and Pansy, which may fail to survive the winter in severe climates if planted in the fall.

The late bloomers which usually succeed best when spring planting is practiced include: Japanese Anemone, Hardy Aster, Chrysanthemum (both Garden Chrysanthemum and Shasta Daisy), Delphinium, Digitalis, Gaillardia, Hibiscus, Kniphofia (this may also be planted after blooming in summer), Perennial Flax, Potentilla, and Stokesia.

The group which is best adapted to midsummer planting in-cludes: Bleeding-heart, Bearded Iris, Doronicum, Virginia Cowslip, Oriental Poppies, and, of the hardy bulbs, Madonna Lily and Crown Imperial.

So when you are starting a perennial garden, you can do so either in early fall or early spring. Actually there is little to choose between the two seasons especially if you are favored by living in a climate where the temperature does not get below zero. If you start in the fall, there are only a few for which it is advisable to wait until

Planting techniques—bed edges are marked at 1-foot intervals with wooden pot labels; boards protect edges of beds; lime circle indicates plants already set. MALCOLM R. KINNEY

spring—Alyssum, Aster (*A. Frikarti,* especially), and Chrysanthe-mum. If you wait until spring to plant, you will have to forgo for a season the pleasure of seeing the blooms of the hardy spring-flower-ing bulbs and Peonies; but, on the other hand, you will suffer less loss from winter killing. Ideally you should take three bites of the cherry and do some of the planting in the fall, some in the spring, and some at midsummer. The places in which the midsummer plant-ings are to go can be filled temporarily by biennials, such as Canter-bury Bells and Foxglove, which can be removed after flowering and their places taken by the permanent occupants.

PLANTING TECHNIQUES—SPRING AND FALL

I must admit I get considerable pleasure from planting a garden by freehand methods—merely making a rough plan in my head and laying out the plants as I meander along the border. This was the method followed when planting the garden pictured on page 85, but I don't recommend it, especially for those whose gardening experience is limited. One is likely to run into trouble with unfortu-nate color combinations and with tall plants hiding their neighbors of smaller stature, unless a plan carefully made and put on paper is followed.

If you have gone to the trouble of making a planting plan to scale, it is foolish to do the actual laying out of plants by freehand, which might mean reaching the end of the bed or border with 6 feet of it unplanted, or, worse still, with dozens of plants left over. Therefore, some provision must be made to ensure that the plants go into the beds and borders with no more than a few inches of deviation from the plan. The most effective way of doing this is to mark the edges of the planting area at 1-foot intervals.

I find that the ordinary 6-inch wooden pot labels make good mark-ers, though split shingles or something similar could be used. As an additional refinement, which is a valuable aid in locating the position of the plants, I like to put a 12-inch label every 5 feet, numbered 5, 10, 15, 20, and so on. When the bed, or border, is 6 feet or less wide, one can usually estimate lateral distances; but when the width is more than 6 feet, it is worth while to make longi-tudinal furrows in the soil at 2-foot intervals to serve as guides. If the job is being done in the fall, and there has been preliminary planting, for example, of Peony, Oriental Poppy, and Madonna Lilies, their planting stations should be marked by a ring of powdered limestone to avoid encroachment.

Before any considerable work is done, it is desirable to lay boards along the lines of greatest traffic to protect the lawn and bed edges. Inevitably there is a good deal of passing to and fro, and the lawn and the trimmed edges will suffer unless this is done. It is especially necessary when a newly seeded lawn is contiguous to the flower beds, as it was in my own case. If there are any perennials already on the place that are destined to be moved into the new border, they can be attended to first, unless the purchased plants have arrived already.

When the plants are received from the nursery, they should be unpacked at once. Probably some will be wrapped individually in moss and paper; some will be loose and bare-rooted except for the moist packing material surrounding them. The first-named should be arranged alphabetically to facilitate their subsequent placement, and packed upright closely together in shallow boxes. The bare-root plants should be heeled in, also alphabetically, in a nearby shrub border, or in that part of the perennial bed which is to be planted last. The individually wrapped plants may all be laid out prior to planting, which lessens the passing to and fro, but never lay out more than six or so of the bare-root plants before planting them, lest their roots suffer from drying. A cloudy, humid day is best for planting.

PLANTING TECHNIQUES

Plants with deep root systems, such as Anchusa, Peony, and Babys-breath, or those which come in massive clumps, are most conveniently planted with the aid of a spade. Two persons can do this most efficiently—one to dig the holes and shovel in the soil around the roots, the other to hold the plant at the right depth, work the soil among the roots, and make the soil firm around them by pressing it down with his, or her, feet. Broken, mangled ends of thick, fleshy roots, such as those of Babys-breath, Peony, and Anchusa, should be trimmed off with a sharp knife to sound tissue. When the root system is comparatively small, a trowel can be used to make the hole and fill in the soil; the soil can be made firm about the roots with one's hands. (See series of pictures.)

LEFT. Anchusa, whose 9-inch-long fleshy roots disappear into shadow, is held at correct depth for replacing soil (two can do this faster than one). RIGHT. As in all cases, soil is tramped firm around newly planted Anchusa. MALCOLM R. KINNEY

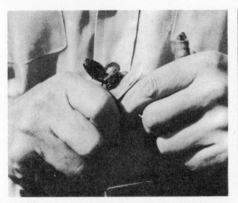

LEFT. Mangled roots of Gypsophila are trimmed to sound tissue. MALCOLM R. KINNEY. RIGHT. In trowel planting hole is made large enough for all roots. Plant is held at right level with one hand; other hand fills in soil. R. A. SMITH

Plants small enough to be set out conveniently with a trowel can usually be firmed by hands alone.

MALCOLM R. KINNEY

Essentials to observe when planting are:

1. Prevent roots from drying by working quickly, and avoid laying out more than half a dozen plants or so at a time if their roots are bare.

2. If roots are bunched by packing, loosen them and spread them in their natural position.

3. Make the hole large enough to contain the roots without crowding.

4. See that the plants are set at the same depth as they were when growing in their previous positions—in general, this will mean that the junction between roots and stems is at, or barely beneath, the surface of the soil.

5. Spread the roots in the hole naturally. In some species the roots tend to spread horizontally, but in general they should point downward, never toward the sky.

6. Work the soil among and over the roots, then make it firm either with the feet or hands. This is important in order to bring the moist soil in close contact with the roots and, in the case of fall planting, to minimize the danger of heaving owing to alternate freezing and thawing in winter.

7. Do not attempt to do the job when the soil is so wet that it is sticky. Under such conditions it is difficult to work the soil in between the roots. Furthermore the inevitable tramping around and making the soil firm over the roots may puddle it, thus injuring the soil structure.

SPECIAL TECHNIQUES—CHRYSANTHEMUMS AND MICHAELMAS DAISIES

Hardy Chrysanthemums almost invariably produce too many shoots for a good garden display. The plant pictured on facing page was set out in June as a single-stem rooted cutting. It was potted in the fall and carried over on an enclosed but unheated porch. Now it is a clump about a foot across, containing over fifty growth shoots. All of these shoots can be used for propagation purposes, but usually in the home garden enough plants can be obtained by using only the strong, rooted shoots from the outside of the clump. Such plants should be turned out of their pots (or dug up from the open ground) and enough of the strongest shoots with roots attached

("Irishman's cuttings"!) should be pulled off and planted a foot apart directly in the garden. It is a good idea to pull off and pot up in 3- or 4-inch pots a few more than are actually needed, just in case some of those set directly in the garden fail to "take." If these are not needed for filling in the garden, they can be set out in a row in the vegetable garden to be dug up in the fall and used as fillers, or they can serve as cut flowers.

LEFT. Chrysanthemum dug from open ground in the fall, carried over winter in a pot. RIGHT. Turned out of its pot, the Chrysanthemum clump is converted into "Irishman's" and unrooted cuttings. MALCOLM R. KINNEY

Although Hardy Chrysanthemums will bloom the first year from cuttings even when set out as late as mid-June, better or more vigorous plants can be produced from rooted shoots or cuttings started early and planted out in early spring. (For method of rooting cuttings, see chapter on propagation.)

Michaelmas Daisies (Hardy Perennial Asters) also are likely to be more satisfactory if given the same treatment, except that the divisions obtained from the outside of the clumps may contain from two to four shoots. Perennial Asters are subject to a wilt disease carried over within the underground parts of the plants. It is possible that this disease, when present, can be by-passed by making cuttings of the strongest shoots in the fall or spring and destroying the old clumps by burning. This is predicated on the assumption that the disease grows more slowly than the shoots, and that tip cuttings can be taken before the disease has reached up into them. These cuttings should be inserted singly in 3-inch pots containing a sifted mixture of equal parts soil, sand, and peat moss. If they can then be plunged in sand in a cold frame heated by subsurface electric cable, rooting will be facilitated. Rooted cuttings or divisions of the larger-growing Asters should be set 3 feet apart; 2 feet will be enough for those of moderate growth.

Japanese Iris: example of excellent division ready for planting.
BROOKLYN BOTANIC GARDEN

Among the plants which are benefited by division every three or four years are Siberian and Japanese Irises, which can be divided in the spring, though there are many gardeners who prefer to do so in September; Armeria and Heuchera, whenever the centers of the clumps have dead areas, or when the latter seems to be pushing itself out of the ground; Phlox, Shasta Daisy, Blue Salvia, and others whose centers have become worn out—all of these and many others can be divided to advantage in spring or fall. In all cases the best way is to dig up the entire clump and make divisions containing from three to nine growth shoots. This is done, not by chopping the

Large Coreopsis clump dug with spading forks. MALCOLM R. KINNEY

Same plant is divided for replanting; two forks back to back aid in separating clump. MALCOLM R. KINNEY

New planting division is set in hole accommodating roots and white underground stems from which new top growth comes. After filling in the soil, plant is gently shaken to settle earth around roots and tramped firm.
MALCOLM R. KINNEY

clump into pieces with a spade, which destroys many of the roots, but by pulling it apart either with the bare hands or, in the case of toughies, by sticking two spading forks, back to back and close together, into the clump and prying it apart. Always select the strong, vigorous pieces from the outside of the clump for replanting and reject the worn-out centers. Whenever possible, improve the soil before replanting by digging in a 2-inch layer of rotted manure or compost prior to resetting. Do not allow the roots to dry out; cover the dug-up clump with moist soil while the planting site is being prepared; and when the divisions have been made, do not waste any time planting them. First consolidate the soil by tramping, then dig a hole large enough to contain the roots spread out naturally, set plant in place, cover the roots with soil, and make it firm.

Plants which resent root disturbance and those which may take ten years or longer to attain their peak should not be moved now or at any time unless absolutely necessary. These include Christmas-rose, Gas-plant, Platycodon, and Peony. Others for which spring division is not desirable include early-blooming plants, such as Chinese Forget-me-not and Rock-cress. Also avoid disturbing Bleeding-heart, Leopards Bane, Oriental Poppies, Bearded Iris, and Virginia Cowslip, which are best attended to during midsummer.

DORMANT PLANTING AT MIDSUMMER

Although August is not the prime transplanting month for most perennials, there are a few that are more nearly dormant then, and, therefore, transplantable with less injury than at any other season except perhaps during the depth of winter when it is not practicable to do it. Pre-eminent in this group are varieties of the Oriental Poppy, *Papaver orientale*. The foliage of these dies down about midsummer and, when the leaves are sere and brown, it is time to transplant and divide if necessary. Because they are deep-rooting, it is desirable to dig deeply—18 inches or so—for two reasons: (1) to get as much of the root as possible; (2) to avoid leaving any pieces of root behind which might grow into new plants and cause embarrassment.

If it is just a case of moving a plant in its entirety to a new location, all that is necessary is to dig a hole wide enough and deep enough to accommodate the roots at the same depth they were before, put them in place, and shovel soil around them to within 3 inches of the surface; and then pour on water to fill the hole. This last serves a double purpose: that of washing and settling the soil among the thonglike roots; and of ensuring that it is adequately moist. When the water has drained away, the remaining soil should be used to fill the hole. If the clump is crowded, it should be divided into pieces containing from one to three crowns by pulling them apart or cutting with a sharp knife and gently disentangling their roots. Unless they are needed to increase one's stock or be given away, any surplus weak crowns should be discarded. Planting is the same as with an undivided plant, setting them with the crowns 3 inches below the surface.

Bleeding-heart, *Dicentra spectabilis,* which has much the same ungainly roots as the preceding, can be handled the same way. Unlike the Oriental Poppies, however, it can be transplanted with little setback in the spring, even after growth has started. Any good crowns that are left over after late-summer transplanting can be potted, stored in a cold frame until January, and then brought indoors to a cool room or greenhouse (50 to 60 degrees). There they will quickly develop their handsome divided foliage and bloom—if you can keep the room cool.

Others of the early "diebacks" are species of Leopards-bane (Doronicum), which can be transplanted to advantage in August if it is necessary to change their location. If they have been undisturbed for three or more years, they should also be separated, setting the divisions about 8 inches apart in groups of at least three. Any strong surplus divisions can be potted and forced indoors as suggested for Bleeding-heart.

The Virginia Bluebell, *Mertensia virginica,* seems to resent root disturbance and hence should not be divided. If for any reason an established clump has to be moved, probably the best time to do it is in August, while it is dormant. Dig it up carefully, trying to get all the roots. It is a good plan to soak the soil thoroughly a day ahead of the operation to improve one's chances of being able to move the clump with an intact ball of soil around the roots.

Although there are many who practice division and replanting of Bearded Irises in June or July, it is perfectly feasible to do the job in August. Actually I once planted a large collection as late as early November and got by—with a respectable show of bloom the following year. But summer planting is preferable because then they make a new root system before cold weather, with consequent less likelihood of "heaving" owing to alternate freezing and thawing in winter. There is some difference of opinion among Iris specialists concerning the correct depth at which to set the rhizomes. One school says that the rhizome should ride in the soil with its top visible, like the back of a duck in water; another says to cover it with an inch of soil, which last is generally preferable. But, when soft rot is prevalent, or if the soil is heavy, the semi-submerged method should be chosen.

STEPS IN
DIGGING UP,
DIVIDING, AND
REPLANTING
BEARDED IRIS

Clump is dug up with
spading fork.

Two and three growth
divisions are separated
from clump.

Old flowering shoot is
cut off.

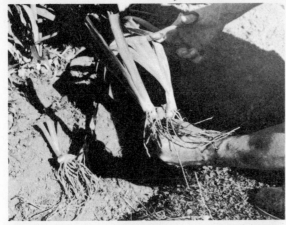

Leaves are trimmed back with shears.

Method of making hole for planting rhizome.

PHOTOGRAPHS: MALCOLM R. KINNEY

LEFT. Planting rhizome on ridge with roots dangling into hole on either side.
RIGHT. Soil is filled in all around and made firm by tramping.

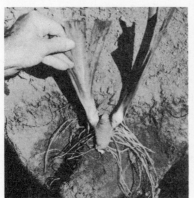

A good technique when planting these Irises is to make the hole for the roots by thrusting the blade of a spade about half its depth in the soil, making a small hole, and then doing the same from the opposite side, leaving a ridge of soil in the center just below the grade. On this ridge the rhizomes of the Irises are set with the roots dangling on either side. The soil is then filled in over the roots and firmed by tramping. (See pictures on pages 74 and 75.)

There are two bulbous plants in particular for which August is the preferred month for planting. These are the Madonna Lily (*Lilium candidum*) and the Crown Imperial (*Fritillaria imperialis*). In the case of new plantings the bulbs should be set in the ground as soon as you can prevail on your dealer to send them to you: the Lily because it is its habit to develop a basal tuft of leaves in the fall, and the Fritillaria because the bulbs seem to deteriorate if kept long out of contact with the soil.

Most gardeners are rightly reluctant to disturb an established clump of Madonna Lilies; but when they become so crowded that the blooms deteriorate in number and size, separation and replanting are in order. This should be done as soon as the leaves and stems become brown (Elwes says, "within five weeks after flowering"), digging them up with the roots attached and replanting with no more than 2 inches of soil over the top of the bulbs, spacing them about 8 inches apart. If the soil is very acid, mixing ground limestone with it at the rate of half a pound per square yard will be helpful. The Crown Imperial needs a rich soil, and deeper planting than the preceding. It is a good plan to remove the topsoil to a depth of 6 inches from the planting area; spread a 2-inch layer of rotted manure in the hole, dig it under, make soil firm by tramping. Then set the bulbs, and cover with the soil initially removed.

Of the plants mentioned above only Iris, Madonna Lily, and Oriental Poppy are commonly offered for sale by commercial people at the ideal time for planting, so, as far as the rest are concerned, the counsel of perfection is applicable only when replanting from existing clumps in your own garden.

Peony clumps usually increase in size and beauty for many years after they are planted. There may come a time, owing to depletion of nutrients in the soil, when the flowers diminish in size and quantity. When this happens, it is time to dig up, divide the clump, and either improve the soil or start in a new location. Late in September

Madonna Lilies can be transplanted with the least injury during August.

PHOTOGRAPHS:
STEENSON & BAKER

Bulb which has divided into two is separated by pulling apart with hands.

While some Lilies thrive when bulbs are planted deeply, Madonna Lily bulbs should have no more than 2 inches of soil above them.

STEPS IN
DIGGING UP,
DIVIDING, AND
REPLANTING PEONIES

Dig up the entire clump with a spade, keeping the latter away from the center to avoid injury to the crown. Shake off the soil or wash it off with a stream of water from the hose. Pointed whitish knobs which appear in the photograph above are the growth "eyes" from which will come next year's stalks. *They must not be injured.*

Some three- to five-eye divisions can be pulled off with the hands; others must be cut apart. Soil removal enables you to see what places to cut.

PHOTOGRAPHS: R. A. SMITH

A four-eye division set in hole. It is essential that the soil beneath the roots be firmly tamped (to prevent future subsidence) and that none of the eyes is more than 2 inches below the surface. The angle at which photograph was taken makes one eye seem to be deeper than the recommended 2 inches.

When the right depth for the clump has been determined, fine topsoil is worked in between and over the roots so as to be in full contact with them. Tramping will then pack the whole thing firmly and eliminate all of the sub-surface air pockets which would handicap plant. Cut off stalk stubs.

is a good time to do this. Dig up the plant, remove the soil from the roots (wash it off with water from the hose if necessary), and with a strong knife carefully cut the rootstock apart into pieces each having from one to five eyes, the number depending on whether you want to increase your stock. The divisions should be replanted immediately in stations prepared by digging a hole 2 by 2 feet. Mix rotted manure with half the soil removed, put it in the hole, and tramp it down firmly. Then put in an inch or two of unmanured soil, set the division in place, the eyes not more than 2 inches below the finished grade. Then fill in the soil around the roots and as you are doing it mix a couple of handfuls of bonemeal or 5-10-5 fertilizer with the soil in such a way that it is not in contact with the roots. If the soil is acid (below pH6), mix pulverized limestone with it to bring it up to the neutral point, which is pH7. Sometimes it is difficult because of the nature of Peony roots to work the soil properly in among and around them. In such cases necessary firmness and intimate contact between soil and roots can be achieved by putting in only enough soil to cover the eyes barely, and then pour in a couple pails of water. When the water has drained away, the remainder of the soil can be filled in.

So much for dormant planting in spring, midsummer, and fall. When it is a matter of transplanting actively growing plants during summer months, it is necessary to take certain precautions.

PLANTING ACTIVELY-GROWING PLANTS

First, unless nature has helped out with a good rain, the soil around the roots must be thoroughly soaked with water. Do this the day before, so as to avoid having to work with muddy soil. Next, in the new location, dig a hole of adequate size and the shape of the root ball, and put the soil removed in a wheelbarrow. (The size of hole needed can be estimated fairly accurately after one or two trial runs have been made.) Make the slant of one side of the hole to correspond to the angle at which the spade is thrust into the ground when digging up the transplant. To insure getting an unbroken ball of earth when digging the plant, thrust the spade vertically to its full depth into the soil on three sides of the clump to be moved. Remove the spade by pulling it out without disturbing the soil. Then, on the untouched side, again push the spade into the ground and bear down on the handle, which will lift out intact a squarish "ball" of

First step in moving a *blooming* Phlox clump is to soak the ground around the base the preceding day. Cut around the root area with a clean, sharp spade to loosen the plant. MALCOLM R. KINNEY

The clump to be moved is lifted on the spade and lowered into a previously prepared planting hole sufficiently large to accommodate the root mass. Earth removed from the new hole has been put in wheelbarrow to use in filling the original hole. MALCOLM R. KINNEY

roots and soil (see photo above). Carry the plant on the spade to the previously prepared hole, place the back of the spade against the slanting side of the hole, raise the handle to vertical, pull out the spade, and make the soil firm around the roots by tramping on it. The soil removed in making the hole can be wheeled around to fill that from whence came the clump.

When the clump is too large to permit the use of this technique, make a trench three quarters of the way around the clump, exposing some of the outer roots; thrust the spade in the soil of the undisturbed area, bear down as described previously, and carry the ball on the spade to the new location (see photo on facing page). It is wise to wait until the dormant season to move any clump that is too heavy to handle in this way.

STEPS IN MOVING AN ACTIVELY GROWING PHYSOSTEGIA PLANT

A large clump is prepared for moving by opening a spade-width trench three fourths of the way around the root ball. Once this space is cleared around the root mass, it is easy to dig up the plant. MALCOLM R. KINNEY

Physostegia is planted in a hole previously prepared for it and liberally watered. Note that the shoot tips are already wilting as a result of moving. MALCOLM R. KINNEY

Not a bridal veil! Old window curtain provides shelter from sun and wind to minimize transplanting shock. Overnight the wilting (as seen at left) disappeared. MALCOLM R. KINNEY

When planting is finished, give a thorough soaking with water (see photo on page 81), and if the plant wilts, as did the Physostegia, put a stake in the center of the clump and drape it with cheesecloth or, as I did, use a discarded glass curtain (see photo on page 81). Although this plant looked very ill a half hour after the transfer (notice the drooping shoot tips in photo on page 81 left), it was entirely recovered by the following morning and went on from there to give a normal display of flowers.

Young plants of Viola, English Daisies, and Canterbury Bells can be transplanted with a strong trowel, otherwise using the same techniques as outlined above.

Unseasonable plantings of this kind should be attempted only in the case of plants which have a compact and fibrous root system. Examples are the Phlox and Physostegia pictured here, taken from a reserve planting in the shrubbery border to fill vacancies in the flower garden. Among other amenable plants are: Astilbe, Chrysanthemum, Canterbury Bells, Coral-bells, English Daisy, Globe-flower, Kniphofia, Pansy, Plantain-lily, Primula, and Viola.

CHAPTER SEVEN

What Can You Expect?

This chapter is somewhat of the nature of an intermission, seeing that it consists in the main of a report of what happened in the case of the garden planned and planted to provide illustrative material for this book.

As we have seen under some circumstances it is possible, by a combination of fall, spring, and summer planting, to complete the making of a perennial garden so that it is in full working order during the first growing season. For example: when there are no extensive changes of grade to be made, beds or borders can be prepared early in September and, allowing a month or so for the soil to settle, a major part of the planting can be done in October, leaving only the late-blooming plants, such as Chrysanthemum, Japanese Anemone, Mist-flower, Ceratostigma, and so on for planting the next spring.

But, in the case of this particular perennial garden, for several reasons it was considered undesirable to do this. You may remember that considerable grading was necessary, and the fill varied from none at all to 3 feet. Because of the difficulty of obtaining help it was not possible to get the garden ready for planting until the middle of May, even though grading was started two months earlier. Therefore, it was decided to put in a temporary planting only, deferring until the fall the making of the truly perennial garden. The reasons back of this were: there was some doubt as to the amount of settling that would occur in the filled areas, which might require another partial regrading later; and it was too late to plant some of the perennials for their best welfare.

The chronological story of what was done goes something like this: at the end of April, before the lawn area was graded, single plants of seven or eight Phlox varieties were set out to get a line on their color and behavior; also, several varieties of Dianthus and Viola were planted for the same purpose, together with Heliopsis Summer Gold, Rudbeckia Goldsturm, Delphinium Rose Pink Sensation, White Liatris, and others. On May 15 a few previously ordered perennials arrived and were planted. These were largely kinds new to me in this location, and were set out for the purpose of giving an inkling on what their behavior might be in this soil. Included among these were White Bleeding-heart; *Penstemon grandiflorus* and P. Pink Sprite; *Thalictrum Rochebrunianum;* various Violas; Fringed Loosestrife (*Steironema ciliatum*), Southern Turtle-head, Pyrethrums in variety, and Shasta Daisies. Then there were some old stand-bys that happened to become available, including Chrysanthemums and Hybrid Delphiniums.

The mixed border makes a sturdy show. This view shows top of low retaining wall. STEENSON & BAKER

AUTHOR'S
PERENNIAL
GARDEN
IN ITS FIRST YEAR
—EARLY FALL

View of entire garden looking south, one month later.

PHOTOGRAPHS: MALCOLM R. KINNEY

Another view—mostly annuals.

About a week later seeds of annuals—Cleome Helen Campbell, Celosia Purple Plume, Cosmos Fiesta, Zinnia Persian Carpet, and Scabiosa Coral Moon—were sown in the curved beds, in which practically no perennials had been planted. Instead of broadcasting the seeds in the usual way, they were planted three or four in a clump in stations representing their final positions. This allowed me to eliminate much hand weeding by hoeing in between the clumps, each of which was marked with a small piece of wood shingle. The seedlings, when large enough, were thinned out to leave only one at each station.

When all this was done, the planting was still sparse, but I had no chance to do anything about it until the second week of July. Then I visited a nearby florist and bought up for little or nothing a sufficiency of his remainders of annuals—plants such as Marigold and Petunia, and a few bedding plants of Heliotrope, Begonia, and Pelargonium to fill in the vacant spots.

Chrysanthemums in bloom viewed from opposite side of garden from preceding page. MALCOLM R. KINNEY

Close-up of groups of annuals and perennials: front, Marigold, Armeria, Heliotrope, Chrysanthemum; middle, Coleus, Delphinium; rear, Chrysanthemum. MALCOLM R. KINNEY

On the whole the results were good. I was able to decide that some of the Phlox varieties were wanting in some respect, and these were discarded. I came to the conclusion that the Turtle-head and Fringed Loosestrife would be more useful along the wild-flower path, and they were so moved. The good behavior of Heliopsis Summer Gold, Rudbeckia Goldsturm, and Viola Royal Purple, to mention only a few, indicated that they were worthy of prominent places in the permanent planting.

There were flowers from May onwards; by the end of August the garden looked well furnished, and during the early part of October it was a blaze of color. On October 15 everything was reluctantly but ruthlessly ripped out so that the garden could be planted in accordance with Plans 5, 6, in Chapter Five. This "slum" clearance was not a complete loss, however. The Chrysanthemums were "flatted" and put in the cold frame to provide planting stock for next year; other perennials were used as temporary fillers in the shrub planting surrounding the garden; and the Veterans' Hospital at Castle Point benefited by armful on armful of beautiful cut flowers.

The following year was its first year as an "all-perennial" garden, and I am glad to report that it was as successful as it could be under the circumstances. Of course you cannot expect the perennial garden to be at its best the first year. Some of the plants so hopefully set out, especially if they are purchased from a distant nursery, will fail to grow, leaving gaps which must be filled. Some will grow too vigorously and prove to be too large for the space assigned them. Others will fall short of perfection either because they are kinds which are slow to recover from transplanting injury or because your particular soil and location do not suit them, or because they were planted at the wrong season. Inevitably there will be some that are unfortunately placed as to color; and you'll notice some that could be more effectively placed in another part of the garden. All of these factors operated in connection with our perennial garden.

The hazards of travel proved too great for Iceland Poppy. Both the original shipment, more than a week in transit, and the replacement received the following spring failed to survive even though they were good plants carefully packed and planted. I believe the only way to succeed with Iceland Poppies is to raise your own plants from seed or buy them locally. The same is true of Golden-tuft (Alyssum).

Christmas-rose (Helleborus) and the Gas-plant (Dictamnus), notoriously resentful of transplanting, did not make enough growth to be effective.

I attribute the poor growth of Hardy Asters, including Wonder of Staffa, to my failure to practice what I preach—namely, to set out late-blooming plants in the spring. As I described in Chapter Six, there are four main transplanting seasons for perennials: spring for late blooming—Asters and Chrysanthemums; mid to late summer for

Bearded Iris, Oriental Poppies, Madonna Lilies, Leopards-bane, and Virginia Bluebell; early fall (September) for Peonies, Japanese Iris, and Siberian Iris; October and early November for hardy spring-blooming and early summer-blooming plants such as Oenothera, Border Catmint, and Coral-bells. When you are starting a new garden, there is always the temptation to take a chance and finish the job at one crack, but it is better to proceed according to Hoyle.

The Bee-balms, rather surprisingly, failed to make really vigorous growth. Tentatively I attribute this to my dry sandy soil and root competition of nearby Sugar Maples, but time will tell and I shall leave them for another year. On the other hand gray-leaved plants such as Border Catmint and *Veronica incana* have done exceptionally well for themselves, which suggests that I should, another year, include some Blanket-flower (Gaillardia) in the planting—something I should have thought of in the first place.

The Golden Columbine, although it made a good early display, was disappointing in the length of time it remained attractive. Probably it does not get enough sun in its present location, but as I cannot think of anything else I would rather have in its place, it will be allowed to stay another year to give it a chance to improve. Perhaps room will be found in a sunny spot for a few additional plants which might behave better.

Some of the dark-colored flowers—Anchusa and a deep purple unnamed Iris—in the remote curved borders were ineffective when seen from the house. This could be corrected by substituting light blue or white Delphinium for the Anchusa and planting the yellow Iris Elsa Sass in place of the dark-colored variety.

Anchusa seemed to me to grow too large and coarse for this small garden—it could be replaced by *Delphinium belladonna* Cliveden Beauty. An unnamed variety of Coral-bells planted in the front of the border grew to a height of almost 3 feet; it was later transferred in full bloom to a vacancy in the rear of the border. Apparently it never knew it had been moved, for it did not wilt and continued to bloom in its new location. The practice of moving herbaceous plants in bloom or when they are about to bloom can in many cases be done, if necessary, with but little injury to the plants. Phlox and Physostegia used as "fillers" in the boundary shrub planting were so moved in July to take the places of defunct Asters and others as described on pages 80 and 81.

AUTHOR'S GARDEN
IN ITS SECOND YEAR—LATE JULY

ABOVE. Looking north. BELOW. Looking northwest. MALCOLM R. KINNEY

In spite of an abominable growing season the plants and garden in general gave satisfactory performances. This is not the habitual griping attitude attributed to farmers and gardeners—it really was a bad growing season. In these parts the spring was cold and wet with intervening harsh, dry winds. The worst spell of weather came at the height of the Iris season when the flowers became waterlogged and then were ripped to tatters by wind. Then there was a drought in July, which also happened to be the hottest on record in this region. In spite of this there were flowers from the first of April onwards. Crocuses and Glory-of-the-snow were at their best by mid-April; by May 1 the Daffodils were in their prime and Tulips were in bud. Unfortunately a deer, by eating off all the flower buds from a clump of strategically placed Tulips in one of the two curved beds at the rear of the garden, caused the ensemble to look terribly lopsided. Toward the end of May the Tulips, Heuchera, Oriental Poppies, Pyrethrum, and Violas were taking over; to be followed in June by Peony, Peach-leaved Bellflower, and Delphinium. During this period, Heuchera Rosamundi was surprisingly good in color, freedom of bloom, and endurance; and toward the end of the month, Gypsophila Bristol Fairy was performing its function of hiding the ratty and messy Oriental Poppy foliage. In July, Phlox, Heliopsis, Rudbeckia, Platycodon, Carpathian Bellflower provided the highlights, with Helenium, Lobelia, Aster, and Chrysanthemum promising for the future.

But on July 27 disaster struck the garden in the form of a hailstorm of unprecedented virulence. You can see the results pictured on page 92 (compare this with the photograph above). However, Nature is a great healer, and less than two weeks after the storm struck there was evidence of revival. So I was not entirely surprised to see the garden presentable again before the first frost of autumn.

About two hundred additional bulbs of Narcissus were planted in the fall, mainly to liven up the shrubbery screen surrounding the garden. The following year these, plus the natural increase of those planted previously in the garden itself, made a much more effective display. Non-bulbous perennials, too, grew more luxuriantly, so that by summer the garden looked really stable, and the boundary shrub planting was beginning to fill out and become effective. But then trouble came in the form of an unprecedented drought and the ill-starred lawn which the preceding year had been ruined by Japa-

Looking southeast. MALCOLM R. KINNEY

"Look here, upon this picture, and on this . . ." *Hamlet,* III:iv

Same view, twenty-four hours later—complete devastation! (See text, page 91.) MALCOLM R. KINNEY

nese-beetle grubs became almost entirely sere and brown. We heard of wells in the neighborhood drying up which had never been known to fail before, so we did not feel justified in using water for the garden, thinking that if we did, the Frees might have to forgo bathing and drinking. But, even so, thanks to a sprinkling of drought-resisters (see list on page 328) the garden remained presentable; and a good display of Chrysanthemums in the fall, some of them moved in from the reserve garden, restored our spirits.

AUTHOR'S GARDEN
IN ITS THIRD YEAR

Early May—*Doronicum caucasicum, Brunnera macrophylla,* Hemerocallis, Boxwood, *Epimedium niveum.* MALCOLM R. KINNEY

Late May—Iris and Dianthus coming into bloom. MALCOLM R. KINNEY

Late May—Iris, Madonna Lilies in bud, Oriental Poppies in bloom, Dianthus, and Viola. MALCOLM R. KINNEY

Now to answer the question posed as the title of this chapter: "What can you expect?"

In the first place your soil will probably be richer and more retentive of moisture than mine, which is not inherently good, and overlies molding sand so that water passes through it rather too freely. You, if you are unfortunate enough to live in a Japanese-beetle area, will be warned by my experience and grubproof your lawn at the time it is made, instead of taking a reckless chance as I did. And the chances are that you will not be subjected to two seasons of drought (if you are, your watering facilities will likely be better than mine) and a disastrous hailstorm. So don't be deterred by my tale of partial woe, because I am sure that you will get great satisfaction from your perennial garden, as I did, in spite of hail and no water. Of course there will be some setbacks: if there were none, gardening and life, in general, would be intolerably humdrum.

CHAPTER EIGHT

Edgings—Inanimate and Living

In this chapter we shall consider the pros and cons of edging materials, primarily as they affect flower beds and borders. The kind of edging to be used is a matter for the individual to decide on the basis of personal preference and the character of the layout.

An inanimate or dead edge as opposed to a living edge is often the best answer to the problem of providing a suitable line of demarcation between flower borders and walks, or lawns and walks.

In the fifteenth century the shank bones of sheep were among the inanimate edges used. These were "stuck in the ground, the small end downwards, which will become white, and prettily grace out the ground." This suggests that our forefathers did not mind a charnel-house atmosphere in their gardens, and that mutton was much more plentiful than it is today.

Other inanimate edges, more practical in these times, include wood, metal strips (zinc, aluminum, or steel), stone or slate flags set on edge, natural uncut rocks, tile, terra cotta, or concrete curbing.

The character of walks is related to the kind of edging used and each must be considered together. Often the edge of the walk itself may provide an effective and practical line of demarcation. This is especially true of concrete walks, the most utilitarian but not necessarily the most beautiful or pleasant to walk upon. However, that "concrete look" can be minimized by adding mineral pigments of the color desired (not more than 5 pounds per 100 pounds of cement, however), and by scoring the surface.

If there is a lawn area on one side, concrete walks should be laid so that they are level with the grade on the lawn side and an inch or two above soil level on the side nearer the flower border. This raised edge may be provided by means of a concrete curb or, preferably, when conditions permit by grading the soil surface to just below the walk. The concrete itself should be 3 inches thick, laid on a cinder foundation or its equivalent about 9 inches deep. Walks of this nature permit plants to grow to the extreme limit of the front of the border because there is no danger of their being lopped off by lawn mowers or clippers. The planting can be either formal with a line of edging plants or informal with a variety of plants some of which deliberately are allowed to encroach on the walk.

Rectangular flagstone walk needs no other edging. GOTTSCHO-SCHLEISNER

Informal brick walk provides own edging. GOTTSCHO-SCHLEISNER

Except for their usually better appearance flagstone or brick walks have much the same qualities and edging potentialities as concrete walks. Flagstone walks may be of cut stone, square or rectangular, laid in either a regular or random pattern; or the stones may be the irregular kind known as crazy paving. The last-named demands a border of similar stones laid on edge to make a really effective edge, either flush with the grade or slightly raised according to circumstances. Flagstones may be set in concrete and grouted with cement, or laid on a dry foundation and the interstices filled with sand.

Brick walks properly laid are both pleasing and effective when suitably located. The edges may be bricks stood on end, or laid edgewise, either set flush with the walk or slightly raised. Like flagstone walks, they may be cemented or laid on a sand bed. Their lack of flexibility (it is difficult to lay a brick walk along a curved line) is their chief defect.

A foundation similar to that suggested for concrete walks is necessary, or at least desirable, for brick and flagstone walks. I have, however, known flagstones to be fairly successful when merely laid on the surface of sandy, well-drained soil.

Although I have seen and admired a garden in which there was no

Gravel walk with no definite line of demarcation. JESSIE TARBOX BEALS

definite line of demarcation between the gravel walk and the flower border, with clumps of Nepeta, Ajuga, and Dianthus occasionally encroaching upon the walk, gravel, cinder, or earth walks, in general, usually need something in the way of edging to prevent commingling of the soil of the border with the gravel of the walk. There is a variety of material available.

One of the most pleasing edgings to a perennial border I have ever seen was of rather blocky rocks of various sizes projecting about 6 inches above the surface and interplanted with easily grown rock plants such as Cerastium, Dianthus, and Veronica. In this case the border was raised about 6 inches above the level of the walk. If a more formal setting is needed, the edging can be metal strips about 3 inches wide held in place by metal stakes, driven at least a foot in the ground, flush with the upper edge of the strip, or paving tiles can be used set on edge with the major portion below ground.

Sometimes tiles are available made especially for edging purposes with the top edge ornamented, often in cable pattern. Usually, however, the less obtrusive the edging material the better is the general effect. Tiles, except perhaps in a frost-free region, will need to be reset periodically owing to heaving as one of the effects of winter. This, of course, could be obviated by putting in a foundation and setting them in concrete. But before doing this, however, be very sure that you will never want to change the location of the walk or the flower border, an exhortation which applies also to builders of concrete, flagstone, or brick walks, if they are laid in cement.

When flower borders have to be made across a slope, usually they are terraced to obtain level areas. In such cases it is often desirable to make the lower edge in the form of a wall from 1 to 3 feet high. This may be of bricks or cemented masonry, or a dry-rock wall may be constructed which offers a splendid opportunity to insert plants in the chinks. When edges of this nature are used, it is desirable to avoid grass walks in their proximity because of the difficulty of using the lawn mower close to the rocks. If for any reason it is necessary to have a lawn coming up close to the rock wall in this way, you are faced with two alternatives, for either you will have to get down on your hands and knees and clip the grass with shears, or you will have to maintain a strip of cultivated ground between the lawn and the wall to permit the use of a lawn mower. Otherwise you will have to reconcile yourself to an untidy mess of long grass.

Walks of tanbark, like those of gravel, need a defining edge except when they are used in a woodland or wild-flower garden. An appropriate edging to keep tanbark in place is wood strips about 3 inches wide and an inch thick held in place by wood or steel stakes. Such an edging can be fairly permanent if wood resistant to decay, such as cypress, is used; or, other lumber treated with Cuprinol. Don't be tempted to use creosote as a preservative, as it is toxic to plant life. If, for any reason, it is desirable to define a walk in a woodland section, slabs (rough outside pieces cut from logs) can be used laid flat with the bark showing. Or you can follow the lead of King George V, who had the Azalea beds in the royal gardens at Windsor bounded by logs about 6 inches in diameter cut to suitable length. However, not everyone has access to material of this kind. Doubtless, too, some would be apprehensive lest the slabs or logs might be hiding places for sowbugs, slugs, and similar vermin. On the other hand such critters are likely to be bothersome in any case and it may be an advantage to know just where they are likely to hang out and apply remedial measures there rather in the vicinity of the plants.

As a lawn edging, either in association with a gravel walk or flower bed, probably the best of all is a metal strip set flush with the grade. Next best is a concrete or stone curb. Never, if you can avoid it, use rough stone or rock edging in conjunction with grass—it is tough on the lawn mower and anathema to the operator.

LIVING EDGES

The use of living plants to make a neat line of demarcation between the walk (or lawn) and flower beds is often preferable to dead edges of wood or stone. Sometimes, however, it has the disadvantage of requiring considerable work in maintenance. Furthermore it must be recognized that living plants are not static and the edge may grow out of bounds to such an extent that complete renovation is the only remedy.

The most commonly seen edging for flower borders is a grass lawn. Strangely enough, though, it is among those which require a great deal of attention to maintain properly. Unless they are carefully watched, perhaps pruned or staked, the flowers lop over and either are chewed up by the lawn mower or smother the lawn grass. When the latter occurs it is a matter of "truing up the edge" in spring or fall either by patching with sods or by expanding the flower border.

A mown grass edging should be at least 2 feet wide to permit easy use of the ordinary, side-wheel-drive lawn mower. You'll find of great help a "trimmer and edger"—a one-wheel mower which cuts a 6-inch swath clear to the turf edge without trespassing on the flower border. A 3-inch metal strip set flush with the lawn grade helps to keep the edge neat and cuts down trimming time (if you can find or pay for the metal).

So much for grass. Among the requirements for a more formal kind of living edge are: winter hardiness for the location, ease of growing, reasonable freedom from pests. Its growth should be naturally compact, and capable of being kept down almost indefinitely by shearing to a height and spread of less than a foot. The cost should be within reason. Among the shrubby evergreens that may be considered, with due respect to climate and other limitations, are the following:

Edging Box (*Buxus sempervirens suffruticosa*) approaches the ideal in regions where it is hardy—climates no more severe than that of Philadelphia. The Korean Box (*Buxus microphylla koreana*) is hardy in Massachusetts. The initial cost is rather high because close planting (4 to 6 inches) is desirable. If you can wait a couple of years, it would be cheaper to acquire a stock plant or two and raise your own. It is easily propagated by cuttings about 4 inches long

Grass edging with Germander along a concrete slab walk.
J. HORACE MCFARLAND COMPANY.

inserted in a shaded cold frame in summer. In England the common method of propagating Edging Box (and of keeping it down to size) is to dig up an established edging (one about 10 inches high) in spring, divide it into rooted pieces, and reset them 4 inches deeper than when previously growing.

Both kinds are naturally compact and slow-growing and if sheared lightly in spring before growth starts and again in summer to shorten new shoots, they may be kept to the desired small size for many years.

Germander (*Teucrium chamaedrys*) is an evergreen subshrub with small oval leaves which, untrimmed, may grow to a height of 10 inches, or more, with rosy-purple flowers. John Parkinson (*Paradisi in Sole, Paradisus Terrestris,* first edition, 1629), in connection with its use for making the "thrids" in knot gardens, says of Germander: "The rootes doe so farre shoote vnder ground, that . . . they will spread into many places within the knot, which if continually they be not plucked vp, they will spoile the whole knot it selfe; and therefore once in three or foure yeares at the most, it must be taken vp and new set, or else it will grow too roynish and combersome."

It might help to prevent it from growing "too roynish" if every year a spade is thrust into the ground alongside the edging to cut off and remove the far-ranging "rootes." This practice, combined with clipping, might, however, reduce its winter hardiness—normally it comes safely through the winter in Massachusetts. Germander was, because of its aromatic qualities, formerly used as a strewing herb and was a reputed remedy for gout. For these reasons it is an exceptionally appropriate edging in herb gardens.

Ivy, either English (*Hedera helix*), Baltic (*H. h. baltica*), the hardiest kind, or the strong-growing Irish (*H. h. hibernica*), is particularly useful in the shade, but can be grown in full sun in sheltered spots where the winter temperatures seldom go below 10 degrees; if shaded from winter sun they can survive 10 or more degrees below zero. The technique of planting is to set pot plants with shoots 2 to 3 feet long so that the tips of one plant reach to the base of the next to make a narrow row. Smaller plants can be used by setting them about a foot apart. The shoots are pegged down to hold them in place. Future care involves prevention of lateral spreading by pruning off wandering shoots. If contiguous to a grassy area, a cultivated strip at least 3 inches wide should be maintained between the grass and the ivy.

Lavender (*Lavandula officinalis*) is an excellent plant for a sunny location in rather poor, well-drained soil provided an ultimate height and spread of a foot or slightly more is not undesirable. In order to keep it from increasing in size too rapidly it should be sheared *lightly* just before growth starts in spring and again at flowering time—either at height of bloom, if the flowers are to be used for sachets, or when the flowers fade. For a low edging Compacta or Hidcote or Nana should be used.

Lavender-cotton (*Santolina chamaecyparissus*), although Rehder assigns this to Zone VII, which extends from southern New Jersey to Tennessee, has been known to survive the winters in Zone V, around Boston. Here again, as in the case of Lavender, a sunny situation and a well-drained, rather poor soil are partially controlling factors. Lavender-cotton is a compact little subshrub with narrow, pinnate leaves, densely covered with whitish wool. I would not dare recommend it for northern states, but for more favored climates it is excellent and, because of its aromatic foliage, it is especially appropriate as an edging in herb gardens.

Pachysandra (*P. terminalis*) is a gregarious plant, never really happy when growing alone. Because of this it is desirable, when planting it as an edging, to set the individual plants 4 inches apart in two or three rows. This, if plants are purchased, may cost about $4.00 or $5.00 a foot, so those whose budget is limited should, as in

Pachysandra and grass with informal flagstones. MALCOLM R. KINNEY

the case of Boxwood, obtain a few stock plants of fairly large size and insert cuttings in a shaded cold frame in August, which will provide rooted plants to set out the following spring. Like English Ivy, it will grow in sun or shade, preferably the latter, and the problem in keeping it to size is one of preventing too much spread. This can be solved by periodically thrusting a spade into the ground alongside the row and heaving out the encroaching underground shoots. Although it can be grown right up to a grass verge or lawn area, it is preferable to keep a narrow strip of cultivated soil between to avoid injury when mowing.

Perennial Candytuft (*Iberis sempervirens*) grows to about a foot when in bloom. Its height can be reduced 6 inches by shearing as soon as the blooms fade; the lateral spread is more of a problem than the height, but can largely be controlled by cutting back after blooming. The variety Snowflake is more compact than the species; Little Gem and Purity grow to about half its size. Although they will grow in half shade, full sun is preferable; hardy in Massachusetts.

Thyme. The Common Thyme (*Thymus vulgaris*) is sufficiently diminutive (about 5 inches tall and 6 inches wide) to be used as an edging plant without the necessity of trimming. Plants should be set 4 inches apart (in a sunny location only) in well-drained, sandy soil, limed, if necessary, to bring it near to the neutral point (pH7). Plants can be raised from seeds, the progeny of which may show some variations; any especially desirable forms can be propagated by cuttings. Although it is supposed to be hardy in Zone V, I have known it to winter-kill in Zone VI to the southward, so do not plunge too heavily until you have tried it on a small scale.

Wormwood. Two species of semi-evergreen, subshrubby Artemisia, are valuable edging plants for dry, rather poor soil in sunny situations. *Artemisia pontica*, Roman Wormwood, has silvery, feathery foliage. Although it is reputed to grow to 4 feet, the form most commonly seen under this name is low-growing, seldom exceeding a foot in height and it may be kept down even more by periodical shearing. A defect is its tendency to spread too exuberantly, but it can be curbed by thrusting a spade into the ground around the edge and digging up and picking out the offending shoots. A. *Schmidtiana nana*, sometimes called Silver Mound Artemisia, grows 4 to 6 inches tall in a mound a foot or more across. Its handsome silvery, finely-divided foliage has a satiny sheen. It can endure zero weather and seems more likely to suffer during open winters with mild weather alternating with moderately cold spells.

Box Barberry (*Berberis Thunbergi minor*) is the only deciduous shrub I can think highly of as an edging plant. This is a reduced replica of the Japanese Barberry, which, by shearing once or twice annually, can be kept down to a height of less than 10 inches for a number of years. It is hardy and, when in leaf, has somewhat the pictorial value of *true* Box.

EDGING WITH HERBACEOUS PERENNIALS

So far we have been dealing chiefly with shrubs and subshrubs. Now let's take a look at some suitable herbaceous perennials. Ideally a herbaceous edging should be evergreen or mostly so, low-growing, robust but not so rampant that curbing it becomes a continuous chore. The plants should be chosen with care to fit the location in respect to sun or shade, and fitted to the size of the border.

Some of these plants are especially valuable where the flower bed is somewhat higher than the walk, with a more or less abrupt slope of a foot or so down to it, because their dense growth and extensive root systems are capable of protecting the soil to prevent erosion. Here are a dozen or so which have most if not all of the qualities mentioned above.

Thrift or Sea Pink (*Armeria maritima*) is a plant whose value for edging has been recognized by gardeners for centuries. It is an evergreen and is especially valuable for sandy soils. It makes a close mound of tufts of grasslike foliage with deep rose flower heads on 6-inch stalks in June. The variety *A. m. laucheana* has brighter, rose-red flowers and is free-flowering over a longer period than the species. Plants should be set 6 inches apart in a row. After a few years dead patches are likely to appear in the clumps; the best way to handle this situation is to dig up the entire edging in the spring and reset it.

Pinks. There are several low-growing species of Dianthus, mostly of the mat-forming kinds, which can be used for edging. Representative of these are Maiden Pink (*D. deltoides*), a green-leafed species; the Cheddar Pink (*D. gratianopolitanus*), better known as

D. caesius, which has glaucous foliage; and the Grass Pink (*D. plumarius*), which has slightly glaucous foliage. All of these species are available in many garden varieties. These Pinks should be set 6 to 9 inches apart according to the size of the transplants. Seed heads of all kinds should be sheared off after flowering and also any shoots which are too wide-spreading. Removal of seed heads is in the interest of neatness and prevention of seeding, which may result in numerous unwanted seedlings.

Alpine Strawberry, *Fragaria vesca.* Those who like to combine beauty with utility may be interested in using one of the varieties of Alpine Strawberry as an edging plant. The best known of these is called Baron Solenmacher, a runnerless kind which grows to a height and spread of 6 to 9 inches. Its foliage is fairly good and it is handsome in flower and fruit. Although it is a perennial, it is desirable to renew the edging every two or three years by raising seedlings so as to keep it young and vigorous.

Moss-Phlox (*P. subulata, P. nivalis,* and hybrids) are the mat-forming Phloxes with mosslike foliage which is obscured by the profuse bloom in April or May. Since the colors of some of the varieties are rather blatant, it is desirable to select plants from a nursery when they are in bloom. Suggested for consideration are the following: Camla, clear pink; Blue Hill, pale blue; Maysnow, white; Vivid, pink with dark eye. Plants should be set in fall or spring about 3 inches apart. Usually it is necessary to dig up and replant every three or four years so as to prevent them from spreading too widely.

Stonecrops. Of the multitudinous species of Sedum there are two that stand out for their value in holding the soil and preventing erosion on a sloping edge. These are S. *hybridum,* with yellow flowers in spring and late summer; and S. *spurium,* which has pink blooms in late June or early July. The more deeply colored forms of S. *spurium* are preferred—*splendens, coccineum,* and Dragons Blood. For quick coverage rooted shoots should be set in a triple row 3 inches apart each way.

Lambs-ears, Bunnies-ears, or Woolly Woundwort (*Stachys lanata*), an old-time favorite, has leaves that are so thickly covered with white wool that the green coloring beneath is almost completely obscured. Small purple flowers on 1½-foot stems are insignifi-

Edging of *Sedum spurium* in author's garden. MALCOLM R. KINNEY

cant, and when the plant is used as an edging, flower stalks might as well be removed before they are fully developed. It is a good-tempered, easily grown plant which quickly fills in if set 8 inches apart.

Mother of Thyme or Creeping Thyme (*Thymus serpyllum*), although technically a subshrub, is a prostrate species ordinarily grouped with herbaceous plants. It forms closely matted clumps which periodically need attention with a spade to prevent them from wandering too far. There are three varieties which are preferable to the species for our purpose: var. *albus*, with dark green foliage and white flowers; var. *coccineus*, with crimson flowers; and the Woolly Thyme, var. *lanuginosus*, which seldom blooms and is grown solely for its gray foliage.

Speedwell. There are two Speedwells well adapted for edging purposes; one, *Veronica incana,* has almost white foliage and 18-inch spirelike inflorescences of blue flowers in June; the other, *V. rupestris,* is a dwarf, tufted plant no more than 6 inches tall with racemes of deep blue flowers. There are also pink and white forms of this variety which I think are inferior to the blue. *V. incana* should be set 9 inches apart and *V. rupestris* 6 inches.

SEMI-SHADE AND SHADE

The Carpathian Harebell (*Campanula carpatica*) will grow in full sun or partial shade. For semi-shady spots compact varieties such as *nana* or Blue Carpet are preferred. These have violet flowers starting in late June; they are at their best in July with scattered bloom until frost. *C. carpatica* may grow to about a foot high and even wider; dwarf forms are about 8 inches high; they should be set from 8 to 12 inches apart.

Epimedium. The Epimediums demand partial shade for best results. They are an exquisite but neglected group, the beautiful spurred flowers developing in early spring along with the pinnate leaves, which have bronze tints in spring and fall; semi-evergreen in favored locations. One of the best is *E. grandiflorum* (*macranthum*) *niveum,* with white flowers, growing to about 1 foot tall. The English name is Barrenwort, which I do not like and therefore do not use.

Bugle. For full or part shade (they also grow in sun) there is probably no better edging plant than one of the Bugle-weeds. *Ajuga genevensis* is preferred over the Carpet Bugle (*A. reptans*) because it is not stoloniferous and therefore can more readily be kept in bounds. Its flowers are bright blue. Set the plants 9 to 12 inches apart in fairly rich soil.

CHAPTER NINE

Aquatic and Water-side Perennials

There may be some who will think that a discussion of water plants is out of place in a book that is mainly about perennials, but most of the plants used to furnish pools and their immediate surroundings definitely are herbaceous perennials, so it seems to me that some mention of them is in order.

While a pool is not an essential part of a perennial garden, it does add a great deal of charm and enables one to grow handsome long-blooming Water-lilies and waterside plants.

The pool should, of course, be adapted to its surroundings—if the garden is formal, the pool should be likewise. Formal pools usually are made of concrete, though brick or stone plastered with cement mortar may be used. If one no larger than 4 x 7 feet will suffice, steel may be used. These last-named are easy to install, needing only the digging of a hole large enough to accommodate the steel lining. It is essential, of course, to make the bottom absolutely level.

Informal pools can be made by merely digging a hole 2 feet deep in the required area with the sides sloping at a 45-degree angle. This is then lined with 6 inches of clay, which must be thoroughly puddled by tamping to make the pool watertight. Or concrete can be used by putting in wire hog fencing for reinforcing, which can be kept off the bottom by an occasional brick laid flat. Use only enough water to make a stiff mix that will not run when put on a 45 degree slope. The concrete must be well tamped and, before it is thoroughly set, it is a good plan to put on a plaster coat of one part cement and two parts sand. In clay-lined pools and usually informal pools, in general, the soil in which the plants are to be set should be spread in a layer 8 inches deep over the bottom. This preferably

Informal pool.
GOTTSCHO-SCHLEISNER

Formal pool with informal planting around coping. Notice water not entirely obscured, thus providing reflecting surface.
GOTTSCHO-SCHLEISNER

should consist of three parts fairly heavy loam and one part thoroughly rotted cow manure. If this is not available, use good vegetable garden soil, adding a 3-inch flowerpot of 4-12-4 fertilizer plus a 3-inch pot of dried blood to each 3 bushels of soil. When planting is completed, smooth the surface soil and cover with 1 inch of sand, which helps prevent the water from becoming muddy.

In formal pools usually it is better to put the soil in boxes, as this is an aid in manipulating the plants and the water is less likely to become roiled. Each box should hold at least a bushel of soil—one 18 x 18 x 7 inches deep will hold slightly over a bushel, and is large enough for one small Water-lily.

Small pools can be filled and emptied (by siphoning) with the garden hose; those in excess of 200 square feet in area should be piped to supply the water and equipped with an overflow and drain.

Hardy Water-lilies may be planted at any time provided there is no ice on the water, but preferably early in the spring. The rhizomes or tubers should be planted horizontally with the growing point even with the surface of the soil and then covered with 1 inch of sand.

SPACING

Much of the charm and value of a pool is lost if the surface of the water is entirely obscured by the leaves of plants. In order to avoid this, it is necessary to avoid planting Water-lilies too thickly. Even the Pigmy Water-lilies may cover a space 3 feet in diameter; and medium-sized ones may reach a diameter of 6 feet.

Suitable varieties for small pools include: Aurora, the flowers of which are yellow tinted with red on the first day, then red-orange, becoming red the third day; odorata minor, white; tetragona, white; tetragona helvola, yellow; and Paul Hariot, yellow changing to pinkish orange to nearly red. All of these are small-growing kinds. Those of medium size suitable for slightly larger pools include: Chromatella, a free-blooming yellow; Escarboule, rich red; Formosa, pink; Gonnere, white; James Brydon, deep pink; and Sioux, coppery yellow to red.

ROUTINE CARE

Once the planting is done, there is very little work for the pond gardener. Weeds are practically nonexistent; insect pests are few.

Aphids occasionally attack the flower buds. A close watch should be kept for these and as soon as they are seen they should be washed off with a spray of water from the hose causing them to fall into the pool where they will provide attractive morsels for the fish. Water-lily foliage is sensitive to insecticides; therefore, their use should be avoided as far as possible. For this reason I recommend hand-picking to get rid of the leaf miners, which occasionally are bothersome.

Yellowing leaves should be removed in the interest of tidiness. A convenient way to do this, to avoid any stooping and stretching and a chance of taking a "header" into the pool, is to lash a sharp paring knife to a bamboo stick. Use this to cut through the petiole below the water line and then to spear the leaf and flick it into a trash basket on the shore.

Green algae sometimes grow in the water and make it look disgusting to some people. Often the water can be kept clean and free of algae by the use of scavengers. These—fish, water snails, clams, tadpoles—can be obtained from water-garden specialists and from dealers in ornamental fish. If this does not suffice, you might try a remedy recommended by G. H. Pring, Superintendent of the Missouri Botanical Garden, which consists of making a solution by dissolving 2 or 3 teaspoons of potassium permanganate in 1 gallon of water, using 1 teaspoon of the solution to each gallon of water in the pool. To determine the number of gallons in the pool, first find the cubical contents—the length, breadth, and depth of the water—convert the answer to cubic feet, and multiply by seven and one half.

PREPARING FOR WINTER

In regions having a mild winter climate where ice is not likely to form more than 2 inches thick nothing need be done in the matter of preparing for winter, but in regions where the water is likely to freeze so deeply that the roots of the plants are endangered it is necessary to take some precautions. The best way to do this in the case of small pools is to bridge the pool with boards and cover them with enough hay, straw or leaves to prevent the water from freezing deeply. When the pool is too large for this, the water should be drained off, the boxes placed close to each other in one corner of the pool and covered with 2 feet, or more if necessary, of dry leaves to prevent the soil from freezing. Put a tarpaulin or roofing paper over the leaves to shed rain which might cause the leaves to mat down into a soggy mass to the detriment of the plants. Whenever possible it is better to carry the plants over winter in Nature's way by a covering of water.

Astilbe—Forget-me-not in foreground. J. HORACE MCFARLAND COMPANY.

WATERSIDE PLANTS

Often in formal pools it is not desirable to clutter up the edge of the pool with other plants, except in those cases when there is a shelf provided for shallow water plants, one constructed inside the pool, where their growth will not obscure the line of the coping. But most informal pools can be improved by planting around them either to aid in hiding an unsightly concrete curb and/or to serve as a background for the pool, or to avoid monotony by variation in the height of plants. A selection of suitable plants follows; others are listed in the Appendix.

Among the hardy low-growing plants which can be planted in shallow water at the edge of the pool are Forget-me-not (*Myosotis scorpioides*), and Floating-heart (*Nymphoides peltatum*), which has small, heart-shaped leaves and abundant 1-inch yellow, fringed flowers. Beware of planting this in a large pool or natural pond, because it is so invasive that it will quickly take possession of the entire water area. It is safe, however, to plant it in a small pool where it can be easily controlled. A good creeping plant which can be set outside of the pool to trail over the edge is Creeping Charley (*Lysimachia nummularia*), a species with rounded leaves and numerous yellow flowers in late spring.

Taller plants which are choice and appropriate for waterside planting include: Astilbe, Filipendula, Hosta; Japanese Iris (*Iris Kaempferi*), Yellow Flag (*I. pseudacorus*), and the Siberian Iris (*I. sibirica*) (see Descriptive List of Perennials); *Lythrum salicaria* (Purple Loosestrife), of which Morden Pink, growing 3 to 4 feet high with deep pink flowers from July to September, is a good garden form. *Hibiscus moscheutos* (Rose-mallow) is a native swamp plant of which there are many giant-flowered garden forms with white, pink, or red flowers. Growing to 5 feet and making bushy plants as much as 4 feet across, they are suitable only for large gardens. Their flowers may be up to 8 inches across. Unfortunately Japanese beetles are fond of their foliage, which must be considered by those who live in areas where these pests are prevalent.

CHAPTER TEN

Fillers and Follow-uppers

ANNUALS, BEDDING PLANTS, BIENNIALS, AND BULBS

Reference already has been made to the desirability of fillers and follow-up flowers, either to take the place of plants which have died or to provide fillers after early bloom has passed. Most desirable subjects for these purposes are annuals, bedding plants, biennials, and tender, summer-flowering "bulbs."

ANNUALS

The way in which these are handled depends somewhat on the facilities available. If you have a greenhouse or even a cold frame, it is possible to start tender annuals and bedding plants—Begonia, Marigold, Petunia, Salvia, Verbena, etc.—under glass and thus gain several weeks of bloom.

The seeds may be started six to eight weeks ahead of the time that outdoor planting is possible. The seedlings should be transplanted singly in 3-inch pots or dirt bands, so that they can be put in their flowering quarters with no setback from root injury. They should be hardened-off to outdoor life by gradually exposing them to air and sun. If planted directly from greenhouse or cold frame without this attention, they are subject to sunburn. When no greenhouse or cold frame is available, plants can be purchased reasonably from florists and commercial garden centers.

There are numerous hardy annuals that can be sown in place, chiefly to follow the spring-flowering bulbs, merely by loosening the surface soil as soon as the foliage of the bulbs begins to wither, using a hand cultivator for the purpose, scattering the seeds, and then patting down the soil. A selection of these will be found listed below.

There are some which self-sow their seeds and, once started, may be expected to come up year after year. In such cases (as with Garden Balsam, Portulaca, and Spider-flower) all that has to be done is to hoe up those which come up where they are not wanted; if needed elsewhere, these misplaced seedlings can be transplanted when they are young if the job is done on a cloudy day when the soil is moist and care is taken to dig them up with as many roots as possible.

Almost any favored annual can be used. Some should be started early under glass to give a long season of bloom; others are best sown in place. Among my favorites are:

Chinese Pink, which may be grown as an annual, but which sometimes may be a short-lived perennial.

J. HORACE MCFARLAND COMPANY.

To start early: Ageratum; Antirrhinum (Snapdragon), a perennial treated as an annual in the north; *Dianthus chinensis Heddewigi* (Chinese Pink); *Helianthus argophyllus* (Silverleaved Sunflower), a tall species suitable for the rear of the border; Petunia, in variety; *Phlox Drummondi* (Annual Phlox); *Sanvitalia procumbens* (Trailing-zinnia); *Tagetes patula* (French Marigold); *Torenia Fournieri* (Blue Wings), good in part shade; Verbena; and Zinnia.

To sow in place: *Celosia plumosa;* Cleome (Spider-flower), Helen Campbell and Pink Queen; Coreopsis, annual species; *Eschscholzia californica* (California Poppy); *Impatiens balsamina* (Garden Balsam); *Lobularia maritima* (Sweet Alyssum), especially Royal Carpet; *Papaver Rhoeas* (Shirley Poppy); and *Portulaca grandiflora* (Rose-moss).

BEDDING PLANTS

Every year when June came around, an old friend used to say to me: "You can say what you like, there is nothing to compare with scarlet Geraniums for dressing up the garden," and I'm inclined to agree with her. The lady, of course, was referring to the House or Florist Geranium (correctly Pelargonium), which does not belong in this chapter at all, seeing that it is technically a tender shrub; but this happens to be the only convenient place to say a few words about how to handle it, so here goes.

Plants grown in pots, preferably in 3-inch size (sometimes it is difficult to plant the larger sizes over bulbs without injuring the latter) can be purchased and set out when danger of frost is past. Sometime in August, if you want to save some to plant the following year, and if you have a sunny window in a cool room where they can be kept over the winter, cuttings can be made. Use terminal shoots cut to 6 inches long, which can be inserted to root in moist sand shaded from the sun. Make a clean cut with a sharp knife through the stem just below the junction of a leaf and remove the lowermost leaf before inserting the stem. The cuttings when rooted should be potted separately in 3-inch pots. Another way of carrying Pelargoniums over the winter, possible only if a moist, frost-free cellar is available, is to dig up the plants in the fall the day before frost is expected and hang them from the cellar rafters. In late winter they should be taken down, cut back to stubs 3 to 6 inches long, and potted in pots just large enough to contain the roots comfortably. They will look very miserable before they are cut back and for a few weeks afterwards, but if the stems are green and succulent, they will come through to produce good-looking plants before it is time to set them out late in the spring.

Other suitable bedding plants include: *Begonia semperflorens* (Wax Begonia); and *Coleus Blumei* (Painted-nettle).

BIENNIALS

These are plants whose life cycle occupies two growing seasons; that is to say they make part of their growth one year, bloom the following year, set seeds to perpetuate their race, and die. Some, however, do not behave according to Hoyle, and thus we have so-called annual strains of Sweet William, Canterbury Bells, and Hollyhock, which bloom the same year if they are sown early; sometimes there are individuals which refuse to abide by their allotted span and linger on as short-lived perennials; and there are others, notably Hollyhock and Sweet William, which may give the impression of being perennial by reason of the fact that they self-sow their seeds, which germinate and come up among the clump. Then, too, there are some plants, such as English Daisies (*Bellis perennis*) and Pansies, which theoretically are perennials, but which under cultivation give better results when they are treated as biennials, and, therefore, the gardener grows them as such.

GROWING BIENNIALS

In most cases this means starting them from seeds annually; ideally in a cold frame with the sash removed and a cheesecloth screen substituted. The seeds may be sown either in a seedbed or a flat; the time of sowing for most of them is June or July, but for Pansies, August is the preferred month. (For fuller discussion of technique for sowing, see Chapter Fourteen—Propagating the Plants.) When the seedlings have made three or four leaves, they are transplanted 3 to 6 inches apart in sandy loam soil, one third of its bulk to a depth of 6 inches composed of leafmold or peat moss thoroughly mixed in. The purpose of this soil mixture is to ensure a friable medium which will promote a fibrous root system, so they can be transplanted without trouble. They are again transplanted late in August or early September either to their flowering quarters in the garden or to a cold frame, depending in part on whether there is a vacancy for them in the garden and partly on whether they are being grown in a region where they need protection during winter.

To some gardeners raising biennials seems to be too bothersome. But Canterbury Bells, Sweet William, and others are so beautiful, and since they bloom at a time during the lull between the early and midseason perennials, they are well worth the extra trouble involved in raising them.

Sweet William, an old-time favorite biennial.
J. HORACE MCFARLAND COMPANY.

Canterbury Bells, one of the showiest of biennials.
J. HORACE MCFARLAND COM-PANY.

Here in tabular form are some of the most important plants grown as biennials.

NAME	HEIGHT	DISTANCE APART	MONTH TO PLANT	MONTH OF BLOOM	REMARKS
Althaea rosea Hollyhock	4–10 ft.	1½–2 ft.	5–8	6–8	Usually perpetuates itself by self-sown seeds.
Bellis perennis English Daisy	6– 8 in.	6 – 9 in.	5–8	4–5	A perennial which is treated as a biennial.
Campanula medium Canterbury Bells	2– 3 ft.	9 –12 in.	6–8	6	Cup-and-saucer varieties have petal-like sepals.
C. medium calycanthema Cup-and-saucer Bells	2– 3 ft.	9 –12 in.	6–8	6	
Digitalis purpurea Foxglove	3– 4 ft.	1 ft.	5–8	6–7	Good for naturalizing in partial shade.
Myosotis alpestris Forget-me-not varieties	6–12 in.	6 – 9 in.	5–7	4–6	Often used among spring-flowering bulbs.
Viola tricolor Pansy	6–12 in.	6 – 9 in.	8	4–6	Liberal use of the flowers for cutting prolongs the period of bloom.

TENDER SUMMER-FLOWERING "BULBS"

There are numerous species and varieties of bulbs, corms, and tubers which cannot endure freezing, which can be used to fill gaps and follow early-blooming perennials. The most important of these are Dahlia and Gladiolus. The hardy summer-flowering bulbs (Lilies) are dealt with in the Descriptive List of Perennials.

DAHLIA

The Dahlia fancier is confronted with a bewildering array of varieties ranging in height from 2 to 6 feet and in flower size from 1 to 12 inches in diameter. The colors are similarly varied and also the form of the flowers—Singles, Anemone-flowered types, Doubles, Formal, and Informal Decorative, Cactus, etc. For our purpose the most valuable kinds are the Miniatures, and Bedding Dahlias (Coltness Gem and Unwin Hybrids), which can be accommodated in a space 2 or 3 feet in diameter and which do not need any special care.

PLANTING STOCK

Dahlias can be planted as tubers, green plants, or seeds. When tubers are used, the old rootstock is divided into individual tubers, each bearing a growth-bud "eye." Cutting is done with a stout, sharp-bladed knife, and all cuts should be dusted with sulphur to prevent the growth of fungi which might cause trouble.

Green plants are obtained by putting the rootstock or a division of it in moist sand at a temperature of 60 degrees, in a sunny window or in a greenhouse. When the shoots are 4 to 6 inches long, they are cut off and inserted in moist sand to root. These rooted cuttings are potted in soil and planted out when danger of frost is past.

Seeds can be started indoors six or eight weeks ahead of the time when frost is no longer expected. Usually it is better to stick to the Bedding Dahlias because the large-flowered, named varieties raised from seeds are likely to be disappointing. The seedlings will develop tubers by the fall and especially good varieties may be dug up and saved over winter by storing the roots in a frost-free place.

TIME AND METHOD OF PLANTING

The time to plant Dahlias in most parts of the United States is from May 15 to June 15. In the South and on the Pacific coast from one to two months earlier is considered a better time.

When planting tubers, dig a hole 1 foot wide and 4 to 6 inches deep; if the plants are to be staked, drive the stake in the hole toward one side before setting the tuber. The tuber should be laid horizontally with the bud end close to the stake and covered with 2 inches of soil; as growth proceeds, the remaining soil is gradually filled in the hole until it is level with the grade. The Bedding Dahlias will need a space 18 inches to 2 feet across, and for the Miniatures it is better to allow about 3 feet.

When setting out green plants from pots, bury the root ball 1 or 2 inches below the surface; when planting out seedlings from flats, plant them down to the first leaf.

GENERAL CARE

Little is needed in the way of pinching and pruning when Dahlias are grown solely for garden display—possibly pinching out the tip of the young shoot when it gets to a length of 8 inches or so is desirable to induce branching. Beyond this all that is necessary is to cut off the faded flowers to prevent seeding and ensure tidiness.

When the foliage has been killed by frost in the fall, the plants may be cut down, the roots dug up and stored in a cool frost-free place for the winter.

GLADIOLUS

By manipulating the time of planting and the use of early, mid-season, and late varieties, it is possible to have Gladiolus in bloom any time from July until frost. (Catalogues of Gladiolus specialists usually give information as to the number of days required from planting to bloom.) By planting them in groups of from five to twenty corms 4 to 6 inches apart it is possible to fill vacant spaces of varying sizes. Furthermore, in view of the comparatively small size of the corms, planting holes can be made with little disturbance to the roots of nearby plants. Then, too, variation in the height of the different varieties from 18 inches to 5 feet enables them to be used either in the foreground, middle, or rear of the border.

PLANTING

In general, corms of medium size, say, about 1¼ to 1½ inches in diameter, are preferred for planting. They may be set out a week or two ahead of the date of the last average killing frost in the locality —usually in New York this is about mid-April—and planting may continue into July. The corms may be set from 4 to 6 inches deep, depending partly upon the size of the corm and partly on the character of the soil—it is possible to set them deeper in sandy soil than in heavy clay soil. When large patches are to be set out, it facilitates matters to loosen the ground with a spading fork prior to planting; otherwise plant them by using a trowel to make the holes. A more pleasing effect is gained if rows are avoided; make the groups irregular in outline and vary the distance between the corms. The insect pest most likely to be bothersome is a species of thrips—a minute, slender insect which causes the flowers to be malformed and blotched with brown. In order to prevent this insect from getting a foothold it is desirable to spray the developing shoots at weekly intervals as soon as they attain 6 inches in height, using a preparation of DDT.

When the flowers fade, they should be cut off, leaving the foliage until it begins to wither, at which time the corms can be dug up, dried, and stored for winter in a cool (50 degrees F.), airy place.

CANNA

The cult of the Canna has fallen on evil days partly as a result of the jibes of the garden-club ladies who say it belongs in the era of mustache cups, shaving mugs, and cast-iron deer. But the Canna has its good points provided it is not displayed filling a circular bed in the middle of the front lawn. Its foliage is bold and handsome, the flowers of the modern varieties are large and showy; so, if you like Cannas and have a gap that needs filling at the rear of the flower border, don't be deterred by uplifted eyebrows, but go ahead and plant a clump of them.

The Canna has a tuberous rootstock which, in the north, is started into growth indoors and the resultant plant set out when danger of frost is past.

CHAPTER ELEVEN

Perennials Outside the Garden

Perennials do not have to be segregated in the garden. Many of them are well adapted to growing under semi-wild conditions (some will actually naturalize themselves) in thin woodland, along a stream, in swamps or dry meadows; and some are excellent for use as ground covers.

A stroll along a woodland walk can be really worth while when it is beautified by clumps of Bloodroot, Foam Flower, Wild Blue Phlox, Moss-Phlox (choose the sunnier spots for this), Dutchmans-breeches, and Columbine. You need not restrict the planting to native flowers. The Eurasian Wood Forget-me-not (*Myosotis sylvatica*), once it is started in a congenial location, can take care of itself and develop into a sheet of clear blue that is sheer beauty. It was this species that started me on my project of naturalizing perennials in the partial shade cast by Sugar Maples. A single plant came up spontaneously—probably a seed happened to be in some soil spilled from a flat of annuals that had been started in the greenhouse. When it bloomed, we were careful to avoid cutting off the flower stalks when mowing in the vicinity, leaving them for seed. The following year there were a dozen plants, all of which bloomed. The original plant blossomed too, in spite of the fact that it is supposed to be an annual or biennial. Another plant which has grown vigorously is the Fringed Bleeding-heart, which comes up here and there from self-sown seeds. This blooms from May to September and has fernlike leaves, and it is with reluctance that we have occasionally to pull it up to prevent it from spoiling less robust plants nearby.

As the season progresses, the tide of bloom is carried on by perennials which are more massive in appearance. Among these are: Day-lilies, notably *Hemerocallis fulva*, which has become naturalized along roadsides over a large part of the East and makes a stunning appearance when in bloom in summer. This has taken over a nearby slope and has to be restrained by mowing around the edges. The Dames-rocket, *Hesperis matronalis*, which was started by scattering a package of seeds in the grass and forgetting about it, now grows to 3 feet every year and its blossoms perfume the surroundings in late spring and early summer. This is a plant which is native to Europe, but which has become naturalized over a considerable portion of eastern North America. The Bugbanes (*Cimicifuga*) are "naturals" for woodland planting. On one occasion I was greatly impressed by Nature's eminence as a landscape architect when I saw a large group of *C. racemosa*, known as Fairy-candles (a much more pleasing name than Bugbane), growing in a wood with a somber background of hemlock. The airy, branched racemes, reaching to a height of 6 feet and clothed with small white flowers, were perfect in their setting. This species blooms in July and August. A related kind, the Appalachian Fairy-candle (*C. americanus*), is not quite so tall and blooms in August and September. Naturally enough I planted some of these, but their behavior has been disappointing. You see, they require a rich, moist soil, which I do not have, and this points up a fact that must be considered by planters, and that is to cut your coat according to the cloth; or, in other words, fit the plant to the kind of location available. The White Snakeroot (*Eupatorium rugosum*), which grows 3 to 4 feet tall and blossoms in late summer and autumn with white flowers, which reminds one of Ageratum, is much happier under these conditions, thriving as it does in poor, dry soil in shade. According to Dr. Wherry, "The foliage contains a poisonous principle which if eaten by cows gets into the milk and may cause a serious, sometimes fatal, human illness." While you are not likely to allow cows to browse in your wildflower garden, I put in this little item in case it might be of interest.

Other appropriate perennials for planting in the woodland include: the Wood Geranium, *G. maculatum* (this is a true Geranium, not to be confused with the tender-to-frost House or Florist Geranium—properly called Pelargonium), which is showy in bloom with 1¼-inch rosy-purple flowers on stalks up to 2 feet tall. The

Early Meadow-rue, *Thalictrum dioicum;* and also the exotic *T. Rochebrunianum,* a Japanese species, which may grow to 6 feet tall with airy, elegant panicles of lavender flowers; Bee-balm, *Monarda didyma,* whose brilliant scarlet flowers are capable of really lighting up a dark corner; Virginia Bluebells, *Mertensia virginica,* delightful in early spring with its pink buds and lavender-blue open flowers. This species resents disturbance, so some thought should be given to its placement to avoid having to move it later.

Virginia Bluebells in thin woodland. MARK NORTON

The Foxglove, *Digitalis purpurea,* although usually biennial in habit, is appropriate and fairly easy to naturalize; *D. lutea* (Straw Foxglove), a true perennial, with creamy or yellow flowers, is another possibility.

STREAM-SIDE PLANTING

Ordinarily I am not wildly enthusiastic about Plantain-lilies except for the fragrant late-blooming, white-flowered *Hosta plantaginea,* often sold as *Funkia grandiflora,* but some years ago I saw a planting of various species of Hosta which excited my admiration. They were disposed along a tiny meandering brook in part shade, a cultural factor which made them so happy that they were really beautiful. By selecting early, midseason, and late species it is possible to have bloom from late spring until the fall. (See Descriptive List of Perennials beginning on page 191.)

Other plants which grow happily when planted along a stream are: Marsh-marigold (*Caltha palustris*), whose brilliant yellow buttercup-like flowers are among the harbingers of spring; Astilbe, sometimes erroneously called herbaceous Spirea, which can thrive only when grown in constantly moist soil. Then there are two native species of Lobelia that are available for stream-side planting. One, the Cardinal Flower (*L. cardinalis*), is cantankerous and may fail to thrive unless it is given an acid, humusy soil (pH5 to pH6) and ample moisture. If your soil does not meet these specifications, it can be modified to conform by mixing acid peat moss about half and half with the upper 6 inches of soil. This species, with its brilliant, pure red flowers in spirelike racemes, is worth a little trouble. Cut it back before its seed matures, and it is more likely to remain perennial. The Great Blue Lobelia (*L. siphilitica*) is an easy doer, but its flowers, though pleasant, are not so showy as the preceding. It will grow in a soil that is slightly acid to neutral.

The Yellow Flag Iris (*I. pseudacorus*) is a species native to Europe and has run wild in parts of the eastern United States. It has handsome foliage and yellow flowers in summer, but it should be planted only with the understanding that it is invasive and may monopolize the entire stream-side unless the fading flowers are picked off to prevent seeding. The Siberian Iris is less rambunctious and more beautiful; the Japanese Irises, while they delight in wet feet, are so flamboyant that care must be exercised to plant them only where they will not be out of keeping with the rest of the plantings.

Of low-growing plants that can be planted at the water's edge there are two that are outstanding—the true Forget-me-not of romance and literature (*Myosotis scorpioides*), and Creeping Charley (*Lysimachia nummularia*). While the last-named is pretty with numerous yellow flowers and never grows more than a few inches tall, it is a great invader and is almost impossible to kill, and this should be taken into account—do not plant it where its vigorous spreading habits are likely to cause trouble in the future.

FOR WET GROUND IN FULL SUN

Perhaps you have a wet spot in the open that cannot conveniently be drained, and, therefore, is unavailable for the general run of garden flowers. Sometimes Nature takes care of such situations by planting Purple Loosestrife, Rose-mallow, and Blue Flag Iris. If, however, there is nothing growing there but colorless sedges and grasses, you might be pleased to introduce some of all of the above. Additional species which will grow in wet locations include: Joe-Pye Weed (*Eupatorium purpureum*), which is a variable species— some individuals being much more effective as garden plants than others. I would suggest that it would be worth while to take a trip to neighboring swamps at the time they are in bloom to pick out a desirable form. Don't forget to throw a spade and a pair of rubber boots in the car—you will probably need these. Then there are Goats-beard (*Aruncus sylvester*); the Irises previously mentioned; Queen-of-the-prairie (*Filipendula rubra*); and Globe-flowers (*Trollius europaeus* and *T. asiaticus*).

FOR POOR, DRY SOIL

If your property happens to be part of an abandoned farm, there is likely to be some submarginal land where nothing grows but Poverty Grass. Such a plot can be made more interesting by planting a group here and there of enduring plants such as the following: Butterfly-weed, *Asclepias tuberosa,* with brilliant orange-yellow flowers in summer. This resents root disturbance and, therefore, is not easy to establish unless it is raised from seeds, which should be planted two or three in a 3-inch pot; when the seedlings are 3 or 4 inches high, transplant them without disturbing the roots.

A good companion is the Eastern Lupine (*Lupinus perennis*), 1 to 2 feet tall with lavender-blue flowers. This is perhaps even more difficult to transplant successfully than the preceding, and the best way to establish it is to gather seeds when they are barely ripe and plant them immediately in the place where they are to stay. Chances of success are greater if some soil taken from near the roots

Bleeding-heart, Foam Flower, and Wild Blue Phlox grow well in partial shade. GOTTSCHO-SCHLEISNER

of the parent plant is incorporated in the planting station to provide the right kind of nitrogen-fixing bacteria for this species.

Other desirable species which can endure poor, dry soil include: False Indigo (*Baptisia australis*), Blanket-flower (*Gaillardia aristata*), and the White or Flowering Spurge (*Euphorbia corollata*), a native perennial, 2 to 3 feet tall. The flowers with conspicuous white lobes are produced in umbels.

Perennial Candytuft on rocky outcrop. MALCOLM R. KINNEY

ROCKY OUTCROPS

Rocky outcrops, while not adapted to general gardening, can be embellished by a suitable planting of perennials. Study the picture on page 131. This area, when a mess of brambles and Japanese Honeysuckle was cleaned off and the soil enriched with manure, made an almost ideal spot for planting of Polyanthus Primroses; notice, too, the planting at the base of the large rock, page 131; here Tulips, Perennial Candytuft, Fringed Bleeding-heart, Coral-bells, Speciosum Lily, and Plumbago provide blooms from spring to fall.

GROUND COVERS

Two of the most valuable ground covers are Trailing Periwinkle (*Vinca minor*) and Japanese Spurge (*Pachysandra terminalis*), which usually are looked on as herbaceous perennials even though, technically, they are subshrubs. The Periwinkle is an admirable plant, with its bright green foliage throughout the year and its clear blue flowers in the spring. In order to secure quick coverage, plants should be set about a foot apart each way. They will grow in sun or shade.

The Japanese Spurge is grown almost solely for the beauty of its lush green leaves. Its flowers are insignificant, but it does occasionally produce a few fruits which are white, looking like gigantic Mistletoe berries. These, while interesting, are not produced in sufficient abundance to be a factor in the decorative scheme. This is a gregarious species and for best results should be planted fairly close —say from 6 to 9 inches apart. Another interesting and beautiful ground cover is the Allegheny Spurge (*Pachysandra procumbens*), which is native in the mountains of Kentucky, West Virginia, and southward. The difficulty in this case is finding a source from which to obtain planting stock—it is another of those cases of a prophet being without honor in his own country, for very few nurserymen sell it. If you do find it possible to get stock for planting, you will be pleased with its abundant flowers, produced on upstanding spikes, the conspicuous parts of which are thick white stamens, coming before the new leaves start in the spring. Some authorities (with whom I agree) say that this is a herbaceous perennial—others call it a subshrub.

There is no doubt whatever about the herbaceous nature of Bugle and Lily-of-the-valley. The first-named is available in two species— *Ajuga genevensis* (the Alpine Bugle); and the Common Bugle (*A. reptans*), both having several garden varieties, differing in color of flowers and in leaf characters. The Alpine Bugle is perhaps the more showy in bloom with the flowers carried in spikes up to 12 inches. The Common Bugle spreads vigorously and is more valuable when quick coverage is required. Flowers of the variety most commonly grown are purplish blue; *A. r. atropurpurea* has blue flowers and bronze colored leaves. The Bugles will grow in sun or shade, in wet or dry soil, though they prefer middle-of-the-road conditions.

Lily-of-the-valley will quickly cover a large area if planted in congenial, moist soil plentifully supplied with humus. Or it will thrive in full sun if planted in deep, moisture-holding soil, but it is naturally a woodland plant and appreciates partial shade.

Tulip, Candytuft, Fringed Bleeding-heart, Coral-Bell, Speciosum Lily, and Plumbago at base of rock.

Narcissus naturalized near barn. PHOTOGRAPHS: MALCOLM R. KINNEY

NATURALIZED BULBS

And we must not forget the possibility of naturalizing the hardy bulbs, both spring- and summer-blooming. Pre-eminent among the spring-flowering bulbs are various Narcissi (see pictures on page 131); these will thrive in full sun or in the shade of deciduous trees. Others that can be used effectively are: Snowdrop; Grape-hyacinth; various species of Scilla, including the Siberian Squill (*Scilla sibirica*), the first to bloom, followed by the English Bluebell (*S. nonscripta*) and the Spanish Bluebell (*S. hispanica*). For summer bloom the native Meadow Lily (*Lilium canadense*), the American Turks-cap (*L. superbum*), and the Tiger Lily (*L. tigrinum*) are available.

Narcissus, Peeping Tom, with fading double-flowered Snowdrop in foreground.
MALCOLM R. KINNEY

It demands considerable skill and imagination to indulge in this kind of gardening and have the results look right. Eschew gardenesque plants—those with double flowers, and kinds which have been highly developed by the plant breeder. Avoid anything in the nature of formal beds and make your plantings in informal groups so that they look at least semi-natural. My own plan when planting them is to dig up an irregular planting area to kill off the existing vegetation. The weeds are kept down during the first season, after which the plants are expected to take care of themselves, except perhaps in some cases when an occasional scything around them is indicated —just enough to enable the subjects to be more plainly seen.

There are many other perennials available for these purposes. If you are interested you should experiment, paying particular attention to native plants.

CHAPTER TWELVE

Routine Care

This starts as soon as the frost is out of the ground in the spring or perhaps a little earlier. Take advantage of a mild, sunny day and amble around with a pitchfork or spading fork and with it loosen up the winter covering or partially remove it above the bulb plantings. But if, by the time you get around to it, the shoots have already made several inches of growth and are blanched by the mulch, remove most of the covering, but leave some shreds and tatters to shade the pale leaves from bright sun until they are properly greened up. When the covering consists of a moderate mulch of no more than an inch or two of fine material such as buckwheat hulls, rotted manure, compost, or peat moss, it may be left as is because the shoots can easily push their way through it. If the peat moss is felted down, it should be loosened so as to permit penetration of rain—a potato hook is a good tool to use for this purpose—but be careful when working among the shoots, because they are easily injured. At this time, if you are feeling strong and vigorous, you can (assuming that the job was not done in the fall—more of this anon) cut back to the ground line the dry stems and leaves of the perennials. Pay particular attention to Peonies and Phlox, which should be cut off just below the soil line: the Peonies, to remove as much as possible of the resting spores of botrytis, a fungus disease which is responsible for blasted flower buds and marred foliage of Peonies; the Phlox, because it is believed that the disease characterized by progressive dying of the leaves from the base of the stems upwards is brought about when new growth comes from the woody, above-ground bases of the old stems. Pull off all the old leaves of the Bearded Irises, leaving only the short, stubby new fans which made

Removing surplus mulch with potato hook. MALCOLM R. KINNEY

Cutting back dead tops in spring. Note tree leaves held by tops and stubs of perennials. MALCOLM R. KINNEY

their start last fall. This is particularly important if Iris borers are infesting the neighborhood, because the eggs are laid on the bases of the old leaves in late August or September. Unfortunately Mamma Moth may lay some of her eggs on nearby vegetation or perhaps on the ground; so, even though you are meticulous in pulling off all the old leaves, it does not necessarily mean that an infestation will be cleaned up. But it does at least reduce the number of borers. Old leaves of Siberian Iris should be cut off close to the ground. This must be done before the new shoots start to grow to avoid injury to them. Although they can force their way through the tangle of old leaves, they do so with difficulty and beholders are offended by the sight of their struggles. Watch for those plants which go into winter with evergreen basal leaves, such as Canterbury Bells, Foxglove, Dianthus, Madonna Lily, Primula, and Viola, for a covering of soggy leaves can be responsible for rotting of the living foliage.

As you make your rounds, watch out for plants which have been heaved out of the ground by alternate freezing and thawing. These should be reset before the roots become dried out as a result of exposure to the winds of March. Also when shoots start pushing, take note of those invasive plants which might be encroaching on their less robust neighbors. Mist-flower, Physostegia, Perennial Sunflower, and some of the strong-growing Daylilies are likely to be offenders in this respect. If a small portion of the outside of the clump is properly placed in relation to its neighbors, well and good —just dig up and remove the remainder. But, if the correct location is the center of the clump, dig it up in its entirety, mix a liberal amount of rotted manure in the vacancy, plant a strong piece of the outer portion, and reject the worn-out center.

During the preceding growing season strong-growing front-line plants, such as *Nepeta Mussini*, probably exceeding their bounds, flopped over onto the lawn and killed the grass. When spring rolls around, the edges of the beds are likely to be ragged and uneven in consequence and need to be trued up. There are two ways of doing this: (1) by extending the border a few inches and stretching a line (or placing a hose if the edge is curved) and making a new edge with a sharp spade—the strips of sod thus removed make an excellent addition to the compost pile; (2) by cutting out bare spots and patching with sods 2 inches thick and at least 6 inches wide taken from an inconspicuous part of the lawn area. The holes thus made should be filled with soil and new grass seed sown immediately.

REJUVENATION

There are some herbaceous plants which, while they are capable of persisting indefinitely, produce a much better effect in the garden if they are divided annually—Chrysanthemums and Hardy Asters. And some need division and replanting every three or four years because the clumps become crowded and too weak, especially in their worn-out centers, to produce a lavish display of bloom. In this group are such plants as Armeria, Phlox, and Heuchera. Some of these may need attention as soon as the frost is out of the ground.

FERTILIZING AND MULCHING

If the winter mulch consisted of manure, about the only additional fertilizer desirable at this time would be a dressing of superphosphate at the rate of about a quarter of a pound for each square yard. But, when covering material poor in nutrients is used, some kind of fertilizing program is desirable to aid the plants to get off to a good start. What this should be depends partly upon easy availability and the cost. Personally I would prefer to use rotted cow or horse manure, or compost in a 2-inch layer, plus superphosphate. This last, ideally, because phosphates move very slowly in the soil, should be forked into it so as to be not too far from the plant roots. My next choice would be a processed and dried animal manure (cattle, sheep, or poultry) obtainable packaged in 5- to 50-pound bags under various trade names. Because these are variable in their nutrient content, it is not practical to make specific recommendations as to the quantity needed; so follow the directions on the bag —usually these fertilizers are applied at the rate of 5 to 10 pounds per hundred square feet. If none of these is conveniently available, a commercial fertilizer with an analysis of 4-12-4 or 5-10-5 could be used at the rate of about half of a pound per square yard. This should be spread evenly and scratched into the surface.

Now you can rest from your labors for a week or two, which were for the purpose of preventing malformed growth and blanched shoots as the result of their attempt to push through the heavy covering. But, as soon as there is no danger of really severe weather, the spring cleaning should start in earnest and the heavy winter overcoats be removed.

What to do with the material removed depends partly on the character of it and your plans for the summer. If you live in a severe climate which necessitates a heavy covering of straw or tree leaves, the covering should be removed and put on the compost pile together with a sprinkling of fertilizer and rotted down for use as a soil conditioner later on. If the covering is of durable material, such as salt-marsh hay or pine needles, it can be removed and stored under cover for future use. If winter covering is no more than 2 inches or so (which is all that is needed in the regions where the temperature seldom gets down to zero) and it consists of finely divided material, such as rotted manure, compost, peat moss, buckwheat hulls or sawdust, it is not necessary to remove it, for it can be lightly forked into the surface soil, or it can be left there and loosened with the aid of a potato hook, a small rake or digging fork, depending upon whether you plan to keep the garden free of weeds by hoeing or by use of an organic mulch plus hand-pulling. There is no great hurry about applying a mulch to help in weed control; if put on too early, it may keep the ground from warming up, so that some of the plants may delay their flowering; and in any case it is a good plan to hoe the surface once or twice to kill off growing weeds. The mulch should be presentable and not constitute too much of a fire hazard (cigarette smokers sometimes are careless in disposing of their butts). This rules out excelsior, straw, and salt-marsh hay. Good-looking materials include buckwheat hulls, peat moss, sawdust, and ground corncobs. The depth of the layer should be about 2 inches, renewed if necessary as the season progresses. One disadvantage of buckwheat hulls is that they may be scattered hither and yon by birds—especially English sparrows—seeking for stray kernels of buckwheat. Since the bacteria and other organisms responsible for the decay of organic matter need nutrients—nitrogen and phosphorus in particular—it is advisable, especially if sawdust is used, to supply extra quantities of these nutrients, so that they are not drawn from the soil to the detriment of the higher plants. Twelve ounces of sulphate of ammonia (or 1 pound of nitrate of soda) and 12 ounces of superphosphate to each bushel of dry sawdust applied to 100 square feet of soil surface should do the trick. When an acid reaction is desired use sulphate of ammonia in preference to nitrate of soda. The entire amount of superphosphate should be put on at the time of the application of the sawdust. But the nitrogen carrier, because it is subject to leaching, should be divided in three parts and put on at six-week intervals. Mulching does to some extent save labor in weeding—it is a means of conserving moisture in the soil, and it helps to maintain its humus content.

SUPPORT THE PLANTS

Unfortunately many of our best-loved flowering plants are not able to withstand the winds and rains that accompany summer storms, so we have to devise some means of supporting them. Fortunately, on the other hand, this is not too arduous a chore, and it can be interesting as well as rewarding. The important things to bear in mind are: the stakes or supports must be applied before the need for them arises; they must be as unobtrusive as possible; and the natural habit of the plant should be maintained. I'm all in favor of using, so far as possible, natural materials which can be found

Twiggy branches suitable to use as plant supports. Left to right—Apple, Peach, Maple. MALCOLM R. KINNEY

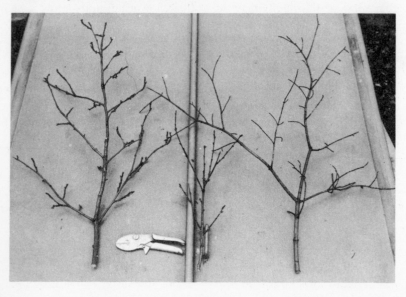

around the place. Among these are twigs and small branches of shrubs and trees, suitable portions of which should be selected and saved at pruning time. These should have 6 to 8 inches clear at the base, so they can be easily pushed in the ground, and the tops should be moderately twiggy. Peach prunings with the tips shortened are excellent. If normal pruning does not provide enough material, two or three Privet bushes can be set in an out-of-the-way spot and cut down each fall. These cuttings should be kept in a dry place, or they may embarrass you by growing when they are set in the ground to supply the supports. These twiggy branches are used to stick in around sprawling plants before they have attained their full growth, so that, as they start to lop over, their shoots are caught in the forked twigs. A little practice, and you will soon be able to apply the brushwood supports so that they are efficient and practically invisible. It may be necessary in some cases, after the supports are in place, to go around them with the pruning shears to clip off projecting twigs. The smaller pieces—those 12 to 18 inches long—can be used with such plants as *Veronica latifolia* (*V. Teucrium*), *Potentilla nepalensis,* and other Cinquefoils; Petunia, Geum, and so on. The heavier, larger branches, 20 to 30 inches long, can be used on Peony, Chrysanthemum, Coreopsis, Oriental Poppy, Rudbeckia, and Heliopsis. If brushwood is unavailable, its place can be taken by putting three to five stakes of suitable length around the clump and connecting them with soft twine. Wire supports can be used for small plants, as will be described later.

A favorite support for Peonies is a hoop on a tripod, which is put over the plants when they are in bud and before the weight of the flowers causes the stems to bend over. If you don't like the purchased metal kind, you might prefer to make your own of Weeping Willow, by tying three to five pliable shoots together to make a hoop which can be held at the right height by resting it on three or four forked sticks or by tying it to stakes.

There is almost always need for slender, straight sticks to support individual stems of Lilies, Iris, Foxglove, Gladiolus, Delphinium, etc., to which they are tied in one or more places. In order to provide the smaller sizes suckers can be cut from overgrown, neglected Lilacs, water sprouts from fruit trees, and by cutting the straight shoots of Hazelnut and Arrowwood. For heavier stakes, such as are needed by tall Delphiniums and the large-flowered Dahlias, you

Oriental Poppy supported by inconspicuous brushwood.
MALCOLM R. KINNEY

Peony supported by brushwood.
MALCOLM R. KINNEY

Weeping Willow can easily be woven into a hoop for supporting Peonies. Hoop
is held in place by forked branches. MALCOLM R. KINNEY

Old Lilac provides plenty of suckers which can be cut to supply stakes to support individual stems. MALCOLM R. KINNEY

may, unless you live in the South, have to rely on boughten heavy (up to ¾ inch) Bamboo canes, or those made from sawn lumber (usually 1 inch by 1 inch or somewhat larger). It is customary to put in Dahlia stakes at planting time to avoid injuring the tubers.

Then there are stakes made of No. 8 or No. 10 galvanized wire, cut into lengths of from 3 to 6 feet, which can be used for supporting individual stems of Lilies (be careful to avoid spearing the bulbs when placing the stake), Foxgloves, and Gladiolus. These are inconspicuous and effective, provided the plant itself is not too heavy. Wire stakes should always have a loop made at the top, bent over at a right angle, to minimize the danger of poking out an eye when bending over to smell the flowers. Fastening materials consist of soft twine, raffia, and covered wire. The ties should be tight around the stake and loose around the plant stem. From one to three ties may be necessary, depending on the length of the stems. The covered wire fasteners have the advantage of ease of application—a couple of twists and the job is done. There are two or three forms of fasteners which can be purchased from seed stores, or you can raid your husband's smoking stand for pipe cleaners, or you can use thin, rubber-covered electrical wire. Browsing around the seed and hardware stores and perusing the sundries pages of seedmen's catalogues will disclose other devices which may appeal to you for supporting plants. There are ringed Tomato supports which can be used for Peonies and other plants that grow in clumps; single stakes with attachable hoops for smaller plants; flexible wire bars with legs of varying height which can be used along the edge of a flower border to prevent Nepeta, Ceratostigma, and similar plants from flopping over onto the lawn, or they can be bent into a half hoop to confine the stalks of Coral-bells.

Another form of wire support used for large-flowered border Carnations consists of No. 14 or No. 12 wire, 12 to 18 inches long, bent into a wide spiral except for 6 inches at the base. These also have the tip looped and turned over. They are pushed into the ground alongside the flower stem, which then is, with a twisting flick of the finger, slid into the spiral which, with the loop at the top, holds it without any tying being needed. If you are really in need of such stakes and are unable to locate a source of supply, they may be made with the aid of a vice and pliers by twisting lengths of wire spirally around a tapering sharpening steel (the kind that Papa uses prior to carving the roast) off which they can easily be slipped.

ENJOY YOUR GARDEN!

Don't, when engaged in these chores, forget to enjoy your garden. Remember you are your own boss and no one (I hope) is going to object if you take time out now and then to enjoy the beauty of some especially engaging plant in bloom or a particularly pleasing combination. If it pleases you, take a chair along and sit down once in a while, light up your pipe, and just look around. On the other hand, if you, unfortunately, constitutionally dislike to be idle, you can kill two birds with one stone by carefully inspecting the garden and transferring your findings to a notebook or to the margins of the plan which, if you followed a suggestion made earlier, will be mounted on stout cardboard. These notes will be varied, such as: plant more of such and such in this place; eliminate so and so because it is ungainly; the color is not pleasing or the plant grows too lushly. Here and there may be inharmonious color combinations; and plants which need to be divided and reset. Note these things when they are fresh in your mind, otherwise they are likely to be forgotten when the appropriate time for action comes along.

No matter how carefully the garden was planned and planted, there will always be something that needs correcting—colors may clash, some plants will be too tall for their location, and some will be too short, some will crowd their neighbors, and some will die and leave a gap to be filled. The growing season is the time to make notes of corrections to be made in fall or spring, when plants are more or less dormant; but in the case of plants which have compact and fibrous root systems transfers can be made during the growing season, even when they are in full bloom or about to bloom. Naturally enough, great care must be taken to insure that the roots are disturbed as little as possible, and that the plants do not suffer from lack of water. The technique of planting in such cases, together with a list of amenable plants, is found on pages 79 to 81.

WATERING

Whether or not watering is necessary depends on the capacity of the soil to hold moisture and the goodness or otherwise of the weatherman. If you can get by without artificial watering, so much the better. Remember that merely sprinkling the surface is useless— enough must be given to wet the soil at root depth, which may be 6 inches or more below the surface. So, except in the case of a small garden when you can spend an evening once a week handling a hose fitted with a spray nozzle, some kind of device is necessary that will enable you to turn on the water and leave it running for an hour or more. This can be a length of porous hose that is laid on the soil so that water drools over it; or a sprinkler that delivers a fine spray of water overhead. There are scores of different makes of these available from seed and hardware stores. I must leave it to you to select a kind that suits your conditions and pocketbook.

CURBING AND PRUNING

There are certain perennials, some of them beautiful and almost indispensable, that must be curbed lest they crowd out their less robust neighbors. Among these invasive plants are: (1) Bee-balm, Boltonia, Coreopsis, Mist-flower (*Eupatorium coelestinum*), and Perennial Sunflower—all more or less late-flowering, which should be dealt with in the spring; (2) a few late-bloomers and late-starters, such as Carpathian Harebell and Plumbago, which require an attitude of watchful waiting, with the gardener ready at any time to amputate offending shoots; (3) spring- and early-summer-flowering kinds, such as Rock-cress, Moss-Phlox, Dianthus, and Sundrops (Oenothera), which should be attended to immediately after their flowers fade.

For Group 1 a spade is the pruning implement used to dig out, root, and branch those parts of the clump which are shouldering nearby, less robust plants. Whenever it becomes necessary to do this, it should be taken as an indication that the clump needs dividing and resetting. A note to that effect should be made as a reminder to do this at the right season. In Groups 2 and 3 a pruning knife is the tool best used to cut out encroaching shoots at or near the base, to avoid giving the plant the appearance of a shorn lamb. If you are hurried, some plants can be restrained by chopping around them with a sharp spade in the same way that surplus pastry is trimmed off when making a pie. This, however, temporarily disfigures a clump, and the better way, if you have the time, is to use a knife to cut the outermost shoots of the clump from below, thus leaving shoots from the center to cover the cut stubs and present a natural outline.

Other plants that will bear watching toward fall are those set out in the vicinity of Oriental Poppies to mask the dying foliage of the latter. As soon as the new leaves of Oriental Poppies start to grow in the fall, the masking plants—Gypsophila, Daylilies, and so on—should be cut back if necessary to give the developing leaves of the Poppy a chance.

When the perennial border is set in a lawn with grass growing up to the edge of it, the plants in its front row must also be carefully watched lest they lop over or grow outwards to smother the grass. If there is a miscellaneous assortment in the front rank, the measure just outlined should be put into effect; if it is a formal, clipped edging such as Boxwood or Germander, hedge shears or hand shears should be brought into use before damage is done.

FADED FLOWERS

Another form of pruning is concerned with the removal of faded flowers in the interest of tidiness, and in the prevention of seeding, to conserve the plant's energies, and to eliminate the possibility of unwanted seedlings. Perennial Candytuft and June-flowering Dianthus should be gone over with hedge shears to remove all flower stalks and, especially in the case of Candytuft, to cut off projecting growth shoots to promote a compact habit of growth. Delphinium flower stalks should be cut off at the base when the flowers fade, and when the leaves begin to turn brown, the entire stalks should be removed to make room for new shoots coming up from the ground. The flower heads of Phlox should be cut off when most of the flowers have faded to inhibit the production of seeds and to stimulate the production of secondary flowering laterals. Individual flowers of Viola should be picked off (if you have time) to prolong blooming, and, if blossoming ceases during hot weather, the plants should be sheared back about one half to favor later flowering.

SURPLUS GROWTH

Many perennials, notably Phlox, Hardy Aster, and sometimes Delphinium, produce so many shoots per clump that many of them are too weak to produce a first-class flower cluster. These weak shoots do not pull their weight and are a drain on the stronger stems. This condition can be remedied by thinning out the weaker sisters in early spring when they are 1 to 2 inches long. Those who have the time (and especially if they're planning to make a killing at the local flower show) should try out the effect of thinning out the weaker shoots of Phlox, Delphinium, Hardy Aster, and Helenium to get more and better blooms on those remaining.

A corollary is the removal of surplus flower buds. Side buds of Peonies, which never amount to much anyway, should be removed as soon as they are large enough to handle, to concentrate the strength of the shoot in the development of the terminal bud. The same procedure is followed with the Carnation (not the cluster-flower type, though), the large-flowered Chrysanthemums, and Dahlias.

PINCHING BACK

This is removing the terminal shoots by pinching them out with thumbnail and finger. This may be done chiefly to promote bushiness or to reduce ultimate height. It is commonly practiced on

Phlox—when new Phlox shoots are well started, thin out the weaklings.

Peonies—side buds, which produce weak flowers, should be removed.

Chrysanthemums when they are set out as single-stem plants in the spring. When the primary shoot has grown to a length of 6 or 8 inches, its tip is pinched out, which stimulates the growth of two or more shoots from the dormant buds below the tip. When these shoots have attained a sufficient length, their tips in turn are pinched out, and this is continued until the required degree of bushiness is attained. Such pinching, however, should not be continued beyond July.

PRUNING PERENNIALS
FOR STRONGER PLANTS,
LARGER FLOWERS

Chrysanthemum—LEFT, pinching out tip induces branching (arrows) to make a more bushy plant. BELOW, disbudding of Chrysanthemum to produce one best flower.

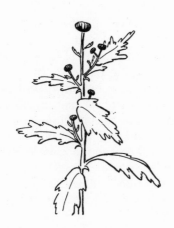

The New England Asters, which normally grow to a height of about 5 feet, may be kept down to half this height by three successive pinchings as the successive shoots attain a length of about 8 inches. Sometimes, too, it may be desirable to leave plants at the rear of the border unpinched and to pinch out adjacent plants in front of them to secure gradation of height.

PRUNING WOODY PLANTS

The pruning of shrubs used as accents and backgrounds must not be neglected. In the early stages this will demand little more than shortening a branch here and there to promote bushiness and symmetry. But, as the years go by and they begin to crowd each other and the perennials, more and more pruning becomes necessary. Except for the "dieback" shrubs, which should be pruned in the spring before growth starts, this usually involves considerable summer pruning, which is more effective in checking exuberant growth than cutting them back during dormancy. Try as far as possible to maintain their natural habit of growth; prune early-blooming plants as soon as the flowers fade, and do not wait until the shrubs are already too large before starting to curb them.

INSECT PESTS

During the early part of the year plant lice (aphids) are the pests most likely to cause trouble, so keep a close watch on your plants (on Heliopsis especially) and get after them with a contact spray, such as nicotine and soap (one teaspoonful of 40 per cent nicotine, one tablespoonful of soap flakes to one gallon of water); or use a proprietary spray following the directions on the container. Another early insect is the leaf miner, which makes the leaves of Columbines unsightly with its tunnels. A spray containing Lindane (there are various proprietary preparations of this kind) is helpful against this pest; or, if you have only a few plants and there are no Columbines growing in adjacent gardens, you may be able to control the pest by picking off the affected leaflets as soon as the beginnings of a tunnel are seen. Toward the end of May or early in June in some regions the gangling beetle, known as rose chafer, is likely to make your life miserable by feeding on the flowers of Peonies, and still later in the season, in Japanese-beetle areas, these beautiful beetles may cause trouble. Hand picking—knocking the insects into a can containing water and kerosene—plus the use of repellent sprays and those containing DDT are indicated to keep these pests from causing too much damage. In the case of Japanese beetles grub-proofing the lawn is an effective way of reducing the numbers of these pests.

FOLLOW-UP CROPS

Unless you are a purist and have an "all-perennial" garden, from April until June you will have to give thought and take action in the matter of flowers to be used as fillers to take the place of early-flowering bulbs. These will be annuals (see list on page 116) or summer-flowering bulbs (see page 121 et seq.). If there is a commercial garden center in your vicinity and you can wait until after Decoration Day, you will be able to get some bargains in started plants of annuals, such as Marigold and Petunia; and tender perennials, such as Begonia and Pelargonium, which can be planted to give you an almost immediate color effect which will persist until frost.

PLANTING

Don't forget those plants which are best when planted or divided, when necessary, outside the normal planting season. These include: Bearded Iris, planted July to September; Oriental Poppies, and Madonna Lilies, planted in August. Directions for handling these and others, including Chrysanthemum, which may be brought in from the reserve garden to provide fall color, will be found under planting techniques in Chapter Six.

The big job in October and early November is planting hardy spring-flowering bulbs to fill any gaps noted last spring; or to replace worn-out groups.

WINTER PROTECTION

I am not convinced that it is desirable to put on the heavy layer of straw 6 inches thick that used to be thought necessary in severe climates. For the past seven years I have been lazy, closed my eyes to the lack of tidiness, and let nature do it. She has done a good job, so far as I can see, for, although we have had two or three fairly tough winters during a seven-year period, with temperature down to

15 degrees, I cannot remember any plant loss that could be attributed to winter injury. So, late in the fall, I do practically nothing to protect the plants beyond putting peach baskets over some of the small shrubs that are on the border line of hardiness; and putting up a length of snow fence along the west side of the garden. The fence causes much snow to be dumped in drifts in the boundary plantings, and a considerable amount is held by the tops of perennials. A few tree leaves are also blown in and lodge among the stems of the perennials. Even Torch-lilies (Kniphofia), which are usually thought of as not thoroughly winter-hardy, have come through satisfactorily with no covering other than their own leaves. Inci-

Author's garden protected by snow fence on west; semi-hardy shrubs covered with peach baskets. MALCOLM R. KINNEY

dentally, Goldfinches appreciate my laziness, for flocks of them appear at the garden in the fall and at intervals throughout the winter feasting on the seeds of Aster, Chrysanthemum, and other late bloomers.

However, some kind of protection is desirable in severe climates for plants such as Canterbury Bell, Foxglove, Madonna Lily, Viola, and others which go into the winter with green leaves. The important thing to avoid is any kind of covering that will mat down into a soggy mess and smother the leaves. So I would suggest first putting a mulch of partly rotted leaves or peat moss *under* the leaves on the soil over the roots after the ground is frozen to a depth of 2 inches. Then, to protect the leaves, put a peach basket over each clump, or, better still, a light covering of evergreen boughs which will aid in holding snow, which is the best possible protection. Fir branches (these can be cut from discarded Christmas trees), pine boughs, or prunings from an overgrown yew are excellent for this purpose. If you are a tidy soul and cannot bear the sight of the admittedly be-draggled appearance of an unshorn perennial garden, and if you have the makings, procedures just outlined could be followed over the entire garden. Or you can put on a loosely applied covering of salt-marsh hay, pine needles, or excelsior, all of which should be removed in the spring. Another alternative is to cover with buck-wheat hulls, flaky leafmold, or peat moss in a layer no more than 2 inches thick; the salt-marsh hay, etc., can be put on in a layer 3 to 4 inches thick. Whatever you do, do not put on any winter covering until the ground is frozen—otherwise you may have field mice making their nests in it and causing trouble.

It is alternate freezing and thawing of the soil that is inimical to the welfare of dubiously hardy perennials. When this condition occurs, plant roots may be heaved out of the ground and growth that is subject to injury when freezing temperatures again prevail may be stimulated during warm spells. A heavy coat of snow is the best possible insulator; it prevents frost from penetrating too deeply and keeps the soil cool enough to inhibit growth. Therefore, endeavor to gather as much snow as possible on the beds by means outlined above. If you live in a region where a snow covering cannot be relied on, a loosely applied mulch as indicated above would probably be desirable.

If the suggestions outlined in this chapter are followed, the perennial garden may be expected to remain in good condition for years. But in five, ten, or fifteen years there will come a time when a complete renovation job is in order. The time lapse depends on a number of things: your own idiosyncrasies—whether you are one of those who crave constant change or whether you prefer to string along with the status quo; the nature of the soil—whether good or bad to start with; and the care with which it was prepared. In any case, after ten or fifteen years the chances are that the garden can be improved by rearrangement to give better balance of incidence of bloom; by the substitution of improved varieties; and the elimination of unsatisfactory performers, plus renovation of exhausted soil. This is hardly a routine job, so let's give a chapter to it.

CHAPTER THIRTEEN

Rehabilitating the Garden

Like marriage, the job of making over a perennial garden should not be entered upon lightly, or the last state may be worse than the first. Ideally you should start a year ahead of the time of actually making the change by carefully noting the defects to be corrected as well as the good things that are to be retained. It is a good plan during this period to visit neighbors' gardens for the purpose of picking up ideas. Also visit nearby nurseries to see plants in bloom, to decide on the varieties you desire; this is especially true of Phlox, whose colors sometimes are difficult to harmonize.

WHEN TO START

A beginning can be made as soon as the hardy spring-flowering bulbs are finished blooming. Tulips, especially, seldom remain effective for more than three years. Those clumps in which the flowers are sparse may as well be looked on as expendable and be dug up and thrown on the compost pile without waiting for the foliage to mature. Other clumps which are reasonably good but diminishing in vigor can be left until their leaves begin to turn yellow before digging them. After a week or so look over the bulbs, throw out the very small ones, and save those which look large enough to bloom. If you have a semi-wild spot in part shade, Narcissus, Squills, Chionodoxa, and Crocus can be planted right away to naturalize themselves; the Tulips can be stored in a cool, airy place under cover until the fall, when they can be planted in the reserve garden to provide flowers for cutting. At this time the flower buds, if any, will be formed inside the bulbs, and by cutting open, longitudinally, a few of various sizes it is possible to get an idea of which ones are worth planting.

Annuals can be used to fill temporarily the spaces occupied by the bulbs; either by seeds sown in place or by setting out young plants.

Next in line for treatment are Oriental Poppies, Bearded Irises, and Madonna Lilies, which, ideally, should all be replanted in August. These present a problem unless you have already made your new plan and know just where they are to go and the plants occupying their places are kinds that you do not want to keep. Of these the Oriental Poppies are the only kind that is likely to suffer badly from being moved later when the rest of the planting is done. The Iris can be moved in late September (I have planted them as late as November and had a fair crop of bloom), and so can the Madonna Lilies if they are dug up with care, not to injure the roots any more than is absolutely necessary.

The major part of the work can be done in late September or early October. First dig up all plants that are to be discarded and throw them on the compost pile. Those which are to form a part of the new planting should be labeled clearly (12-inch wooden labels are good for this) and "heeled in" (planted loosely) temporarily in an unoccupied piece of ground. If they are arranged alphabetically, it will greatly facilitate finding the required kinds when planting. If there is no available ground in which they can be "heeled in," they can be placed in shallow boxes or, if it is more convenient, on a piece of canvas spread out on walk or lawn. In either case cover the roots with moist soil and make sure that it stays moist until they are planted.

Probably some Chrysanthemum blooms will have to be sacrificed. The plants of these should be dug up, planted in shallow boxes, and stored for the winter in the cold frame; in the spring rooted divisions will be taken from them and planted in the garden. The same goes for *Aster Frikarti* and *Alyssum saxatile*, which do not like to be disturbed in the fall, and which probably would fail to survive except when kept under glass during the winter.

Do not, unless it is positively unavoidable, move those plants which resent disturbance such as Dictamnus and Christmas-rose. Peonies also should be left if they are still healthy, free-flowering, and vigorous.

When the planting area is as completely cleared of plants as possible, double-dig the ground as described in Chapter Two, not forgetting to work in an ample supply of partly decayed organic material.

When digging is completed, obtain the services of a weighty person with large feet and get him or her to trample the soil thoroughly to consolidate it, and then rake the surface a little. If heavy rains are experienced between the time of digging and planting (which will consolidate the soil sufficiently), the tramping can be omitted. You are now ready to get on with the planting (see Chapter Six). When you have finished, rake the surface again to take out footprints, and then wait until there is a frozen crust on the surface before putting on a mulch for winter, as described in the preceding chapter.

CHAPTER FOURTEEN

Propagating the Plants

Before you can start propagating any plants, it is necessary to have seeds or living plants with which to operate; there are various sources from which they can be obtained.

First scout around locally. There may be nurseries nearby from which you can get many of the plants needed; and you will have the assurance that they are freshly dug and not debilitated by a long trip by railroad or truck. Another advantage of buying locally is that in some cases (Iris and Phlox, for examples) it is possible to see the plants in bloom so that appealing colors can be chosen. The local florists or garden centers also are a possible source of supply for such plants as English Daisies, Doronicum, Globe-flower, Moss-Phlox, Primroses, and Pansies—plants which, because of their compact, fibrous root systems, can be dug up in bud and sold to give an immediate effect in the garden. But don't be tempted to buy the right plant at the wrong time. Madonna Lilies and Peonies are sometimes offered for sale during the spring months, which are not the best for moving these plants. Don't forget your friends and neighbors—a hint or an outright request for a start of plants usually is well received. By proceeding along these lines it is possible to get most of the commoner plants and perhaps a few rarities. But when a considerable variety of plant material is required, it is necessary to buy by mail from those nurseries which specialize in perennials.

Herbaceous perennials can be propagated by seeds, division, and cuttings of stem or root. To raise one's own plants is not only economical, but the varied processes are of absorbing interest.

PROPAGATION BY SEED

Seeds afford the most ready means of propagating *some* perennials—those that are true species and not garden forms. Those whose ancestry is mixed, those which have been subject to the ministrations of the plant breeder cannot be relied upon to reproduce exactly the parent plants. So, if you were to sow seeds of garden Phlox, Iris, or Daylily, the chances are that not one seedling in a thousand would be equal to the parents. These, therefore, must be propagated by vegetative means, either by divisions or cuttings. But true species such as *Phlox divaricata, Iris pseudacorus, Hemerocallis flava,* and many others can be expected to reproduce from seed with little variation from their parents.

TIME AND PLACE OF SOWING

The former recommendation, based largely on English practice, to sow seeds of perennials in August is not valid in the United States, except for a few, such as Delphinium, when seed of the current year is available. For the great majority of perennials spring sowing is preferable, but there are some, such as Aconite, some Irises, Japanese Primrose, Globe-flower, and a few others, which germinate more freely if they are sown in the fall in a cold frame and exposed to low temperatures during winter.

The seeds must be sown in a prepared seedbed—either in the open or in a cold frame—the latter being preferable because it is easy to protect the seed and soil from washing and beating effects of heavy rains, and the seedlings can be protected from sun. Beds preferably 3 to 4 feet wide should be prepared in a well-drained spot to a depth of 6 inches by forking over the soil two or three times to mix with it a 2-inch layer of sifted leafmold or peat moss. If the soil is sticky clay, a 2-inch layer of coarse sand should also be mixed in. When this has been done, it should be tamped down with the back of the rake and then raked and raked to break up lumps and to remove stones and debris. Drills for the reception of the seeds can be made 3 to 6 inches apart by pressing the edge of an ordinary wood builder's lath, or its equivalent, into the soil to the required depth. This varies according to the size of the seeds—ordinarily it is equal to twice the diameter of the seed. The seed should be sown evenly

Seeds sown in cold frame are labeled with name of plant and date of sowing.
"HOME GARDEN" MAGAZINE

Seedlings ready to be transplanted.
"HOME GARDEN" MAGAZINE

and sparingly (not more than twelve seeds to the inch is a good mark to shoot at) and covered with dry sand. When it is not possible to do the sowing from a walk surrounding the bed, it is desirable to have a 12-inch board, long enough to span the bed, from which to work. This distributes the weight and avoids the nuisance of deep footmarks.

Each row, or fraction of a row, of seeds should be labeled (6-inch wooden pot labels would suffice) with the name of the seeds and date of sowing. When sowing is completed, the bed should be watered with a fine spray and covered to protect the seeds from the elements. If the bed is in a cold frame, the glass sash should be put on, tilted to admit plenty of air, and covered with a double thickness of cheesecloth to temper the rays of the sun. If the bed is in the open, cheesecloth should be tacked to a frame made of furring strips which can be supported a foot or two above the bed by stakes driven in at each corner. It is essential to water carefully to keep the soil constantly moist—neither too wet nor too dry.

The above method is preferred when a large number of a few species are required, and when it is not possible to give daily attention to watering. When no more than a dozen or so plants of each of many different species are required, it is better to sow each in a 3- or 4-inch pot, or in flats, one kind to each row, spaced 2 inches apart, provided you can give them the necessary care. Pots or flats should be filled with a mixture of sandy soil two thirds, of leafmold or peat moss one third; pressed down ½ inch below the rim. When pots are used, the seeds are scattered over the entire surface; in the case of flats they are sown in drills made 2 or 3 inches apart. Otherwise follow the directions given above for sowing in beds.

There are some seeds, such as Achillea, Centranthus, and Thymus, which seem to need light in order to germinate freely. These are best sown on the surface of shallow depressions made in the soil of a flat which is then covered with a pane of glass to keep the surface from drying. When germination is effected, gradually admit air by tilting the glass; after about a week or two the glass can be entirely removed.

Thin sowing will lessen the danger of damage from the "damping-off" fungi. If inadvertently the seeds are sown so thickly that the seedlings crowd each other, they should be thinned out or transplanted immediately. Usually, however, transplanting can wait until two or three true leaves are formed, at which time the young plants can be set out in another bed situated in the open, spacing them 3 to 6 inches apart. If it can be done without too much trouble, it is good to shade them for three weeks with cheesecloth screens until the roots have taken hold in the new soil. Shade lovers, of course, will need this screen all the time unless they are set in a bed where the shade is dappled. Here they may stay until the fall or the following spring, when they may be set out in their permanent locations.

DIVISION

Propagation by division of such plants as Aster, Chrysanthemum, and Peony, which are tolerant, easy subjects, has already been covered in the chapter on planting. There remain to say a few words about those that are pernickety, especially when close division is required to produce a large number of plants.

The plants mentioned above (also Daylily, Phlox, and many others) can be divided and transplanted immediately with little or no setback to the places where they are to bloom; others need special care to ensure that they come through the operation successfully. This involves doing the job at the right time; using a particularly well-aerated soil (a mixture of sand, leafmold, and loam); careful attention to ensure that it is kept constantly moist; and in some cases starting the divisions in the cold frame so that atmospheric humidity can be provided in the early stages to prevent the excessive loss of moisture from the leaves.

Among the plants notoriously resentful of root disturbance is the Christmas-rose (*Helleborus niger*). Anyone having a thriving clump is naturally reluctant to disturb it, but it is possible to increase such a clump without any appreciable injury by digging a hole close to one side of the clump to expose some roots and parts of the crowns, one or two of which can be carefully cut away from the parent plant with the roots attached. The ends of broken or mangled roots should be trimmed off cleanly with a sharp knife, to facilitate absorption of water, and the divisions planted in porous soil in a shaded cold frame which should be kept closed for four or five weeks. Then plant in a permanent location in spring. If a cold frame is not available, an apple box with the top and bottom removed may be put over them and covered with a pane of glass. Be sure that the soil is not allowed to become dry; on the other hand, do not keep it in a sopping-wet condition. Early September is the best time to divide Christmas-rose. Don't forget the mother plant—a shovelful of leafmold and a handful of bone meal should be mixed with the soil removed when digging up the division. The soil mixture should be filled in the hole, made firm, and the surplus spread on the ground beneath the leaves of the plant. Japanese Irises can be divided in spring or fall and the divisions set where they are to bloom, pro-

Gorgeous Oriental Poppies dominate the foreground of this well-balanced garden. GOTTSCHO-SCHLEISNER

STEPS IN DIVIDING
A DAYLILY AND GARDEN PHLOX

A clump of Daylily is dug up preparatory to dividing.

PHOTOGRAPHS: R. A. SMITH

When dividing Phlox pry strong pieces from the outer edges of the clump with a hand fork. Spindling stalks should not be used for propagating purposes unless necessary.

The clump is pried apart with the aid of two spading forks back to back, thrust through it, and separated as shown here.

Further division into pieces of planting size is done with the aid of a hand fork. Notice that each fair-sized division is well supplied with foliage and roots.

Phlox division in place ready for covering, with roots spread in a natural position.

vided each piece contains about six growth shoots. But, if these are to be closely divided for propagational purposes with only one or two shoots for division, it is desirable to do this in early September, reduce the leaf surface by cutting them back one half, and otherwise treat them as suggested for Christmas-rose.

Division of Primrose and Polyanthus may be done in the spring as soon as the flowers fade, as well as in late summer. If it is done in the spring, it is very necessary to give them partial shade throughout the summer and to ensure that they do not lack moisture at the roots.

STEM CUTTINGS

Cuttings should be taken early in the spring when the shoots are 2 to 3 inches long, except in the case of Dianthus and Viola, which are best handled in July and August. Cut them off just below the soil line (see pictures on page 164), insert them in clean, moist sand, and put them in the propagating case with bottom heat enough to raise the temperature of the rooting medium 5 to 10 degrees above that of the air. This can be done by means of soil-heating electric cables; or, on a small scale, by putting the cuttings in a flat 18 x 4 inches which could be stood above a hot-water radiator. It would probably be necessary to raise the flat an inch or two from the radiator by means of wood cleats to avoid having the sand get too hot, and certainly necessary to enclose the flat and cuttings either with glass or poly-ethylene plastic to maintain moist air about the cuttings. When they have made roots about 2 inches long, they should be removed from the sand and potted in soil (two thirds sandy loam and one third leafmold or peat moss), kept in a shady, closed cold frame for a week or two, after which they should be gradually hardened off prior to planting them in the open ground.

It usually is possible to get plenty of young shoots of Dianthus and Viola during the summer months. These shoots should be cut off 3 inches from the tip and inserted in sand in a shaded cold frame. Phlox can be made to produce shoots suitable for use in summer by cutting a clump down to the ground when it is in bloom. Plants raised from these cuttings cannot be expected to bloom until the following year. Delphiniums after flowering is past normally pro-duce basal shoots whether or not the clumps are cut down; these can be used for cuttings.

PROPAGATING
PRIMROSE
AND POLYANTHUS
BY DIVISION
MAY BE DONE
IN SPRING OR
LATE SUMMER

Entire plant should first
be dug up.

Divisions can be made by pulling apart
with hands.

With trowel hole is dug large
enough to contain roots without
crowding. Faded flowers are removed.

Plants must be thoroughly watered as
soon as planting is completed.

PHOTOGRAPHS: STEENSON & BAKER

PROPAGATION OF
CHRYSANTHEMUM
BY STEM CUTTINGS

Shoots 2 to 3 inches long, taken
from stock plants early in spring,
are inserted in moist sand.
MALCOLM R. KINNEY

Six weeks later cuttings are 100 per cent rooted, and ready for potting.
MALCOLM R. KINNEY

ROOT CUTTINGS

Anemone, Summer Phlox, and Verbascum can be increased
readily by means of root cuttings. In order to obtain cuttings the
plants should be dug up in the fall, thick roots selected (one tenth of
an inch or more in diameter), and cut in lengths of 1 to 3 inches.
These should be placed in flats horizontally an inch apart on a half
inch of sand overlying a soil mixture of equal parts of sand, loam,
leafmold or peat moss, and covered with a half inch of sand. Water

PROPAGATION OF JAPANESE ANEMONE BY ROOT CUTTINGS

Roots should be dug up in fall. MALCOLM R. KINNEY

LEFT. Suitable roots for cutting; CENTER. Roots are cut into pieces 1½ inches long and placed horizontally in a flat of soil—surfaced with sand— then covered with ½ inch of sand; RIGHT. Following spring, plantlets develop from the roots. In left foreground is plantlet removed from flat to show development of new roots and shoot. MALCOLM R. KINNEY

them thoroughly and put in a cold frame for the winter. In the spring young plants will appear, which, when they are about 2 or 3 inches high, can be taken from the flat and either potted up or planted in the nursery bed. (See the section on stem cuttings above.)

In Oriental Poppies the timing and technique are somewhat different. They are best propagated in August by cutting the roots to a length of 3 inches and potting them singly and vertically in sandy soil contained in 4-inch pots. (Make sure they are put tip end up—so as to avoid making a mistake, it is wise to cut the top off squarely and the lower end diagonally.)

The pots of cuttings should be plunged to their rims in peat moss or sifted coal ashes in a cold frame and left there until the fall, when those which have started growing can be planted out in the places where they are to bloom—usually eighteen months later.

GRAFTING

The only herbaceous perennials that are commonly propagated by grafting are the double-flowered forms of Gypsophila. Commercially the work is usually done in a greenhouse during winter. When the new shoots are about 4 inches long, sometime in February, they are inserted in slits 1 inch long made about halfway through the root of the understock, which is a single-flowered species (*G. paniculata*). Skin is carefully removed from the lowermost inch of the scion and, after insertion in the understock, is tied in place with raffia and the completed graft is potted in a 2½-inch "long Tom" rose pot. They are then placed in a closed propagating case and after a few days are gradually given increasing amounts of ventilation. Gypsophila can be grafted in a cold frame in August or September if suitable young shoots can be obtained for scions at that time.

CHAPTER FIFTEEN

Shrubs in the Flower Garden

The role of woody perennials in the flower garden already has been touched on briefly. It is now time to go into the subject in more detail to indicate added uses for them and to discuss the kinds most suitable.

When the property is small, say 75 by 100 feet, and some privacy is needed by the owner, usually a boundary planting of fairly tall shrubs together with a few small flowering trees is indicated.

Some of these will need to be "faced down" with smaller shrubs to hide the bare legs of the tall ones. By the time this is done, you will find that there is no room for a lawn area plus a flower garden as such and, as a lawn large enough on which to swing a cat is usually a *sine qua non*, the flower garden must be combined with the shrubbery. This can be done by making a flower border 6 or more feet wide either across the end of the property and/or along one or both sides, depending upon the amount of space left—and, of course, your own ideas as to the relative importance of lawn, flowers, and shrubbery. When the property is fenced or walled, considerable space may be saved by using vines or espaliered shrubs to form a background. The shrubs used should be chosen with care. Avoid being overcome with so much enthusiasm and sentiment when you see Lilacs in bloom that you use too many of them. Remember that their period of bloom is fleeting; that the effect of their foliage is mediocre; and their moldy appearance when they are attacked by mildew is distressing. Follow the line suggested for herbaceous perennials and choose only those which have a long blooming season and/or good foliage throughout the year. Plan, if possible, in the case of deciduous material to use as many as possible of those kinds which have an interesting branch pattern in winter. Make good use of those whose appearance is varied throughout the year with a floral display in the spring, good foliage in summer, and fruits or colored leaves in the fall. Those which in the North are called "die-back" shrubs, because their branches are killed to the ground as a result of freezing in winter, are particularly valuable because: most of them bloom after June, when flowers are scarce in the shrub

East side of author's garden showing shrub grouping on the left. To the right are pillars clothed with Climbing Roses and Clematis. Rose beds in foreground. MALCOLM R. KINNEY

border; they serve the same purpose as any deciduous shrub in winter; the annual cutting back to near the ground line in the spring assures some stability in size. A few choice evergreens, both broad-leaf and coniferous, should be placed in strategic situations because they provide an element of beauty and interest in winter, and they may also give a seasonal display of flowers and/or fruit an added attraction. When space is limited so that a wide background is not permissible, it is necessary to concentrate on those shrubs which naturally are slender or those which permit close trimming, and those which can be grown attached to a wall or fence—either as vines or as shrubs which can be espaliered. After this general survey of the uses of shrubs let us now deal with them more specifically. The approximate ultimate spread, when it differs greatly from the height, is given as a guide in spacing them. It should be remembered, though, that in most cases it will be many years before these sizes are attained.

ONE—PRIMARILY FOR FLOWERS

Buddleia alternifolia has, so far as I know, no English name, so I am going to manufacture one and call it Garland Butterfly-bush, because the wand-like lilac-colored flowering branchlets lend themselves admirably to the making of garlands. It is a shrub which is definitely improved by cutting off the blooming shoots as soon as the flowers are faded: (1) because the dense clusters of small lilac-purple flowers are produced all along the shoots of the preceding year and the pruning promotes a formation of such shoots; (2) it eliminates the drab-looking seed capsules, which, if left, spoil the appearance of the bush in winter. It is a very vigorous grower up to 10 feet; the slender branchlets are clothed with dull green, smallish narrow leaves.

Forsythia intermedia. There are several kind of Forsythia commonly grown, but the most valuable is *F. intermedia* or one of its garden forms. This is another shrub which should be pruned—not so much to promote floriferousness as to make an open, graceful bush by removing annually some of the three- and four-year-old branches. This can be done as soon as flowers fade; or in winter if a primary purpose is to acquire branches for blooming in water indoors. It grows 8 to 10 feet high.

Kolkwitzia amabilis, Beauty-bush. A shrub 6 to 8 feet tall; upright, with outward-curving branchlets, smothered with pink flowers, yellow in the throat. Some individual bushes are more beautiful than others, and it is worth while to keep an eye open for them in your travels and beg a few cuttings of young side shoots which easily root in moist sand in a shaded cold frame in late June. When planted in rich soil, it may be several years before it starts to bloom; it is also more subject to winter injury in good soil so, on the whole, it is better to give it a lean diet and omit fertilizer.

Magnolia stellata, Star Magnolia. Among the earliest shrubs to bloom, the flowers of the Star Magnolia often are blackened by frost or withered by strong dry winds. But, even though you may not get a good display more than once in five years, it is worth growing because the delightfully fragrant white flowers are so beautiful. Its long (4-inch), narrow leaves are not to be sneered at either, because even after enduring dry summers, they remain in good condition well into the fall, when they turn to a rather attractive yellowish tan. It is capable of growing into a small tree 15 feet high; but it is slow-growing and starts to bloom when it is no more than a foot or two tall.

Rhododendron calendulaceum, Flame Azalea, is a variable native species with flowers that run the gamut between yellow and deep orange-red; its foliage turns yellow to orange in the fall. Rhododendron hybrids of the "Ghent," "Mollis," and "Koster" groups, of which there are innumerable named kinds, all showy in bloom, are valuable in regions where they thrive, but some of them are not reliably winter-hardy north of New York City. Visit a nearby nursery when they are in bloom (May and June), select kinds which appeal to you, take them home, and plant them immediately. A well-drained, humusy, acid soil is necessary for practically all Rhododendrons.

Spiraea Vanhouttei, Vanhoutte's Spirea. One of the most commonly planted kinds, this is smothered with clustering snowy white flowers in June, produced on a shapely bush which grows to about 6 feet. Although the small leaves provide excellent blending value, they are inclined to take on a rusty, drab appearance when grown in the impure air of large cities.

Syringa persica, Persian Lilac. This is probably one of the best of the Lilacs for background purposes. It has smallish leaves and a graceful habit; its small, chubby flower clusters are delightfully fragrant. It grows about 6 to 8 feet tall and if given a chance may ultimately extend to 15 feet or more in width. *S. vulgaris* and its varieties and hybrids are perhaps more spectacular in bloom; some are fragrant and in others the odor is faint or lacking. There are hundreds of named varieties and the best advice I can give is that you visit a nursery during lilac time and select the kinds which appeal to you. Lilacs thrive best when the soil is neutral or slightly alkaline; so, if it is strongly acid, don't forget to apply ground limestone to bring it up to near the neutral point.

Viburnum tomentosum, Doublefile Viburnum. This is one of the most handsome of all shrubs when in bloom about the end of May. It has flat-topped clusters of flowers of two kinds—the outer ring very large, showy and pure white, while the inner, fertile ones are small. These flower clusters are produced on almost horizontal branches. Overall, it is a rounded bush growing to 10 feet high. The variety *sterile* (Japanese Snowball), although the best of the Snowballs, is less winter hardy and cannot endure much below zero weather.

TWO—PRIMARILY FOR FOLIAGE EFFECT

Euonymus kiautchovicus. This usually is sold by nurserymen under the name *E. patens.* It has shining deep green leaves and toward the end of summer produces myriads of tiny greenish-white flowers. In mild climates these are followed by ornamental pinkish and orange-red fruits, but north of New York City the growing season is seldom long enough to enable them to mature. It will grow in sun or shade—actually it retains its leaves longer in the North when grown in shade—7 feet high, ultimately becoming much broader.

Neillia sinensis. An unobtrusive, graceful little shrub with slender branches and bright green leaves usually less than 4 inches long. In late May it has racemes of small pinkish flowers which while not showy are pleasant. It is at its best when grown in light shade. Usually about 4 feet tall in the North, in favored locations it may reach 6 to 7 feet in height and spread.

Stephanandra incisa. A favorite "facing-down" shrub of landscape architects, this Japanese species has practically nothing to commend it but its beautiful lacy foliage, which, when grown in full sun, develops bronze-green tones, turning to red-orange in the fall. It is a graceful shrub with spreading slender branches and is reputed to be capable of growing to 10 feet high, though I have never seen it more than about 5 feet in the North. When exposed to much subzero weather, the shoot tips may be killed, necessitating some pruning in the spring.

THREE—MULTI-VALUE SHRUBS

It is from this group that the long-sighted gardener will make most of his selections.

BERBERIS, Barberry. There are numerous deciduous Barberries with decorative flowers, foliage, and fruit. Unfortunately some of them are alternate hosts for wheat rust and in consequence are taboo in wheat-growing regions. One of these is *B. koreana,* a graceful shrub with red-veined, bright green leaves which change to a deep red in the fall. The yellow flowers are in short dense racemes, followed by bright scarlet berries which retain their color well into the winter. It grows to about 7 feet high. *B. Thunbergi* is the Japanese Barberry. This and its varieties are not susceptible to wheat rust. The species is rather dumpy, growing much broader than its ultimate height of 5 to 6 feet. It is densely branched and very prickly, which is an asset when required as a defensive hedge. Beautiful in all seasons, it is especially so in spring when its flowers are displayed among the developing leaves and its scarlet fruits, the latter being retained all winter long. *B. T. var. atropurpurea* has bronze-red foliage useful for color throughout the growing season; *B. T. minor,* a dwarf form which seldom exceeds 2 feet in height, but more in diameter, is known as the Box Barberry, valuable for foreground planting; *B. T. pluriflora* is a narrow, upright variety. (See under "Narrow Shrubs," page 186.)

CHAENOMELES, Flowering Quince—often listed as Cydonia. The Dwarf Japanese Quince (*C. japonica*) has clusters of orange-scarlet flowers, about the same size and general appearance of apple blossoms, before the lustrous leaves appear. *C. lagenaria,* the Japanese Quince, has similar but generally larger flowers; variety *Simoni* excells with large flowers of deep crimson. Both species have good foliage, handsome flowers with many colored forms among the named varieties. Large yellowish Quince-like fruits produced in the fall are reputed to make palatable jelly. *C. japonica* grows to 3 feet; *C. lagenaria* to 6 feet. (See also "Narrow Shrubs," page 186.)

Cotinus coggygria purpureus (*Rhus cotinus rubrifolia*), Purple Smoke-tree. I have been favorably impressed by the behavior of this purplish-leaved variety of the Smoke-tree, with deep purple hairs on the inflorescences which give the smoky appearance. Leaves are held late—mid-November—and, while they are not flamboyant, their color, purple with deep pink veins, is striking. The species *Cotinus coggygria* has gray-purple "smoke" and bluish-green foliage which turns orange-red in the fall. These are capable of growing into broad bushes 10 feet or more high.

COTONEASTER. This genus contains numerous shrubs of varied habit. Among the most desirable for our purpose are: *C. Dielsiana,* a graceful species with arching branches, small glossy green leaves which become orange-red in the fall, and shiny red berries. About 8 feet high. *C. hupehense* has rather showy small white flowers in late May followed by large, bright crimson fruits in August which, however, do not long persist. Leaves become orange-yellow in the fall. It grows about 6 feet tall.

EUONYMUS. *Euonymus alatus,* the Winged Euonymus, forms a rounded mass of deep green foliage about as broad as it is high. The greenish flowers are inconspicuous. It is in the fall that it really goes to town when its leaves become a brilliant cerise. After the leaves have fallen, the fruits—their exposed seeds covered with a red-orange aril, with which the branchlets are spangled—become more conspicuous. During winter there are the curiously winged branchlets that demand interested attention especially when they are laden with snow. There is a form offered for sale under the name "Monstrosus," in which the corky wings are produced in greater abundance. *E. compactus* is a compact version which grows to about 5 feet; *E. alatus* may ultimately reach 8 or 9 feet.

Ligustrum obtusifolium Regelianum, Regel Privet. This is characterized by its horizontal overlapping branches forming a broad, rounded bush. It is attractive in bloom during July with small racemes of white flowers. These are followed by clusters of black berries covered with white bloom so that the over-all effect is gray. Its 10-foot height and spread make it valuable when a large shrub is needed.

Lonicera Morrowi, Morrow's Bush Honeysuckle. Of the numerous Bush Honeysuckles of merit this is perhaps the best one for our purpose. This blooms about the end of May with white flowers changing to yellow followed by ornamental berries (red in the type, yellow in var. *xanthocarpa*) which are produced in June–July and last until August—unless the robins take them. It forms a bush of rounded outline, broader than high, up to 9 feet tall.

Malus Sargenti, Sargent Crab-apple. This is the lowest-growing of all the Crab-apples and is a real triple-promise shrub—laden with white flowers in May, followed by attractive red, somewhat bloomy fruit, and fall foliage which becomes yellow and orange. Usually it does not exceed 6 feet in height, but its ultimate spread may be twice this.

RHODODENDRON. *Rhododendron* (Azalea) *arborescens,* is a handsome native shrub growing to 9 feet or even larger under favorable conditions. Although its white flowers in July are attractive and deliciously fragrant, it is its foliage, which turns red in the fall, and its furnishing value for which it is chiefly grown.

R. Schlippenbachii, Royal Azalea, has a gorgeous floral display with clear pink, faintly brown-spotted flowers in late May. It has broad leaves—produced in clusters at the tips of the branches—becoming brilliantly yellow or yellow and red in the fall; a compact species growing 6 to 9 feet high.

ROSA. There are two Roses which appeal to me as belonging in the present category—Father Hugo's Rose, *R. Hugonis,* and the Altai Rose, *R. spinosissima altaica.* The first-named has single yellow flowers 2 inches across which are produced in profusion about the end of May; these are followed by small red hips. It is a graceful bush about 6 feet high with a spread of 8 feet with arching branches clothed with feathery leaves. The Altai Rose is a geographical form of the Scotch Rose (*R. spinosissima*) with pure white flowers 2 inches across which are admirably displayed among the bright pale green leaves; grows about 5 feet high.

Spiraea prunifolia plena, Bridal Wreath. This rates a place for its display, spread over several weeks, of small double buttonlike white flowers which open early in spring. Its Plum-like leaves, lustrous above, take on warm autumnal tints. With me this forms a tidy bush about 6 feet high, 4 to 5 feet across; interesting in winter with a multiplicity of fine twigs, and conspicuous flower buds ready to start into growth in the spring.

"DIEBACK" SHRUBS

The amount of "dieback" suffered by these shrubs is conditioned by the severity of the winter experienced in the region—in the North they may be killed to the ground, but in mild climates only the tips of the shoots will succumb. Even so, usually it is desirable (unless increase in size is needed) to cut them back almost to the ground in the interest of neatness. These shrubs bloom on shoots of the current season, and all of them, therefore, are summer- or fall-blooming kinds. Essentially they have the same effect in the garden as herbaceous perennials, except that in winter their bare branches have some furnishing value.

Abelia grandiflora, when treated as a dieback, usually grows to about 3 feet; in mild climates it may reach 6 feet. Its small pointed leaves are so shiny that the bush literally glistens in the summer sun. Starting about the middle of June and continuing until frost, the small, white, pink-tinged, fragrant flowers are produced along the side branches. Toward the fall the leaves become bronze, and together with the red-brown color of the persistent sepals present a distinctive color note lasting into the winter.

Buddleia Davidi, Butterfly-bush. There are numerous garden varieties of Butterfly-bush ranging in height from 3 to 8 feet as cutbacks. Ordinarily the comparatively dwarf varieties are preferred for our purpose. If the fading flower spikes are promptly cut off, they may be expected to stay in bloom from July until frost.

Caryopteris incana, Blue-beard, is low-growing and compact, usually about 1½ to 2 feet tall. It has silvery green leaves and from August until frost the upper part of the plant is clothed with clusters of small lavender-colored blooms. The variety Heavenly Blue has deep blue flowers and is more emphatic than the type. Needs sun and well-drained, rather sandy soil.

Hydrangea arborescens grandiflora, Hills-of-Snow. It is better not to attempt to use this except when good moist soil and part shade are available. In such conditions, if it is cut to the ground annually, it will make a rounded bush about 4 feet high with rounded leaves and almost globular heads of snowy flowers in June and July.

Lespedeza Thunbergi, Bush Clover, is often sold under the name *Desmodium penduliflorum.* This member of the great Pea family has rather mediocre foliage, but it is valuable for its late-blooming qualities in September and October, when it produces large panicles of small, rose-purple Pea-like flowers. It grows to about 3 feet high, and as the stems tend to droop over at flowering time, it may be necessary under some conditions to provide some support for them.

ROSA. Roses of the Hybrid Tea and Floribunda groups may be treated as "dieback" shrubs and may be used in the shrub border and as accents in the flower garden itself. However, they are subject to a fungus disease called black spot and varied insect pests, so ordinarily they should be used in a limited way, choosing only those varieties such as Goldilocks, Crimson Glory, and Mrs. Erskine Pembroke Thom, which are not so susceptible to disease; or you could use them in groups large enough to warrant the weekly spraying or dusting which may be necessary to keep them in health. It is well to remember that as shrubs they lack in grace when not in bloom.

VITEX, Chaste-tree. There are two species available for use in the flower garden—*V. Agnus-castus,* of which the variety *latifolia* (*macrophylla* of the nursery trade) is most commonly planted; and *V. negundo,* not commonly offered, of which the preferred variety is *incisa,* because of the softer effects produced by the divided leaflets. Both kinds have grayish-appearing foliage. If grown for flowers *latifolia* is preferred; it produces its showy panicles of small lavender-blue flowers from July until frost.

EVERGREENS

Some evergreens, both narrow-leaf (coniferous) and broad-leaf, are desirable in the flower garden for backgrounds or accents and to provide interest in winter. An added reason for using them is that they furnish shelter and in some cases food (Yew and Juniper) for birds. When the herbaceous garden is enclosed by a hedge, often it is more satisfactory when an evergreen one is chosen because of its year-round effect.

BERBERIS, Barberry. Among the hardiest of the evergreen Barberries is *B. verruculosa,* which almost never exceeds 3 feet in height—as usually seen it is about 2 feet with a 2½-foot spread. The leaves are small, spiny, and shining; its flowers are not very showy, although we welcome them for their fragrance. Another species of entirely different habit is *B. Julianae.* This makes an upright, comparatively narrow bush about 5 feet tall with glossy leaves which may be scorched if exposed to much subzero weather. Flowers are small, yellow, produced in dense clusters. This is not reliably hardy north of New York City.

BUXUS, Boxwood. Before planting Boxwood be sure that its odor is not objectionable to you or your family; to some persons the odor is pleasant, to others it is nonexistent, and to others it is definitely obnoxious, as it is to me. The Common Boxwood (*B. sempervirens*) is a European tree not thoroughly hardy north of Long Lsland, New York. Its variety *suffruticosa,* the Edging Box, which seldom grows more than 12 feet tall, is the kind that is so prominently displayed in the plantings at Mt. Vernon. One of the hardiest, which survives without harm during the normal winter experienced in the mid-Hudson Valley, is *B. sempervirens* var. *rotundifolia.* This makes a compact bush about 5 feet high with large rounded leaves. In spring the developing shoots take on graceful curves. The Korean Box, *B. microphylla* var. *koreana,* about 3 feet tall, is the hardiest of the Boxwoods, enduring the climate of Vermont; Japanese Box (*B. m. japonica*), about 6 feet tall, is hardy in Massachusetts. These, while hardier than the Common Box, are not equal to it in ornamental value.

Chamaecyparis obtusa, Hinoki Cypress. This cone-bearing evergreen is native to Japan. It has deep green frond-like branchlets. The variety *nana,* a dwarf, slow-growing form, is perhaps the most desirable for flower-garden use. It has a picturesque growth habit.

Daphne cneorum, Garland-flower. This grows to about 1 foot high with partially prostrate branches. When it has soil and location to its liking, it may spread to 3 feet or more. Its clusters of clear pink flowers which are produced in the spring, and to a lesser extent again in the fall, are fragrant. The fly in the ointment is that sometimes it is difficult to get it established (I have had best success when starting with small plants), and sometimes it will grow happily for several years and then suddenly die without apparent cause. It needs full sun and a thoroughly drained, sandy, humusy soil with pH of 6.5 to 7.5. In spite of its cantankerous disposition, it is so beautiful that its culture should be attempted.

ILEX, Holly. There are several species of evergreen Holly worthy of consideration. The American and English Hollies are useful when a large-scale shrub or small tree is needed—the latter-named, however, is of dubious hardiness north of Philadelphia. Chinese Holly, *I. cornuta*, is a striking species useful in gardens from Virginia southward. Most valuable for northern gardens are forms of Japanese Holly (*I. crenata*), which grow 15 feet in the South and 8 feet in the North. The variety *convexa*, with the edges of the leaves rolled downward, and variety *microphylla*, with small leaves, both of which are hardier than the type, may be expected to survive as far north as Massachusetts. All Hollies are ordinarily dioecious—that is to say, the male flowers and the female flowers are produced on separate bushes, so when fruits are required it is necessary to have both sexes represented not too far away from each other, usually in the proportion of one male to about ten female plants.

PIERIS, Andromeda. The Japanese Andromeda, *P. japonica*, is a shrub of more than triple promise. The young shoots in the spring take on appealing bronze tones; throughout the summer the rich-looking glossy leaves are a joy; and in the fall the dropping panicles of flower buds are produced ready to open in Lily-of-the-valley-like flowers in the spring. The bush itself is rather narrow in proportion to its ultimate height of 6 or more feet. The native species, *P. floribunda*, which, while perhaps more effective in bloom—the panicles are held erect—is not so generally useful because of its rather dull foliage. It is more dumpy in habit than the Japanese kind and grows usually to about 4 feet high. These, in common with allied plants such as Rhododendron, Blueberry, and their relatives, need an acid, humusy soil which should not be allowed to become too dry.

RHODODENDRON. There are many hundreds of species, varieties, and hybrids of Rhododendron, a few of which are especially valuable in the flower garden. The Carolina Rhododendron, *R. carolinianum*, is one of the hardiest as well as being extremely beautiful. This becomes a rounded bush broader than high (up to about 4 feet in the

North) with leaves about 3 inches long. Its rose-pink flowers are abundantly produced in May or June; there is a variety, *alba,* in which the flowers are white. *Rhododendron obtusum* varieties are in general less hardy (try the Gable hybrids when they become generally available), but are excellent in climates no more severe than that of Philadelphia. This species is supposed to be the progenitor of the Kurume and Hinodegiri Azaleas, available in a bewildering array of colors and forms. The best advice I can give to prospective purchasers is to visit a nearby nursery and select the appealing forms when they are in bloom. Usually none of these is likely to exceed 3 feet in height. Moist, acid, humusy soil is necessary.

Taxus, Yew. Most generally useful of all the evergreens is the Japanese Yew (*T. cuspidata*), of which there are numerous named varieties. Japanese Yew is tolerant of a wide variety of conditions, growing in almost every kind of soil, enduring sun or shade, and is winter-hardy into southern Ontario. It has dense, dark green foliage, against which the pale green developing shoots are seen in effective contrast in the spring. Male and female flowers are produced on separate plants, so, when it is desired to have a display of the scarlet fruits either for bird food or for ornament, it is necessary to have both sexes not too far separated in the proportion of about one male plant to ten female plants. The type is capable of forming a tree exceeding 40 feet in height, but it can be kept down by annual pruning. There are dwarf garden forms ranging from the 1-foot *T. c. minima* to the 6-foot *T. c. nana.* The variety forming a compact cone-shaped bush is a form of *T. media* (a hybrid between the English Yew, *T. baccata,* and Japanese Yew), known as *T. m. Hatfieldi;* and a column-shaped variety with erect branches is *T. m. Hicksi.*

ACCENT SHRUBS

All of the evergreens mentioned can be used, placed at strategic points, to provide accents either in the shrub background or in the flower border itself. The narrow, upright forms are particularly valuable for this purpose: here are a few additional species that can be used.

Chaenomeles (*Cydonia*), Spitfire. This is a variety of the Japanese Quince, with erect stems forming a column about 2 feet wide and 6 feet high. In early spring the branches are clothed with deep crimson, apple-blossom-like flowers.

Daphne Burkwoodi (Somerset). This is a hybrid (*D. caucasicum* x *D. cneorum*) with stiff upright branches clothed with narrow leaves which in mild climates are retained all winter. Its clusters of fragrant, rose-pink flowers are abundantly produced in May. As with *D. cneorum,* success is more certain when young stock is planted.

Hydrangea quercifolia, Oak-leaved Hydrangea. The leaves of this species, reminiscent of those of some Oaks, vary in length from 5 inches to 1 foot or even more; the stout young branches with the developing growth buds are a warm rusty tan in color. In the fall and up to the end of November the foliage takes on deep coppery tones in effective contrast with the gray woolly leafstalks. This is a shrub which will endure part shade, but the color is more intense in full sun. It blooms in June. The panicled flowers, which are rather dirty white, changing to pastel pink and red-purple, are not especially attractive. In mild climates it may grow to 8 feet, with an even greater spread; in the mid-Hudson Valley it seems to limit itself to about 3 feet with a spread of 5 or 6 feet. I like it for contrast with smaller-leaved shrubs. One trouble it has is that it is subject to Japanese-beetle attack.

Picea glauca conica, the Dwarf Alberta Spruce, is a dwarf, narrow cone-shaped form with crowded leaves and branchlets. Slow-growing, it is seldom seen in heights greater than 6 feet and about 2 to 3 feet across. I have seen this used effectively to mark the corners where walks intersect in the flower garden.

Prunus Amanogawa is a narrow, upright Japanese Flowering Cherry which has the same form as Lombardy Poplar, though otherwise differing in almost every respect. It is clothed in May with clusters of semi-double, pale pink flowers which are slightly fragrant. Its ultimate height is about 20 feet, but it starts to bloom when it is no more than 4 to 6 feet high. A very striking, worth-while kind when properly placed.

Juniperus excelsa stricta, Spiny Greek Juniper. The Juniper sold under these names is a narrow, spirelike or cone-shaped variety.

Dwarf Alberta Spruce is useful for accents. In foreground perennial Flax and Dianthus. J. HORACE MCFARLAND COMPANY

Usually seen in specimens less than 6 feet tall, it is capable of reaching a height of 20 feet. The foliage is glaucous, giving a somewhat silvery effect. Similar forms are found among the Common Juniper (*J. communis*)—sometimes in the wild—and these can be similarly used if they are more conveniently available. Junipers are subject to attacks by spider mites, which seem to be more prevalent when the plants are crowded, so this must be taken into account when planting.

FOR WALLS AND FENCES

What to use as furnishing material depends a great deal on the character of the wall or fence. If the structure itself is good-looking, and the color is suitable as a background for the flowers, it should not be entirely obscured by planting—just a trace of foliage here and there will suffice. For brick and masonry walls those plants which climb by aerial rootlets or by adhesive disks are preferred. Among these are Euonymus, Hedera, and Parthenocissus.

Euonymus Fortunei, Wintercreeper, is among the hardiest of the evergreen vines, but even so, it is subject to injury if the foliage is exposed to sun in winter in severe climates; therefore, north of New York City it is better to plant it only on a north-facing or shaded wall. There are numerous varieties, all of which are susceptible to attack by Euonymus scale insects.

Hedera helix, English Ivy. This is an extraordinarily variable species, with many varieties which are not always constant in their appearance. The variety most commonly sold is the Irish Ivy (*H. h. hibernica*), a vigorous grower with large leaves without the white veins characteristic of *H. helix* and its variety *baltica* (supposed to be the hardiest of all) and others. Baltic Ivy is hardy in Boston, the others perhaps somewhat less so, but much depends on their orientation and the amount of shelter. I would suggest that if an appealing variety is growing locally, a good plan would be to beg cuttings from the owner—select young side shoots about 10 inches long in August and plant them at the base of the wall, in the expectation that they will root and climb.

Parthenocissus (*Ampelopsis*) *tricuspidata*, Japanese Ivy or Boston Ivy. This thrives in sun or shade and clings easily to any surface by means of its adhesive disks. Variety *Lowi*, Geranium Creeper, is preferable, as it is less rampant; the leaves are smaller and more distinguished-looking with red veins and stalks. Japanese Ivy is a favorite food of Japanese beetles—a fact that must be considered in areas where this pest is prevalent.

Other methods of furnishing brick or masonry walls include the use of shrubs with flexible branches which are trained and fastened to the wall. In most cases considerable annual pruning is necessary to keep the shrub in balance and to prevent it from extending too far out from the wall.

Some way of fastening the branches to the wall must be devised. This may be done by means of tightly stretched wires spaced about a foot apart on brackets extending 3 to 6 inches from the wall; by means of a wooden trellis; by passing a strip of leather or cloth around the branch and nailing it to the wall with special-type nails; or by patented supports which are attached with a special cement to the wall.

Among shrubs suitable for such training are: *Chaenomeles lagenaria*, Japanese Quince, in variety; *Cotoneaster horizontalis*, which, as its name implies, ordinarily grows horizontally, but I have seen made to grow vertically on a wall in the Oxford Botanic Garden, where it was extremely effective; *C. salicifolia floccosa*, which has lovely arching branchlets clothed with Willow-like leaves, especially effective in the fall when laden with its bright red fruits; *Kerria japonica pleniflora*, a member of the Rose family, with golden-yellow double flowers in summer, and in winter conspicuous green branches. This grows best in partial shade and in climates where temperatures seldom approach zero. In severe climates the stems lose their attractive green color in winter. The double forms of Flowering Peach are excellent for the purpose, as also is the so-called Flowering Almond (*Prunus triloba*), which, if the shoots are cut back annually as soon as the flowers fade, produces abundant wand-like growths extending almost at right angles from the wall clothed in due time with double, Peach-like flowers.

FENCES

The character of the fence largely determines the nature of the material used to embellish it. Wooden post and rail fences, those of the hurdle type, and board and trellis fences, or combinations of these, make admirable supports for choice plant materials such as Clematis and Roses. The following are especially good Clematis species: *C. montana rubens*, Anemone Clematis, is clothed with pink flowers in May. This blossoms on the old wood and is, therefore, not suited for growing in regions where winter temperatures are so low as to kill the shoots made the preceding year; therefore, it is better to choose from the following if in your region the temperature frequently falls below 10 degrees. *C. tangutica*, Golden Clematis, grows to about 8 feet and has numerous slender branches with many small, lantern-shaped yellow flowers followed by clusters of feathery achenes (seeds) which themselves are decidedly ornamental. *C. texensis*, Scarlet Clematis, grows to about 6 feet, with glaucous leaves and urn-shaped, fleshy scarlet flowers 1 inch long abundantly produced over a long period in summer and fall. This is the handsomest American species.

Among the best of the large-flowered Clematis hybrids, and the easiest to grow, are: *Jackmani*, with rich, deep violet-purple flowers; *Henri*, with white flowers 6 inches across; Mme. Edouard André, purplish red; and Ramona, with medium-blue flowers. All of these bloom on shoots of the current season, so even if they are killed to the ground in winter, they are still able to bloom during the ensuing growing season.

ROSES

Of Pillar and Climbing Roses, there is an embarrassingly large number from which to choose. You probably have your own favorites, but if you haven't, as a starter I would suggest: Climbing Goldilocks, a yellow variety which has a tendency toward everblooming; Climbing Cecile Brunner, with tiny pink flowers of exquisite form and handsome foliage; Climbing Summer Snow, with white petaled, semi-double, 2-inch flowers blooming recurrently throughout summer and fall; Doubloons is a hardy variety, with large, buff-yellow flowers; Dream Girl has large, fragrant flowers, with tones of pink and salmon; and New Dawn is an ever-blooming counterpart of Dr. W. Van Fleet, except that it is not so rampant.

Climbing vines are better suited on chain-link and cattle fencing; but if given a little help, they can also be trained on walls and the

Good companions—
Clematis Lawsoniana
candida and Rose
Climbing Cecile Brun-
ner planted together to
climb on pillar. AUTHOR

Clematis Ramona grow-
ing on hurdle fence.
ALICE CHANDLER

kinds of wood fences we have been discussing. Among the best of the climbing vines are: *Akebia quinata,* Five-leaf Akebia, which is grown primarily for the furnishing value of its clean, elegant foliage. It has fragrant flowers of purplish-brown and rosy-purple which are mostly hidden by the foliage and thus pass unnoticed. The fruits are large—up to 3 inches long, pale purple-violet in color, covered with a waxy bloom; but in my experience they are not commonly produced unless the fruits of the female flowers are hand pollinated. The fruits are said to be eaten in Japan, and so far as I'm concerned, the Japanese are welcome to them. To me the insipid unpalatability of the pulp surrounding the seeds (the edible portion) is forecast by the unappetizing appearance of the mass, which reminds me of the loathsome-looking sea slugs which I have on occasion encountered in Bermuda waters.

Polygonum Auberti, China Fleece-vine, is one of the best for quick coverage. It endures neglect, poor soil, city conditions, and hard pruning. It is good that it does endure hard pruning, because it grows rampantly and must be cut back from time to time lest it overrun everything. It has clusters of white, pink-tinged flowers during summer and fall.

Wisteria sinensis, the Chinese Wisteria, is the species most commonly planted, but W. *floribunda,* the Japanese Wisteria, is somewhat hardier, capable of growing and thriving almost to the northernmost part of Vermont and New Hampshire, whereas the Chinese species is dubiously hardy north of Massachusetts. Other differences are in the lengths of the flower clusters—from 8 to 20 inches in the type species *floribunda,* 3 to 4 feet in its variety *macrobotrys,* as compared to the 6- to 12-inch length of the clusters of the Chinese kind. The flowers open gradually from base to the top in *floribunda,* while in *sinensis* practically all of them open at the same time. These species are strong-growing vines and should not be planted except when there is a large expanse of fence to be covered—unless you are prepared to restrain them by pruning, most of which should be done during the growing season in summer.

NARROW SHRUBS

When space is limited, and it is desired to have a large variety of shrubs, naturally narrow kinds should be used rather freely. Among these are: *Berberis Thunbergi pluriflora* (True Hedge Column-berry), a columnar variety of the Japanese Barberry; *Chaenomeles* Spitfire; *Juniperus excelsa stricta;* and the narrow, upright forms of the Common Juniper (*J. communis*); *Picea glauca conica; Prunus* Amanogawa (see accent shrubs above for descriptions).

The above is a selected list of the many hundreds of kinds of shrubs—to me they are the cream of the crop—but doubtless you have your own favorites which I have not mentioned; and nothing I say or refrain from saying will prevent your use of them, which is quite as it should be.

SUMMARY

When flowering shrubs are used, in addition to providing a green foil against which the border flowers are effectively displayed they can often be combined during their blooming season with herbaceous perennials in a pleasing picture. For example: Forsythia and Purple Crocus; Vitex and Rudbeckia; Caryopteris and Chrysanthemum; Daffodils and Flowering Quince; Beauty-bush and Columbine. A mixed shrubbery is more varied and, therefore, more interesting than a hedge; so when there is room to accommodate it, it is preferable. It can serve as a windbreak without the danger of making a stagnant air pocket, which sometimes may occur in a small walled garden.

SPACING

The spacing of the shrubs presents a problem that can be solved by compromise. If they are set close enough to give an immediate effect (immediate, in this case, meaning a year or two), the expense is considerable and they quickly become so crowded that the characteristic habit of the individual is lost, and, unless one is vigilant in pruning, some will be smothered by their stronger-growing neighbors. Close planting may be adopted with the intention of removing alternate plants when they begin to crowd, but this does not affect the expense element, and there are few who have the will power to dig up the surplus bushes before they become so crowded that the habit of the permanent shrubs is distorted. Then, too, it must be remembered, there is another waiting period before the plants assume a more natural shape and fill the gaps. In the meantime

When small shrubs are spaced with future growth in mind, the effect is too open, even for ordinary visual purposes, let alone the requirements of a background for a perennial border such as this. MALCOLM R. KINNEY

there's a misshapen mess for the owner and his friends and enemies to contemplate.

If, on the other hand, the spacing is sufficient (10 to 15 feet for the larger shrubs), so that they can display their characteristic habit of growth for at least a few years before they touch, the planting inevitably looks spotty, inadequate, and for several years fails of its purpose. So it seems to me that the best policy to follow is that which gives fairly liberal spacing to the permanent occupants plus the use of expendable fillers—bulbs, annuals, and herbaceous perennials—to overcome the sparse appearance. Therefore, strong growers such as Forsythia, Viburnum, and Beauty-bush could be set 8 to 10

Herbaceous plants such as Cleome, Daylilies, and Iris complete the background corner. This area is the mirror twin of the one opposite.
MALCOLM R. KINNEY

feet from their nearest neighbors; medium and/or slow growers such as deciduous Azaleas, Enkianthus, Oak-leaf, and Hills-of-Snow Hydrangea, Inkberry, Japanese Barberry, Vanhoutte's Spirea, and Mountain-laurel, 5 to 7 feet; and small ones such as Warty Barberry (*B. verruculosa*), Rose Daphne (*D. Cneorum*), Caryopteris, and most "dieback" shrubs, 3 to 4 feet.

EXPENDABLE FILLERS

Hardy spring-flowering bulbs should be used freely. Scatter a few dozen Siberian Squills or Chionodoxa among the Forsythias; and early Daffodils throughout the planting. It will be two or three seasons before they are smothered by the shrubs. If you are Scotch, you can dig them up when dormant as soon as they become endangered and plant them elsewhere.

Seeds of annuals can be sown in place to follow the bulbs. Suitable kinds which will almost take care of themselves include: Cleome Giant Pink and Helen Campbell, Calliopsis, Flowering Tobacco, Nasturtiums of the semi-trailing group, Love-in-a-mist, and annual Larkspur. Or, with but little more work, plants of Marigold, Petunia, and Zinnia may be started indoors and set in the soil above the bulbs when danger of frost is past; or Gladiolus corms may be planted between the clumps of bulbs.

All the gaps in the shrubbery can be filled with bulbs and annuals; again, some or all of them may be used to accommodate surplus herbaceous perennials. These can stay until their function has been fulfilled and they are crowded out by the growth of the shrubs. Then they can serve as a reserve or be given to friends, or you can dig them up to fill vacancies in the fall garden. Some are so adaptable to transplanting that they can be moved even when they are about to bloom or in bloom.

Bulbs are never likely to grow so rampantly as to imperil the well-being of the shrubs. If during the first year or two annuals and herbaceous perennials should show any tendency to encroach on the domain of the shrubs, they must be restrained.

When wide spacing of shrubs is made and you do not like the "expendable filler" plan, the ground between should have a cover of vegetation to prevent erosion and limit the need for cultivation to small circles around the bases of the shrubs. This can be lawn grass kept down by mowing; or more interestingly with a ground cover of low-growing plants such as Trailing Myrtle, Pachysandra, Ajuga, English Ivy, etc.

CHAPTER SIXTEEN

Descriptive List of Perennials

This is a descriptive listing of the most important perennials. For further information concerning botanical relationships of the plants listed here, and for additional species, consult the Appendix, beginning on page 267.

The height and time of bloom as given in this and the tables of the Appendix are approximate because so much depends on the environment. Climate and soil may exert a profound influence on the behavior of plants, as does the skill, or lack of it, of the gardener.

ACHILLEA, Yarrow, Sneezewort. This is a varied group of herbaceous perennials. Some of them are dwarf rock-garden kinds with silvery foliage and are not too easy to grow. Some are valuable in the perennial garden especially in dry, sunny places; these include: A. *filipendulina*, Fernleaf Yarrow, 3 to 5 feet high, with rather flat clusters of blatant yellow flowers. The variety sold as Golden Plate probably belongs here. Of entirely different appearance is A. *ptarmica*, Sneezewort, a white-flowered species which sometimes spreads rather too freely, grows about 1½ to 2 feet tall. The double-flowered variety sold as A. *p.* Snowball and sometimes as A. *p.* Boule de Neige is reputed to be the best. It blooms over a long period and can be used for cutting. There is one sold as Achillea "Taggetea," which grows to about 18 inches and has pale yellow flowers in clusters. This I think is a rather charming plant, but I have never been able to locate it botanically. There is one called A. *taygetaea*, which, however, grows only to 8 inches high.

ACONITUM, Aconite or Monkshood. This is a group of perennials with showy, hooded flowers related to Delphinium. I have never had

Distinctive flowers of Aconite or Monkshood, *Aconitum Fischeri*.

J. HORACE MCFARLAND COMPANY

real success with them in climates with hot summers, but in the mountainous regions where the nights are cool and in Maine and Nova Scotia they give a wonderful display from June (*A. napellus*) to October (*A. Fischeri Wilsoni*). These should be kept well away from the vegetable garden because of their poisonous nature— fatalities have resulted when the roots have been dug and used by mistake for Horse-radish.

A. autumnale grows from 4 to 5 feet, with deep blue, almost navy-blue flowers in August and September; *A. Fischeri* has flowers which may be pale blue or white, growing up to 6 feet tall; *A. napellus*, with blue flowers, is a variable species, extremely poisonous, with many garden varieties including *A. n. bicolor* with blue and white flowers. A deep, rich soil and partial shade are desirable for Aconites.

AJUGA, Bugle. The Bugles are easily grown low plants, some of them suitable for ground covers in the shade, and some for edging and for planting in the front row of the border. They seem to be indifferent to soil; they will grow in full sun if the soil is kept suitably moist, or in partial shade.

A. genevensis, Alpine Bugle, is the showiest of the Bugles, with bright blue flowers produced in whorls on terminal spikes during May and June. The Carpet Bugle, *A. reptans*, is a rapidly spreading kind, with several garden varieties, some with distinctive foliage and some in which the flower color differs from those of the type which are blue.

ALYSSUM, Golden-tuft, Madwort. Although this is a genus containing about a hundred species, most of them are weedy and not very attractive; some are definitely rock-garden plants and there is only one, to my way of thinking, that is worthy of inclusion in the perennial garden. *Alyssum saxatile* is a species which displays its yellow flowers in mounds about 1 foot tall at the end of April or the beginning of May. There is a compact form, *A. s. compactum*, and a pale yellow variety, *A. s. luteum* (citrinum of the trade), whose color to many is greatly preferable to the glaring yellow of *saxatile*. I have tried twice to establish it here without success. I attribute my failure not to any shortcomings of my own (naturally!), but to the fact that the plants came from a distance, were more than a week in transit, and the confined and airless condition of the packing case was more than their leaves could endure. My suggestion is that planting stock should be obtained locally, preferably in early spring; or you can raise your own from seed sown in May or from cuttings in July.

ANCHUSA, Alkanet. In general these are coarse, bristly perennials, harsh to touch, but redeemed by their clear blue flowers. They are not particular as to soil, provided it is well drained; they need full sun to do their best. *A. myosotidiflora* of catalogues is correctly *Brunnera macrophylla* (see page 201 for description). *A. azurea*, Italian Alkanet, is the one most commonly grown, but its size and tendency to spread by its self-sown seeds limit its usefulness in small gardens. Better kinds (you may have to hunt for them because they are not commonly offered by nurserymen) are: *A. Barrelieri*, which grows to about 2 feet and has blue flowers with white tube and yellow throat; and *A. caespitosa*, Tufted Alkanet (Blue Stars), usually about 1 foot tall, but more across because of the way its stems spread outwards. It blooms from May until July and sometimes in August with blue, white-eyed flowers.

ANEMONE. This is a large genus of value in varied cultural situations. Some—*A. alpina*, *A. baldensis*, and *A. vernalis*—are Alpines suited only for culture in the rock gardens; others such as *A. blanda*, *A. nemorosa* and *A. sylvestris* are charming woodlanders; and *A. canadensis*, *A. carolinianum*, and *A. quinquefolia* are natives suitable for naturalizing. Varieties or hybrids of the Florists' Anemone, *A. coronaria*, *A. fulgens*, and *A. hortensis*, are grown, usually in greenhouses, for cut flowers during the winter. Among the best for culture in the perennial garden are the following: *A. hupehensis*, which starts to display its pale, pastel purple flowers in August and is supposed to be an early-blooming form of Japanese Anemone, *A. japonica*. This is like a little girl who had a little curl! It is a magnificent fall flower in situations to its liking, but does not succeed in every garden. It needs a cool, moist but well-drained, humusy soil in partial shade. There are several garden varieties—semi-doubles and color forms—but to my mind the best is variety *alba*, with 3-inch single white flowers with yellow centers. I will admit that sentiment enters into my evaluation of this variety, because I remember as a small boy enjoying the beauty of these pure white flowers that were growing in the back yard of our home in Cambridge, England. However, it still is a wonderful variety, striking when seen against a dark evergreen background or when associated with the fall-blooming Monkshood. Another species which is well worth hunting for, which you will probably have to do to get it, is the Snowdrop Anemone, *A. sylvestris,* which grows to about 1½ feet, with pure white fragrant flowers up to 1½ inches across in May and June. There is a double-flowered form of this species, which is even more delightful.

ANTHEMIS, Golden Marguerite, St. Johns Daisy. These are herbs with strongly aromatic, finely divided leaves. The true Chamomile, *A. nobilis,* belongs here. This is a rather weedy-looking character, in former times much valued as a "Yarb" in rural districts; on occasion it was used to quiet fretful babies. The kinds most valued for perennial garden culture are St. Johns Daisy, *A. Sancti Johannis,* and the Golden Marguerite, *A. tinctoria.* The first-named differs from the Golden Marguerite, in addition to technical characters, by having deeper orange-yellow flowers. Both kinds grow between 2 and 3 feet high, and are long-blooming from May to September. They are at their best in a sunny location in well-drained, moderately rich soil.

AQUILEGIA, Columbine. So far as Columbines are concerned, the fly in the ointment is a leaf miner which tunnels between the upper and lower surfaces of the leaves, makes them look horrid, and debilitates the plants. But in those regions where this pest is not prevalent or can be circumvented by frequent spraying with an insecticide containing Lindane the airy grace and long-blooming habit of the Columbines make them a "must." Most gardeners prefer the long-spurred hybrids because of their large range of color, but personally my preferences lean toward the species such as *A. caerulea,* the Colorado Columbine; *A. canadensis,* the Common American Columbine; *A. chrysantha,* the Golden Columbine; and *A. flabellata,* the Fan Columbine. It is sometimes difficult to get the true Colorado Columbine—many seeds sold under this name are from hybrids. One way of being sure of getting what you want is to obtain seed collected from the wild in the Rocky Mountains. However, you can't go far wrong with Columbines; practically all of them have some claims to beauty—it is merely that some are better than others. Except for the diminutive Alpine kinds, which are inclined to be fractious under cultivation, Columbines are easy to grow in any fairly good garden soil in full sun or partial shade. Their chief short-

Among the Rockies' famous flowers is Colorado Columbine, *Aquilegia caerulea*, blue and purest white, with amazingly long and graceful spurs.
KATHLEEN MARRIAGE

comings are the aforementioned miner and their promiscuity—they hybridize easily, self-sow their seeds, which germinate, and unless you are careful to get rid of them, your select hybrids will change into a mess of mongrels. For information concerning other species and varieties—and for the height, color, and time of bloom of those mentioned above—turn to page 270.

Arabis albida, White Rock-cress. The double-flowered form, *flore pleno,* is infinitely preferable because of its long-lasting qualities, remaining in bloom from the second week of April until mid-May. Somewhat hoary, carpeting foliage remains attractive until hard frost. It is a valuable edging plant that needs sometimes to be restrained or renewed from cuttings or divisions. It is often sold as *A. alpina.*

ARMERIA, Thrift, Sea-pink. The Thrifts botanically are a mixed-up lot, but we, as gardeners, should not be unduly concerned about this because the most commonly grown kind, Lauche's Thrift, *A. maritima Laucheana,* is so easily increased by division that it is propagated this way by the nurseryman so that it remains true. This variety, to my way of thinking, is greatly superior to the straight species in that the flowers are a stronger color—deep crimson rather than a somewhat washed-out rose-pink—and they are more freely produced over a longer period. The Thrifts produce numerous small flowers in large heads on leafless stalks. They need full sun to be at their best and thrive in a sandy, well-drained soil. Lauche's Thrift is an excellent plant to use for formal edgings, but it will have to be taken up and divided and replanted whenever, after a few years, plants begin to show dead spots in the center.

ARTEMISIA, Wormwood. This is a large genus of annuals, biennials, perennials, and shrubs, most of them with aromatic and bitter-tasting leaves. It contains such well-known plants as Absinthium, Tarragon, and Sagebrush, all shrubby in habit. Best for the perennial garden are silver-leaf kinds such as *A. albula,* usually sold as Silver King Artemisia; *A. Stelleriana,* the Beach Wormwood; the silvery, satiny-leaved *A. Schmidtiana,* which grows up to 2 feet; and its variety, *nana,* which makes a mound up to 1½ feet across and about 1 foot high, which is sold as Silver-mound Artemisia. Their silvery-gray foliage provides an effective foil for flowering plants and serves to separate warring color elements in the border. All of them grow well in poor, dry soil and sunny locations except for *A. lactiflora,* which thrives in the ordinary soil of the border. This is a fine, upstanding plant for the rear of the border, growing up to 5 feet high, with large panicles of tiny creamy-white flowers.

ASTER, Starwort, Michaelmas Daisy. Another varied group ranging in height from 6 inches to 6 feet and flowers from ½ to 4 inches across. It includes the Alpine Aster, New England Aster, and Michaelmas Daisy. Among the most satisfactory for border use are the following: *A. amellus,* Italian Aster, and its varieties; especially King

Aster Mount Everest. Plants are tall and in the fall are covered from top to bottom with white flowers. J. HORACE MCFARLAND COMPANY

George, which has blue-violet flowers 3 inches across during July and August on a plant 2 feet tall; *A. Frikarti,* a hybrid between *A. amellus* and *A. Thompsonianus,* of which Wonder of Staffa is the best-known kind. These species and their derivations are sometimes difficult to establish—spring planting is very definitely preferable for

Aster Violetta (Dwarf) has flowers of deep, rich blue.
A. B. MORSE COMPANY

them. Varieties of the New England Aster, *A. novae-angliae*, are admirably adapted for growing in wet spots, though they will also thrive under ordinary flower-garden conditions. Good garden varieties are: Mt. Rainier, 3 to 4 feet, white with yellow disks; and Survivor, 4 feet with deep pink flowers very lovely in bloom. It is a good plan to cut off about 3 inches of the shoot tips when they are about 1 foot tall; it does improve their appearance, but I don't know why. There are scores, perhaps hundreds, of named garden varieties of the New York Aster, A. *novi-belgi,* most of them raised in England. American breeders are also selecting new forms so that the list of names is in process of change and augmentation. Here are some excellent named varieties including some of the newest, but don't stay with them if you see better kinds flowering in a nursery. Alcida, moundlike habit, 2 feet high, garnet-purple flowers; Aquilla, broad cone-shaped habit, 2 to 2½ feet, pale blue semi-double flowers; Beechwood Challenger, 3 to 4 feet, crimson-red single, free-flowering; Blue Gem, 5 feet, deep blue semi-double, probably the best blue; Gay Border Blue, 5 feet, blue with yellow eye, good for cutting; Hilda Ballard, 5 feet, silvery mauve, large, double; Mt. Everest, 3 to 4 feet, white, small eye; Plenty, 3½ to 4 feet, semi-double, soft blue flowers 2 inches across; Queen Mary, 3 to 4 feet, rich blue tinted with lavender; Violetta, 3 feet, rich deep blue.

Amellus and Frikarti varieties are valuable for their long-blooming habits in summer; New York Asters with their prevailing blue or purple flowers can happily be associated with yellow and bronze Chrysanthemums in the fall.

There is a group of Dwarf Perennial Asters, A. *hybridus nanus,* developed originally soon after World War I by workers for the British Imperial War Graves Commission, who needed a hardy dwarf edging plant for use in military cemeteries. These never exceed 2 feet in height and some are only half this size. Among them are: Constance, 9 inches, shell-pink flowers; Little Red Boy, 1½ feet, 2 feet across; Pacific Amaranth, 1 foot, red purple; Pacific Horizon, about 1 foot, blue flowers; and Niobe, which is really dwarf, only 6 inches tall, with white flowers.

These hardy Asters thrive best in a deep soil enriched with leafmold or rotted manure. They need rather frequent division, say every two or three years, in order to have them at their best, and they also need room to grow. I once saw in England a border of Michaelmas Daisies, probably 100 x 30 feet, each plant standing 3 feet from its neighbor and only three main shoots allowed to grow on each plant. The effect was sparse and one had a feeling of wastefulness of space during the early part of the season, but in the fall the effect was breath-taking when the plants had grown to touch each other.

ASTILBE, Florists' Spirea. There is often confusion between this genus and Spirea, in spite of the fact that they belong in different plant families, and many nurserymen list them under Spirea in their catalogues. They have compound leaves and feathery panicles of tiny white or pink flowers. After trying them here for five years I am now thoroughly convinced that they are not for me—our soil is too poor, dry, and sandy, consequently whenever their flowers are just about to become effective, along comes a June drought and they look miserable for the remainder of the year. However, in rich, moist soil in partial shade they are handsome plants in and out of bloom and most rewarding.

A. *Arendsi* is a hybrid race with A. *Davidi*, a 6-footer, as one of the parents. The hybrids run from 2 to 3 feet tall, with flowers which may be white, through rose to purplish in color. Variety Fanal, with coppery foliage and garnet-red flowers growing to 2 feet tall, may belong here. *Astilbe japonica* and its varieties are the ones that are commonly forced into bloom for Easter by florists and sold as Spireas. The species has white flowers; the variety *rubens* has rosy crimson flowers; those of Peach Blossom are light pink; Queen Alexandra, deep pink. All of these are very much worth while if you can give them the conditions necessary for their good health as outlined above.

BOLTONIA. I have not been able to find any real vernacular name for Boltonia, in spite of the fact that B. *asteroides* is native from Connecticut to Nebraska and southward. It is one of those "Ho-hum," colorless personalities, looking something like a hardy Aster with numerous ¾-inch white to purplish flowers, which is useful for naturalizing. It is capable of reaching 8 feet in height, but usually is seen from 5 to 6 feet. B. *latisquama* is a better species for the flower garden with larger pink to purple flowers on a smaller plant 4 to 5 feet high. Both may spread themselves too vigorously unless curbed annually.

Brunnera macrophylla, Dwarf Anchusa, is a lovely thing in bloom, with airy sprays of small, deep, true-blue flowers in April and May rising from among its broad, heart-shaped leaves. My original plant

Clumps of Spring Snowflake with Brunnera shoots barely visible (photographed March 20). MALCOLM R. KINNEY

Foliage of Snowflake now partially obscured by Brunnera, coming into bloom (photographed April 23). MALCOLM R. KINNEY

Brunnera in full bloom, Snowflake no longer visible (photographed May 8). MALCOLM R. KINNEY

of this was acquired by accident, coming as it did among a clump of Spring Snowflake from a friend's garden. They are admirable companions; the Snowflake is in full bloom when the leaves of Brunnera are just pushing through; by the time the Snowflake has finished its bloom, Brunnera is starting and its leaves cover the unsightly, fading foliage of the Snowflake, remaining in good condition until the fall.

CAMPANULA, Bellflower. This is a large genus of annuals, biennials (see Canterbury Bells, Chapter Ten), and perennials. Many of them are especially adapted to the rock garden—some of these are cantankerous and difficult to grow. There is no difficulty, however, in growing the following in ordinary garden soil provided it is not extremely acid—no lower than pH5.5. Here are the kinds that seem to me to be the most useful:

C. carpatica, Carpathian Harebell. This is a tufted plant with cool-looking, violet-blue flowers 1½ to 2 inches across, freely produced in July and, usually, a scattering of bloom thereafter until frost. There is a white-flowered form (variety *alba*) and a compact one known as Blue Carpet. *C. glomerata*, Clustered Bellflower, is an erect species growing 1½ to 2 feet with its purple flowers in dense clusters; the variety *superba* (is this the same as *dahurica?*) has violet flowers in larger clusters. *C. lactiflora* is handsome in bloom with flowers the color of skimmed milk. Usually grows 3 to 4 feet high, but I have seen it 6 or more feet in British Columbia. *C. persicifolia*, Peach-leaved Bellflower, is one of the most beautiful Campanulas with blue flowers on erect stems to 3 feet tall, which in exposed locations may need support; the variety Telham Beauty, with enormous single, clear blue flowers, is probably the best variety; one known as Moerheimei has semi-double white flowers. These varieties should be propagated by division or cuttings rather than by seeds.

CENTAUREA, Bachelor Button, Cornflower, Knapweed. This genus contains annuals and perennials, most of the latter rather weedy-looking. There are, however, several which have some good points (see tabular list in Appendix), but the only worth-while one that is easily obtainable is *C. montana*, Mountain Bluet or Perennial Cornflower, which grows 1½ to 2 feet with deep blue flowers twice the size of the annual Cornflower, but unfortunately not abundantly produced. Blooms from June to September.

Ceratostigma plumbaginoides, Blue Leadwort, Larpent Plumbago. It is amazing that with the nomenclatorial handicap possessed by the Blue Leadwort it has made any headway at all in our gardens. Doubtless its sterling qualities of clean-looking foliage and clear, deep blue flowers in late summer and fall have endeared it to many gardeners. It forms a mass of foliage on wiry stems 6 to 12 inches high. If you don't find it listed in your catalogue under Ceratostigma, try looking for it as *Plumbago Larpentae*. It is a late starter in the spring, so don't be alarmed if you are unable to discern any sign of growth when everything else is burgeoning.

CHRYSANTHEMUM. A couple of books would be necessary to cover properly the merits of this genus—one dealing with the Garden and Florist Chrysanthemums (actually there are several already written on this subject), the other to concern itself with Pyrethrum, Shasta Daisy, and a host of intriguing species.

Ceratostigma or Plumbago—valuable for its late-blooming flowers of blue. (Note butterfly in right foreground.) MALCOLM R. KINNEY

LEFT. Chrysanthemum, Pink Spoon. RIGHT. Chrysanthemum, Silver Moon, single. J. HORACE MCFARLAND COMPANY

Chrysanthemum, Lavender Lady, decorative.
J. HORACE MCFARLAND
COMPANY

C. coccineum, Pyrethrum, Painted Daisy. These are characterized by almost fernlike, divided foliage, and showy single or double blooms of crimson, lilac, pink, or white on stems 18 inches to 2 feet long in late May and early July. In some favored climates it is possible to get scattered flowers thereafter if the old flower stalks are kept cut off. They are excellent for use as cut flowers. Planting, in a sunny spot, should preferably be done in spring rather than in fall. Following are varieties which appeal to me: Eileen May Robinson, single pink; Helen, rose-pink, double; Huntington Scarlet, the best red; Mrs. C. S. Beckwith, double, white; Silver Tips, red petals, white tips, double.

C. arcticum, C. coreanum, C. morifolium, C. nipponicum (a subshrub). All of these may enter into the make-up of the modern Garden Chrysanthemum. You will find them listed in catalogues as Hardy Chrysanthemums, Northland Daisies, Korean Chrysanthemums; as Ameliamums, or Azaleamums or Cushion 'Mums; and many commemorate the name of the originator or place of origin—De Petris, Kraus, Minnesota, New Hampshire, U. S. Dept. of Agriculture, English, etc.

In the catalogues of the specialists Chrysanthemums often are further divided into Singles, Anemone-flowered, Decorative, Pompon, Button, Spoon, Spider, etc. Northland Daisies were derived largely from *C. arcticum;* Korean Chrysanthemums from *C. coreanum.* Ameliamum, Azaleamum, and Cushion 'Mum belong in a group which originated from a variety known as Amelia; they are characterized by an early-blossoming habit on low-growing, spreading plants—usually no more than a foot high, up to 2 feet and even more in diameter.

The Korean Chrysanthemums, like the Northland Daisies, are reputed to be better able to withstand severe winters than the general run of Chrysanthemums; this is true also of the Minnesota and New Hampshire varieties. English varieties in general are characterized by having large flowers, but many of them bloom too late to be satisfactory in those regions where early frosts are the rule. This is a fact that must be taken into account by those who live in such regions and early-blooming varieties chosen; for, although the flowers of Chrysanthemum can endure light frost, when the temperature gets much below 28 degrees, flowers are likely to be injured.

There are hundreds, perhaps thousands, of named varieties of garden Chrysanthemums; new names are listed each year and many of the older ones are discarded, so it is somewhat futile to recommend specific varieties. However, the following are kinds so good that they can be expected to be available for a number of years, even though no one dealer is likely to carry all of these: Allegro, 2 feet, October, pink and coppery salmon, double; Apricot Glow, 2½ feet, one of the Cushion 'Mums; Autumn Lights, 2 feet, October, coppery bronze; Avalanche, 1½ feet, late September, large-flowered white; Bokhara, 2 feet, early October, rosy crimson; Canary, 2 to 2½ feet, September, yellow; Charles Nye, 2 feet, deep yellow pompon, compact; Judith Anderson, 1½ feet, early October, deep yellow, button pompon; Fred F. Rockwell, 2 feet, early October, bronze and orange-scarlet; Korean Princess, 2 feet, October, red to pink, gold center, anemone-type; Lavender Lady, 2½ feet, early October, lavender; Olive Longland, 2 feet, mid-September, apricot; Pepita, 2½ feet,

September–October, crimson-red flowers; Seagull, 2 to 2½ feet, September, white with cream centers; Summertime, 2 feet, late July to frost, golden-yellow single flowers.

You can order plants from catalogue descriptions and get them by mail in the spring; or you can select varieties in full bloom in the fall at a nursery, load them in the trunk of the car, tote them home, plant them, and enjoy them right away. This may seem a rather expensive way of acquiring a collection, but you are certain of what you are getting, and if you have facilities for carrying them over winter in a cold frame or if you live where they are perfectly hardy outdoors, you will have plenty of propagating stock from which to raise a dozen or more plants from each in the spring.

Chrysanthemums grow best in soil which is rich and thoroughly underdrained; whenever possible it is desirable to prepare it by spreading a 2- or 3-inch layer of partly decayed manure in the fall and digging it in deeply. If this is not possible, use thoroughly decayed manure in the spring, or, if this is unavailable, put on a ½-inch layer of dried, ground cattle manure. Practically all Chrysanthemums make a better display when they are divided each year in the spring and started anew from single, rooted shoots (an exception is variety Summertime, which needs dividing only once every three years). Another method which is desirable when large numbers of plants are required, but is possible only when greenhouse facilities are available, is to take cuttings in March, insert them in sand. When they are rooted, pot them up into small pots of soil and set them out in April (see also Chapter Fourteen, Propagating the Plants).

As soon as the young plants start to grow, they will be benefited by the application of a 5-10-5 fertilizer at the rate of about 4 to 6 ounces per square yard, scattered on the soil and scratched in with a cultivator, being careful to avoid injuring the roots in the process. A further application at the expiration of another six or eight weeks will be of advantage.

The Cushion Chrysanthemums usually do not need any pinching to induce branching, but for the ordinary kinds it is usually desirable to pinch out the tips of the shoots as soon as they attain a length of 6 inches, to induce buds to start to grow from below; when these buds in turn have attained a length of 6 inches, their tips should be pinched back too. Usually this is sufficient to produce enough stems to make a bushy plant; if not, continue the pinching, but not later than July or flowering may be delayed too much. Chrysanthemums which grow in excess of 2 feet high almost always need some kind of support to prevent them from being toppled over by a wind. My favorite support is twiggy branches stuck in around the plants before they have attained their full height. (See pages 138–39.)

Aphids are likely to make their appearance on the young growths of Chrysanthemums; sometimes they can be eliminated by the pinching which is done primarily to promote branching; if, however, they get beyond this stage, they should be sprayed with a good contact spray.

Chrysanthemum maximum vars., Shasta Daisy. This species from the Pyrenees has given rise to a number of single and double garden forms known as Shasta Daisies. These, when they grow well, are excellent both for garden display and for cutting, with flower heads which in some varieties may attain a diameter of 5 inches. They bloom on stems 2 to 3 feet tall in June and July, and if they are cut rather freely for indoor use, they give a scattering of blooms until frost. They do not succeed in every garden. I suspect that different varieties may demand certain conditions in order to do well. For example, in my garden, Mark Riegel, a single variety with flowers which are supposed to be 4 to 5 inches across, was a dismal failure; while Wirral Supreme, a double-flowered form, grew very well indeed. I suggest it would be a good plan to obtain one plant of each of several varieties such as Aglaya, Esther Reed, Jenifer Reed, Majestic, Mark Riegel, and Wirral Supreme and propagate those that give the best performance. This can be done by digging up the clumps in the spring, which should be done every other year in any case, separating them in much the same way you would garden Chrysanthemums, and replanting them.

COREOPSIS, Tickseed. The two species most commonly grown in gardens are *C. grandiflora*, with the upper leaves three- to five-parted, 2½ feet tall; and *C. lanceolata*, with all the leaves entire, which grows 2 feet tall. Both of them are similar in their floral appearance. There is a double-flowered form of *C. lanceolata* (*flore pleno*); the plant sometimes called *C. lanceolata grandiflora* does not belong with this species at all, but is really *C. grandiflora*. Although long-blooming, with showy 2½-inch yellow blooms, they may become too obstreperous in small gardens, sprawling as they do and spreading by self-sown seed. They are well adapted for planting in a semi-wild garden and goldfinches appreciate them because they are so fond of eating their seeds. Another species of entirely different appearance is *C. verticillata*, Thread-leaved Tickseed, 2½ feet, which, while not showy, scatters its blooms over a long period and is always pleasant-appearing because of its finely divided leaves, which look almost fern-like. The Coreopsis known as Golden Shower belongs here.

DELPHINIUM, Larkspur. To most people the name Delphinium suggests the towering races and strains developed originally, it is believed, from *D. elatum;* but of late years, especially, many species have been used in hybridizing to produce the modern Delphinium. There are many others among the three hundred or more species of Delphinium that are suitable for garden display, including the annual kinds, *D. ajacis* and *D. consolida* (which the Delphinium Society prefers to designate as Larkspurs); *D. cheilanthum*, the Garland Larkspur; *D. nudicaule*, the Red Larkspur; and *D. cardinale*, the Scarlet Larkspur.

I have never seen or attempted to grow *D. cardinale*, the Scarlet Larkspur native to Southern California, but from its description it must be a striking sight in bloom with brilliant scarlet flowers on a plant ranging from 3 to 8 feet high. A writer in *Delphinium, the Book of the American Delphinium Society*, suggests that the way to grow it in the northern states east of the Rockies is to dig up the plants as soon as the leaves begin to wither and store them (presumably in soil) in a warm, dry place for winter and plant them outdoors as soon as the ground is suitable to work the following spring.

D. cheilanthum is the Garland Larkspur, the species from which the Belladonna and Bellamosum races have been developed. These, while less spectacular than the tall, aspiring hybrid Delphiniums, have considerable value as garden plants and in general seem to be more truly perennial under adverse climatic conditions. Belladonna grows 3 to 4 feet tall with pale blue flowers; Bellamosum, 4 to 5 feet with deep blue flowers; Moorheimi has white flowers.

D. elatum, Candle Larkspur. It is believed that this species played a major part in the development of the kinds of perennial Larkspurs which most people think of when Delphiniums are mentioned, but

Delphinium, tall hybrids, and Roses. GOTTSCHO-SCHLEISNER

several other species, including *D. cardinale* and *D. nudicaule*, enter into the make-up of the modern Delphinium. It is interesting to know that in England, where distances are short and, therefore, shipments of plants can reach their destination without undue delay, there is a tendency to sell clones, propagated vegetatively by division or cuttings, under names such as Lady Eleanor, Bridesmaid, Watkins Samuel, etc. In this country the general practice is to sell seeds of strains such as Pacific Hybrids, Pudor, Leonian, Offernan hybrids, etc., rather than to sell named varieties which have been vegetatively produced. These strains come fairly true to type from seeds.

I'm afraid I'm a broken reed when it comes to recommending which strains to buy. You see, the lavender, pinkish kinds and the 6- to 8-footers leave me completely cold, and I would be perfectly content with those 5 feet or less in height such as would be represented by Delightful, deep blue; Enchantment, a medium blue with a white eye; Peace, pure white with a cream-colored "bee." There are some who maintain that the English strains (Blackmore and Langdon, Kelway and Watkins Samuel) are more truly perennial than are the American strains; others are on the opposite side of the fence and say that the reverse is true. My suggestion is that you raise several strains and then decide which kind you like the best.

D. grandiflorum (*chinensis*), the Chinese or Bouquet Larkspur, a favorite of mine, grows 2 to 3 feet tall, with a branching habit, and has divided leaves and clear blue flowers from June to September; in the variety album the flowers are white.

A deeply prepared, moist soil is desirable for Delphiniums; they do not appreciate excessive acidity, so if the soil has a reaction below pH6, ground limestone should be applied to bring up the soil to neutral—pH7.

If seeds of the crop of the current season are available in July or August, they may be sown immediately. The seedlings can be wintered in a cold frame or outdoors in mild climates and the following spring planted out in the garden where they will bloom the same year.

No difficulty will be experienced in germinating seeds in spring if they are stored over the winter in an airtight container at a temperature of about 45 degrees in the family refrigerator. If sown in the greenhouse in February and the temperature maintained between

55 and 65 degrees, the seedlings will come along quickly and bloom toward the end of the summer. If a greenhouse is unavailable, they can be sown out-of-doors as soon as frost is out of the ground in the spring.

Spacing should be 2 feet apart for the tall varieties; 1½ feet for the Belladonnas; and 1 foot for the Chinese Delphinium. A 2-inch mulch of organic matter (see Chapter Two) on the soil will be beneficial in helping to keep the soil cool and in conserving moisture. When the flowers on the main stalk have faded, they should be cut off down to the laterals, which will carry on for another week or two. When these fade, they should be cut off also; and when the leaves begin to turn brown, the entire stalk should be cut down to within a few inches from the ground.

DIANTHUS, Carnation, Pink. The recognized species of Dianthus run into the hundreds and the named garden varieties are innumerable— one American catalogue lists seeds of over thirty species, varieties, and strains of Dianthus, and an English catalogue more than sixty. If you should obtain, sow, and grow any or all of these, you will be

Cottage or Grass Pink, *Dianthus plumarius.*

J. HORACE MCFARLAND COMPANY

Button Pink, *Dianthus
latifolius* Beatrice.
J. HORACE MCFARLAND
COMPANY

Cottage or Grass Pink,
Dianthus plumarius Old
Spice.
J. HORACE MCFARLAND
COMPANY

likely to find considerable variation in the progeny obtained from any one package—even of those which are ostensibly species. This might interest or exasperate you, according to your temperament. You can, however, in any case be reasonably sure that all the seedlings will have something to commend them, in flowers, foliage, or fragrance—or all three. Any that have especially appealing qualities can be propagated and perpetuated by cuttings and division. If you wish to keep those good kinds pure and unmixed, flowers should be removed from them as they fade (and from their neighbors) to prevent seeding, because self-sown seeds are likely to germinate and crowd out those you want to keep.

Perhaps the most important group for the perennial garden includes the kinds often listed in catalogues as "Hardy Garden Pinks" —like our family dog, they are of somewhat doubtful ancestry. In catalogues such varieties as Mrs. Sinkins, Her Majesty, and Miss Gladys Cranfield are usually listed under *Dianthus plumarius*—the Cottage, Scotch, or Grass Pink. L. H. Bailey in his valuable book *The Garden of Pinks* lists them under *D. caryophyllus*, Carnation, although he says that "many of them have strong marks of *D. plumarius*." These Pinks generally are quite hardy and persistent.

D. Allwoodi, Allwood's Pinks. This is a hybrid strain attributed to *D. caryophyllus* x *D. plumarius*, which are stocky plants growing about 12 inches tall with large pink, or rose colored flowers. The Cheddar Pink is *D. gratianopolitanus*, which nurserymen, understandably enough, usually prefer to list under *D. caesius*, a synonym. This is a mat-forming Pink usually low-growing, not more than 9 inches high, with rose pink flowers and handsome glaucous foliage attractive at all times. The Maiden Pink, *D. deltoides*, is another mat-forming kind with growth that is almost turflike; this has rather small flowers freely produced on stems about 8 inches high. *D. deltoides* Brilliant has glowing crimson-red flowers. Both the Cheddar Pink and the Maiden Pink can be used in the forefront of a border or when a broad edging is required—their habit is so spreading, though, that it is difficult to make them toe a narrow line.

D. caryophyllus, Carnation. Here belong the classes known as Grenadin Carnation, reputed to be the hardiest of all; and the Marguerite Carnation. These, in some strains, approach the greenhouse Carnation in size and habit of growth. You will find them listed in catalogues under such names as "Super Giants," "Chabaud Giants," etc. Sometimes they are catalogued as Annual Carnations, because they can easily be raised from seed to bloom during the same season, but they are true perennials and can endure subzero weather if protected with evergreen boughs or something similar.

D. *chinensis* var. *Heddewigi,* Rainbow Pink. These usually are classed as annuals in the seed catalogues though they really are short-lived perennials and may persist for three years or even longer. They start blooming three or four months after the seeds are sown and continue until frost. Their brilliant flowers are large, often parti-colored and fringed, and long-lasting when cut.

D. *latifolius,* Button Pink. These grow to a height of about a foot, with single or double flowers an inch or more across ranging in color from white through pink to crimson-scarlet according to the variety. They are produced in clusters somewhat similar to those of the Sweet William. They bloom the same year from spring-sown seeds. Beatrice, a clear pink, Rock Raven Red, and Silver Mine, a pure white variety, give a good range of color in this group.

D. *plumarius,* Cottage, Scotch, or Grass Pink. These in general are more winter-hardy than the Caryophyllus types, although, in most cases, I suspect that Caryophyllus enters into the make-up of the many named garden forms found in catalogues listed under *Dianthus plumarius.* Among the good ones are Bristol Jewel, white and crimson; Dinah, rose and maroon; Essex Witch, pink; Her Majesty, double, white; Old Spice, salmon pink, like most of them, excellent for cutting; and Salmon Unique, salmon pink.

DICENTRA, Bleeding-heart, Dutchmans-breeches, Squirrel-corn. The old-fashioned Bleeding-heart, *Dicentra spectabilis,* has long been a favorite in gardens, and rightly so, for its rosy-red and white flowers pendent from gracefully arching branches are delightful in late spring. Unfortunately the foliage so beautiful in spring and early summer is, during dry summers, likely to become shabby by the middle of August, which suggests the desirability of having companion plants nearby such as Blue Sage, *Salvia farinacea,* or Snapdragon to mask its dilapidation. The white-flowered form (*alba*) is not entirely white, and in my experience has a delicate constitution. The white Californian Bleeding-heart, *D. formosa* Sweetheart also seems to be somewhat fractious, but in gardens where it grows well it is a charming plant for partial shade. The Plumy Bleeding-heart,

D. eximia, is noteworthy for its lush, fernlike foliage and its long-blooming habits—it is seldom without flowers from April to frost. Bountiful, said to be the result of a cross between this species and *D. oregana*, is another free-blooming form with Fuchsia-red flowers, and gray-green glaucous foliage. Dutchmans-breeches (*D. cucullaria*) and Squirrel-corn (*D. canadensis*) are early-blooming species suitable for naturalizing in the shade; their foliage dies down soon after blossoming is finished.

Burning-bush, Fraxinella or Gas-plant, *Dictamnus albus*.
J. HORACE MCFARLAND COMPANY

Dictamnus albus, Dittany, Burning-bush, Gas-plant, Fraxinella. To 3 feet, June. Although this species is not as long-blooming as most of the plants listed, it has so much garden value as an accent when in bloom, and its foliage is so good the rest of the season that it cannot be omitted. Personally I prefer the white flowers of the type to the red-purple varieties. *D. a. caucasicus* is strong-growing, with large racemes of rosy-pink flowers. Give preliminary thought to their placement, for once in position they resent moving.

ECHINOPS, Globe-thistle. I am afraid I cannot warm up to these plants, which to me are harsh to the touch and coarse-looking. But the ladies, especially the arrangers, see great beauty in their globular heads of bloom—steel-blue in *E. ritro,* and pale blue in *E. sphaerocephalus.* The height, 5 to 7 feet, of the last-named makes it of value for background planting in a large garden; *E. ritro* is more modest and grows to about 3 feet. There is one sold as Taplow Blue, which has larger flower heads of an intense metallic blue. The Globe-thistles are easy to grow if planted in ordinary garden soil in a sunny location.

Globe-thistle, *Echinops ritro.* GOTTSCHO-SCHLEISNER

EREMURUS, Foxtail-lily, Desert-candle. Doubtless my lack of warmth toward Foxtail-lilies stems partly from the time when I was a journeyman gardener in England, one of my jobs in the spring being to cover the developing leaves of Foxtail-lilies with cloth as a protection against late spring frosts. Worse still, I had to remove the cold, clammy covers the following morning. Now I read of the experience

Foxtail-lily or Desert-candle, *Eremurus himalaicus.*
J. HORACE MCFARLAND COMPANY

of a man who lives in a region where frosts occur in May and sometimes even in June who says, "We never protect our Eremurus, and
they have never been seriously damaged"! However, I will admit
that they are spectacular in bloom—*E. robustus* may make a stalk
looking like a hoe handle 10 feet long which in its "Foxtail" carries a
thousand or more flowers almost the size and color of Apple blos-

soms. They are still not common in gardens on this side of the Atlantic, so if you want to astonish your friends and neighbors, and cut a dash at the garden club flower show, by all means try your hand at growing some of them. The first of them to bloom is *E. himalaicus,* which usually blooms in May with white flowers on 4- to 6-foot stalks; this is followed by *E. robustus,* pink; and the Shelford hybrids, which may be from yellow to peach in color on slender stalks 5 to 8 feet tall.

Foxtail-lilies should be planted in the fall, preferably in sandy loam in a sunny location. Dig a hole 6 inches deep, a foot wider than the spread of the octopus-like roots. Put back a shovelful of soil in the middle of the hole and tamp it down to make a mound high enough to allow the crown of the plant to sit 2 inches below the surface with the tips of the roots sloping down to the 6-inch depth. The roots are extremely brittle, so, to avoid breaking them, cover carefully with soil up to within 1 inch of the grade, and instead of making it firm by tramping, pour in a couple buckets of water; when the water drains away, put in the rest of the soil.

ERYNGIUM, Eryngo, Sea-holly. I have never seen any Eryngiums in this country that aroused me to real enthusiasm. I don't know whether it is that the good kinds I used to see in England never are planted here, whether I am more critical as the years roll by, or whether these ancient eyes are so dim they are unable to observe beauty where it exists. The group as a whole has spiny leaves, branching inflorescences with numerous small blue flowers closely crowded in globular or ovoid heads surrounded by rufflike bracts. The Sea-holly, *E. maritimum,* is really spectacular in spite of its small size—1 to 1½ feet when it is thriving. It has fleshy, three-lobed, spiny, pale blue (almost white) glaucous leaves; the flowerheads also are pale blue, subtended by bracts which are similar to the leaves but in miniature form. Many, many years ago I took a day's excursion to Hunstanton (pronounced "Hunston") on the east coast of England and I was much impressed by the way this plant grew in nothing but seashore sand. If I had a seashore garden, I would make a determined effort to obtain seeds of this in view to raising it and planting it there—frankly I don't know how I'd go about it because I have not been able to locate any commercial source for seeds of this species.

Chinese Wallflower, *Erysimum asperum*. J. HORACE MCFARLAND COMPANY

Erysimum asperum, the Siberian or Chinese Wallflower. There seems to be some doubt concerning the nomenclature of the plant grown in gardens as Chinese Wallflower and sold as *Cheiranthus Allioni*, which, according to *Hortus II*, apparently belongs to *E. asperum*. It is a free-blooming plant about 1 foot tall in spring with a scattering of flowers until the fall. The flowers are orange or yellow and look like small Wallflowers.

Yellow Spurge, *Euphorbia epithymoides*. J. HORACE MCFARLAND COMPANY

EUPHORBIA, Spurge. There are two species of Euphorbia of value in the perennial garden—*E. corollata,* Flowering Spurge, growing to 3 feet with umbels of flowers with white appendages that look like petals, blooming in July–August; and *E. epithymoides* (*polychroma*), Yellow Spurge, which makes mounds 1 foot high of umbellate flowers, often with yellow leaves immediately beneath them.

FILIPENDULA, Meadow-sweet, Dropwort. On looking over the four preceding genera I seem to have damned them with faint praise, which will never do as a general policy. So here is a genus that I am really enthusiastic about, one that is worthy of more consideration by perennial gardeners. Filipendula used to be included with Spirea, a name by which it is still listed in many nursery catalogues. The genus is characterized by having large, feathery panicles of small blooms.

F. hexapetala, Dropwort, has a tuberous rootstock, finely divided, fernlike leaves, and white flowers in panicles rising to 3 feet. There is also a form, *flore pleno,* with double flowers. *F. palmata,* Palmate Meadow-sweet, is a species native to Siberia and Kamchatka. Its leaves have a large, terminal palmate leaflet with seven to nine lobes, often quite hairy beneath. When well grown, it may reach a height of 4 feet but usually it is seen from 2½ to 3 feet; the flowers are pale pink, ultimately changing to white; needs a moist soil plentifully enriched with cattle manure. *F. rubra* is the Queen-of-the-prairie, which may grow to 8 feet, but is usually not more than 6 feet; has flowers of Peach-blossom pink in large clusters. Its variety *venusta,* sold as Martha Washington Plume, has deep pink flowers. *F. ulmaria,* Queen-of-the-meadow, grows from 5 to 6 feet. Its leaves are white tomentose beneath with a large, three- to five-lobed terminal leaflet, and lobed lateral leaflets; the flowers are white. This is a Eurasian species, naturalized in Northeastern America; there is a double-flowered form known as variety *plena.*

All of the above, except for Dropwort, which does not like a too wet soil, grow best in deep, rich, moist soil plentifully supplied with humus. They are suited for the rear rank in the border and are well adapted for planting in wet meadows and along the sides of streams.

GAILLARDIA, Blanket-flower. There is only one perennial species that is generally grown in gardens—*G. aristata,* native from Minnesota and British Columbia to New Mexico. It is a sun lover which in the Northeastern states sometimes fails to survive the winter if grown in rich, heavy clay soil. It is particularly valuable in dry, sandy soil and is an exceptionally good garden plant in New Mexico and under similar conditions in the Southwest. To some its red and yellow flowers are too gaudy but it does provide color over a long period, blooming as it does from June until frost, if you prevent it from seeding by cutting off faded flowers. Its hoary foliage is sensitive to prolonged moisture and it resents confinement in a packing case for more than a day or two. Because of this it is advisable to obtain plants locally or raise them from seeds. If sown early in the spring they will bloom the same year. There are several named garden forms including: General George Patton, dark red and yellow; Mr. Sherbrook, rich golden yellow, which eliminates the Indian blanket appearance; Ruby, a deep rich red; and Giant English hybrids with varicolored flowers about 4 inches across. Good forms of these can be propagated by division in the spring.

GEUM, Avens. The one drawback to the cultivation of the garden forms of Avens is their lack of hardiness—some of them cannot be relied upon to come through severe winters in a climate more severe than that of Long Island, New York. This is unfortunate because they have showy blooms and good foliage throughout the growing season.

Most of the garden Geums are forms of *G. chiloense,* a native of Chile. Fire Opal is orange-scarlet with flowers that may be up to 3 inches across. It is reputed to be hardy and is worth a trial by those who live where tough winters are experienced. Another possibly hardy one which I saw growing in northern Vermont is called Red Wings, with 2-inch, semi-double, bright scarlet flowers with yellow stamens; Lady Stratheden has rich golden-yellow flowers; Mrs. Bradshaw is similar, with large double flowers of orange-red.

They should be planted in early spring in a sunny location; soil should be fairly rich and must be kept moist during the summer.

GYPSOPHILA, Chalk-plant, Babys-breath. This is a genus of annual and perennial herbs—some quite dwarf and suitable for rock gardens; others are among the most valuable plants for the perennial garden. The name Chalk-plant is indicative of soil preferences; if a test shows that the reaction is lower than pH6, ground limestone should be applied to bring it up to pH7 or pH7.5.

Among the best kinds for a perennial garden are: *Gypsophila paniculata,* Bristol Fairy, a double-flowered form with myriads of small flowers, which in my experience is far more effective than straight *paniculata* or its double form known as *flore pleno.* Usually these double-flowered forms are grafted on roots of *G. paniculata.* There are several forms assigned to *G. repens,* a species native in the Alps and Pyrenees, which are suitable for planting in the perennial garden. Among the best of these is *G. repens Bodgeri,* a pale pink, double-flowered form which grows to 1½ feet high.

The Gypsophilas should have a well-drained soil in full sun. Their place should be chosen with care because they resent moving after they are thoroughly established.

HELENIUM, Sneezeweed, Helen's Flower. The Heleniums are a floriferous group of plants blooming in late summer and early fall. They are valuable not only for garden decoration but also for cut

The deep blue of Anchusa forms the background for this perennial border.

Avens, *Geum chiloense* Fire Opal. J. HORACE MCFARLAND COMPANY

flowers. In general the flower colors of mahogany, gold, and yellow suggest that the onset of fall is near. Heleniums are related to Sunflowers. *Helenium autumnale,* a species native from Quebec to Florida and Arizona, is one of the most tolerant of all the perennials; it is capable of being grown all over the United States except in southern Florida. There are numerous garden forms ranging in height from 2 to 6 feet. *H. a. pumilum magnificum* grows to about 1½ feet with golden-yellow flowers which sometimes start toward the end of July and continue until September; the Bishop is a similar form; Chippersfield Orange, 4 feet, has large heads of copper and gold; Peregrinum probably belongs here; it grows to 3 feet, with dark mahogany rays, the edges faintly marked with gold; Riverton Beauty, 3 feet, has lemon-yellow rays with a dark purplish-black disk; Riverton Gem, 4 to 5 feet, is gold and red.

H. Hoopesi is a species native to the Rocky Mountain regions to Oregon and California. It is one of the showiest of all with golden-yellow blooms up to 3 inches across. It, however, is not nearly so tolerant of various soils and climates as *H. autumnale* and I must confess I have never had much success with it. It probably needs cool nights and rich soil—it is not recommended for the Midwestern states.

HELIANTHUS, Sunflower. These are mostly coarse perennials too large for a small place; some of them are invasive and need replanting annually to keep them in bounds. *H. decapetalus* and its double-flowered form *(flore pleno); H. mollis,* the Ashy Sunflower, with gray leaves, blooming from July to September, growing 4 to 5 feet tall, are probably the best bets for small gardens. *H. rigidus* and *H. r.* Miss Mellish, an improved form, grow 6 to 8 feet tall, blooming in August and September. Giants of the genus suitable for summer hedges or in the background of wide borders are *H. Maximiliani,* 10 to 12 feet; and *H. salicifolius,* 8 to 10 feet. Both of these are late, blooming as they do in September and October. The last-named has elegant Willow-like leaves which droop artistically from the towering stems. This, if room can be found for it, is worth growing for its foliage effect alone. All of these Sunflowers bear yellow flowers.

HELIOPSIS, Orange Sunflower, Oxeye. These, like the Sunflowers, are rather coarse perennials. There are only three that I recommend for the garden of moderate size; these are *H. scabra* Gold Greenheart,

H. scabra incomparabilis, and Summer Gold. All have double flowers of bright, rather harsh golden yellow; those of Gold Greenheart with more petals than *incomparabilis,* the center ones are green when the flowers first open; Summer Gold is long-blooming. All are subject to infestations by large red aphids which I assume are the same species as those commonly seen on Golden Glow. These must be watched for and sprayed with nicotine and soap or other contact insecticide, repeating as often as is necessary.

HEMEROCALLIS, Daylily. There is enough variety among the modern Daylilies, of which there are thousands of garden varieties, to suit anyone's taste. There are midgets no more than a foot high and giants which rear up to a height of 5 feet. Their flower size varies from 2 to 6 inches or more. In time of blooming there are some which start in mid-May; and while the full tide of bloom is in mid-summer, there are some which carry on into the fall. In color the range is from cream through yellow and orange to red, with pastels, blends, and bicolors in profusion; many have fragrant flowers. Climatically they can be grown almost anywhere in the United States; are not particular as to soil—any that will grow vegetables will do; they will grow in sun or shade and they are remarkably free from pests. The smaller kinds can be used as companion plants to hide the frowzy, fading foliage of the spring-flowering bulbs; July and later flowering varieties can effectively follow Iris, Peony, and Poppy: tall, strong-growing kinds are useful as accents; and all are of great value as fillers among shrubs, and can be naturalized in semi-wild surroundings. Cream-colored, yellow, and orange forms are the best for association with other perennials. Delicate pastels and pinkish varieties are likely to suffer in contrast with strong-colored perennials such as Blanket-flower.

Of the species the following especially appeal to me: *H. flava,* the Lemon Daylily, blooming in May with clean, yellow fragrant flowers on 3-foot scapes; the Tawny Daylily, *H. fulva,* which has run wild along the roadsides in many parts of the East and offers a brave show of orange-red flowers on 4- to 5-foot stalks in July and August. This one is a little too rampant for flower-border use. The Thunberg's Daylily (*H. Thunbergi*) blooms at the same time as the preceding with lemon-yellow, 3-inch flowers on stalks 3 feet high. Other species and varieties are listed in the Appendix.

Following is a selection from the "Hundred Day Lily Favorites of 1952" chosen by the members of the Hemerocallis Society. According to Mrs. Merrill Ross, chairman of Awards and Honors Committee of the Society, the following dates are designated by early, intermediate, summer, and late. When hyphenated the seasons indicate different times of bloom in various sections. For instance "summer-late" indicates that the variety blossoms in summer in warm areas and late in more northerly sections. Those listed below for the most part are taken from among the first fifty of the "Hundred Favorites"; most of them are moderately priced at $2.00 each or less.

BESS VESTAL, 36″, broad-petaled red, summer

BLACK PRINCE, 38″, maroon red, intermediate-summer

BOLD COURTIER, 38″, bicolor, rose and yellow, intermediate-summer

CABALLERO, 36″, bicolor, vermilion and yellow, early-intermediate-summer

COLONIAL DAME, 34″, yellow, banded light apricot, intermediate-summer

DAUNTLESS, 35″, cream-yellow, rose-tinted center, intermediate-summer

DOMINION, 38″, red, intermediate-summer

GARNET ROBE, 38″, garnet red, early-intermediate-summer

GAY TROUBADOUR, 40″, bicolor, red and yellow, summer-late

HESPERUS, 46″, lemon-yellow, summer-late

HYPERION, 48″, lemon- and canary-yellow, summer

MISSION BELLS, 40″, clear yellow, free-flowering, summer

MRS. HUGH JOHNSON, 34″, red, free-blooming, intermediate-summer

NARANJA, 36″, orange, early-intermediate-summer

PAINTED LADY, 36″, yellow blended with coppery-cinnamon, summer-late

PATRICIA, 30″, pale lemon-yellow, green throat, intermediate-summer

PINK CHARM, 40″, deep coral-pink, intermediate-summer

POTENTATE, 40″, deep purple, summer-late

REVOLUTE, 38″, ruffled flowers, light yellow, summer-late

SU-LIN, 35″, bicolor, orchid-pink and light yellow, intermediate-summer

The above are large-growing kinds. There are some of us who like the smaller varieties, which usually have more flowers per plant. Among them are:

ACHIEVEMENT, 24", yellow with red blotch
APRICOT, 24", apricot yellow, May
BEAUTEAU, 22", yellow
BIJOU, 24", orange and red, summer
FAVORITE, 24", bright red
FIREFLY, 24", red, early summer
GARDEN CHARM, 22", golden yellow, early summer
RED DIAMOND, 24", summer

Although Daylilies, toughies that they are, can grow practically anywhere and endure almost incredible ill-treatment, they do respond to kindness and an occasional pat on the back. So if you want them to do their best for you, prepare the soil for planting by digging it at least a spade's depth and mixing in it a 2-inch layer of organic matter. Plant them in the fall or spring, preferably in full sun, although dappled shade is not too bad. Keep weeds from encroaching by putting a mulch on the soil and by pulling out all strays. Soak the soil with water if possible once a week during dry spells. Some strong-growing kinds will need replanting every three or four years.

HEUCHERA, Alum-root, Coral-bells. Although about twenty-five species of Heuchera have been described, most of them from western North America, only two species, *H. sanguinea*, and *H. brizoides* (a hybrid, probably between *H. sanguinea* and *H. micrantha*), are commonly grown in gardens. *H. sanguinea* is a tufted plant with rounded leaves, lightly lobed and toothed, with ciliate (looking like eyelashes) margins. These are mottled in the spring and remain green all winter long. The inflorescence has an airy grace, consisting of a slender stem 1 to 2 feet tall, topped by loose clusters of small, bright red, bell-shaped flowers. There are many named garden forms including Matin Bells, coral-red flowers on stiff stalks, 1½ feet; Perry's White; Rosamundi, my favorite, which is long-blooming (almost two months), with pink blooms on stems of about 1½ feet.

Heucheras thrive best in fairly rich soil with ample humus; they should be transplanted every two or three years, or whenever the center of the clump begins to die. While they will grow in part shade, they usually thrive best in a sunny location.

HOSTA (*Funkia*), Plantain-lily. If you like Plantain-lilies they are excellent plants, provided they are not asked to endure dry soil and the competition of tree roots. The two outstanding ones in my opinion are the August-blooming, white-flowered, *H. plantaginea,* a noble plant when grown in rich soil and partial shade; and *H. Sieboldiana,* whose flowers are not so much, but which redeems itself from mediocrity by the distinction of its large seersucker-like leaves of glaucous blue-green. Shade is essential for best results with this species. *H. lancifolia albo-marginata,* with white-margined leaves, is frequently used as an edging plant.

IRIS, Fleur-de-lis. Containing upwards of two hundred species and innumerable garden varieties, the Iris is one of the most important

Fragrant Plantain-lily, *Hosta plantaginea.* JESSIE TARBOX BEALS

genera for the perennial garden. Varying in size from the 4-inch height of some of the *pumila* varieties to the 40-inch or more height of some of the Tall Bearded kinds, they exhibit a striking range of color including white, blue, brown, red, yellow, orange, green, and varied tones and blends. There are two great divisions of Iris—the rhizomatous kinds, with which we are chiefly concerned, and the bulbous group, which is mostly early spring flowering. The rhizomatous group is further divided into Bearded or Pogoniris (having lines of conspicuous, often highly colored hairs along the lower part of the falls), the Beardless, or Apogoniris, and the Crested Iris, or Evansia Iris, characterized by a central ridge on the lower half of the falls which may be saw-toothed or likened to a cockscomb. The Bearded Irises include subgroups—Tall Bearded, Intermediate, and Dwarf Bearded, plus the Aril Irises (of which more will be said later) and hybrids of these with the Tall Bearded forms.

The most popular of these, of which there are thousands of named varieties, is the Tall Bearded group. They are easy to grow, demanding only plenty of sun and no permanently wet feet—which means that the soil must be well-drained. They can be transplanted any time when the ground is not frozen, but the approved period is shortly after blooming is finished—in late July, August, or September (for technique of transplanting, soil preparation, etc., see Chapter Six). They should be taken up, divided, and replanted every three or four years.

Here is a baker's dozen of good, moderately priced varieties, chosen for beauty and variety of color, and suitable for the beginner to cut his teeth on. There are hundreds more good ones to be found in catalogues of specialists ranging in price from 35¢ to $25.00.

BLUE RHYTHM: Dykes Medal winner. Cornflower-blue, with silvery overtones; fragrant well-formed flowers, good habit, introduced 1945, 38 inches.

BLUE SHIMMER: Has large blossoms; white ground, suffused and dotted with blue-violet, 1942, 38 inches.

BRYCE CANYON: A blend of copper and brown marked with henna; conspicuous yellow beard; large, fragrant flowers of good proportion, 1946, 36 inches.

CHINA MAID: An old-timer, with large blooms which are a blend of golden-bronze, pink, and lilac, 1936, 40 inches.

FAIR ELAINE: A handsome fragrant bicolor with pale Primrose-yellow standards and deep golden-yellow falls; orange beard, 1938, 40 inches.

GREAT LAKES: Dykes Medal winner. Clear sky-blue self; large fragrant blooms on well-branched stems, 1938, 40 inches.

GUDRUN: Dykes Medal winner. A free-blooming, fragrant white variety; stands up well against strong winds, 1930, 36 inches.

LADY MOHR: Large blooms with oyster-shell white standards; the falls are white, suffused chartreuse, with red-violet blotch and veins, 1944, 36 inches.

OLA KALA: Dykes Medal winner. The best deep yellow Iris with almost orange tones, 1943, 42 inches.

PINK CAMEO: Clear soft pink with tangerine beard, 1946, 38 inches.

SOLID MAHOGANY: A rich, velvety deep bronzy red mahogany; a handsome, well-formed bloom, 1944, 36 inches.

TIFFANJA: Buff and brown; falls white, with buff edging. Large flowers of good substance, 1942, 42 inches.

WABASH: Dykes Medal winner. White standards; deep red-violet falls margined with white; yellow beard, 1936, 39 inches.

INTERMEDIATE IRISES. These are "betwixt and between" the Tall Bearded and the Dwarf Bearded in size and time of blooming. These seem to have gone almost completely out of fashion. I've looked through the catalogues of a half-dozen Iris specialists without finding any of them listed. If you are interested and if you should come across any of the following, they are among the best. Autumn Haze, Black Hawk, Chrysoro, Eleanor Roosevelt, Kochi, Red Orchid, Zua.

DWARF BEARDED IRISES. These are well adapted for planting in the rock garden, but they have their place too in the small perennial garden, growing, as they do, no more than 9 or 10 inches tall (some of them half this size), and blooming in April and early May. Some varieties have a second period of bloom in the fall. Here is a selection which gives a good color range. Alinva, 7 inches, red-purple self with dark beard; Autumn Queen, 9 inches, snow white, blooms in spring and fall; Blue Flash, 5 inches, bright pale blue; Blue Mascot, 5 inches, clear medium blue; Harbor Lights, 6 inches, rich yellow;

Dwarf Iris, *Iris pumila*. BROOKLYN BOTANIC GARDEN

Olive White, cream-colored, spring and fall bloomer; Sass Dark Ruby, 7 inches, red-purple, gold beard; Tampa, 6 inches, red-toned flowers on slender stems.

ARIL IRISES. These include the Regelia, Pseudoregelia, and Oncocyclus Irises, which differ from the Bearded Irises in having seeds each with a conspicuous aril—a growth partly or wholly covering them. Let me say at once that Oncocyclus and to a lesser extent the Regelia Irises are not easy to grow unless you have a climate similar to that of Southern California. I have grown *I. Hoogiana* and *I. Korolkowi*, two "straight" Regelias, plus a half-dozen hybrids between the Regelia and Oncocyclus groups, in the mid-Hudson Valley. They did well for a couple of years planted on a slight slope in poor sandy soil overlying molding sand, giving the perfect underdrainage necessary for their successful culture, but then they fell on evil times. I got myself involved in a multiplicity of other plants, so the Irises were neglected, became smothered with weeds, and, although six years later some of them were still alive, they never did anything to amount to much after the first two years. In the Northeastern states they start to grow early in the fall, which means they are injured by severe winter weather. This perhaps could be overcome by digging them up when the foliage begins to turn yellow, keeping them dry in sand until late in the fall before planting them; then they should be covered with 4 or 5 inches of straw to protect them during winter. The most tolerant species in the Oncocyclus group is the Mourning Iris (*I. susiana*), a spectacular species with flowers borne on stems about a foot long which have a gray ground color profusely marked with purple-black lines and spots. Of the Regelias, *Hoogiana* and *Korolkowi* seem to be the best ones to attempt to grow. Most of us, however, will be content to take our Oncocyclus Irises diluted with Pogoniris, which has been done with great success, combining some of the unique coloring of the "Oncos" and the good-tempered tolerance of the Tall Bearded. Among the best of these are: El Mohr, rich red-violet; Lady Mohr, oyster white and chartreuse-yellow; Mohr Beauty, similar to El Mohr, but light yellow in color; Peg Dabagh, rich violet-blue; William Mohr, pale lilac with violet veins; and Yarkand, described as a blue version of William Mohr. Some of these are, at the time of writing, rather expensive, but I expect they will come down in price soon.

Mourning Iris, *Iris susiana.*
MRS. EDWARD L. KERNOCHAN

Regelia Iris, *Iris Hoogiana.*
MARK NORTON

Regelia-Oncocyclus Iris, Parthenope. MARK NORTON

BEARDLESS OR APOGON IRISES. These in general need different conditions from the preceding. Although they will grow in the ordinary moist soil of the flower border, they can also endure wet feet and are well adapted for waterside planting. Planting and division if necessary may be done either in early spring or in the early fall.

THE SIBERIAN IRISES (*I. sibirica*) have tall, slender stalks, with the flowers rising above the grasslike foliage. They bloom along with the last of the late Bearded Irises; the Japanese are later and bloom in July.

Among the best of the Siberian Irises are: Caesar's Brother, the darkest-colored Siberian, black pansy purple, 36 inches; Cool Spring, pearly blue flowers, 30 inches; Eric the Red, wine-red flowers on 42-inch stalks; Helen Astor, the falls rosy red with a white halo touched with blue; Snowcrest, tall, large-flowered white; Tropic Night, the best real, deep blue, 40 inches; Tycoon, large flowers of violet-blue, 38 inches.

JAPANESE IRIS (*I. Kaempferi*). These grow best in a somewhat acid soil—pH5.5 to 6.5. A sunny location is best for them, though they will thrive in part shade. Up until flowering time they need abundant water at their roots; after this they can get along quite well in moderately moist soil. They should not be disturbed any more than is necessary, which is when the center of the clump begins to die. When this happens, it is wise, sometime in September, to dig up the clump, separate the strong divisions from its periphery, and replant them. That pesky little insect pest known as thrips sometimes is bothersome; it probably can be kept under control by spraying or dusting the developing foliage and at about ten-day intervals thereafter with DDT. The best forms of Japanese Iris are really spectacular. When well grown, they may attain a height of 3 to 3½ feet, and the flowers may be almost a foot across with the "petals"—three, six, or nine of them—held almost horizontally, so that they are most effective when one is able to look down on them.

The names of the numerous garden forms are in a mess. Some dealers retain the original Japanese names, some translate them into English, and a few apparently have said, "A plague on both your houses," and have invented new ones. The following are good when and if obtainable: Betty F. Holmes, double, white with lemon-yellow throat; Blue Giant, soft deep blue; Dominator, single, deep

Japanese Iris, *Iris Kaempferi*.
BROOKLYN BOTANIC GARDEN

blue with narrow white stripes; Gold Bound, double, white, gold-banded; Mt. Hood, double, light blue with darker shades, orange center; Pink Pearl, double, pink and violet. There are some nurseries which offer a good strain of seeds of Japanese Irises; these, if sown early in the spring, can be grown along to bloom the following year. This affords an inexpensive way of obtaining considerable variety of these lovely flowers.

LOUISIANA IRIS (*I. fulva, I. foliosa*), etc. These are not much grown in the North though many of them have proved to be hardy in New England. *Iris fulva, I. foliosa, I. hexagona, I. giganticaerulea,* and others, native of Louisiana and other Southern states, probably enter into the make-up of named garden forms. They are valuable for planting in wet ground, but they will also thrive under normal flower-garden conditions. Among those offered for sale are: Abbeville Reds, which are collected plants in varying shades of red; their height is about 36 inches. Abbeville Giant Yellow, these too are collected and have soft creamy-yellow flowers; a little taller than the preceding, they rise to a height of 40 inches. Caddo, this hybrid has been described as "vibrant red-bronze" with a "large almost circular signal patch on the heavy-substance petals"; it was given an H.M. by the American Iris Society in 1950, also the Mary Swords Debaillon Award. Mary S. Debaillon, collected and named for Mrs. Debaillon because it was her favorite Iris: "It resembles a tremendous orchid with sepals (standards) of lavender-rose and petals (falls) orchid-pink with a broad yellow signal"; 36 inches.

SPURIA IRIS. This subsection includes *I. spuria*, a variable species, and *I. ochroleuca*, which some authorities believe to be a form of *spuria*. The garden forms are tall, up to 5 feet, with stiff, swordlike leaves. The flowers are reputed to be long-lasting when cut. Available kinds include: Ochroleuca Gigantea, white standards, yellow falls mottled with white; Golden Nugget, rich golden-yellow flowers; Azure Dawn, lavender-blue with pale yellow patch; Dutch Defiance, large blue flowers with a yellow patch on the falls; Lord Wolseley, russet-flame coloring; and Sunny Day, tall, gleaming yellow.

CRESTED IRIS. This is a small group with only a few garden forms. *I. cristata*, the Crested Dwarf Iris, is a native plant with pale lavender-blue flowers nestling among the leaves, which ultimately grow to length of about 9 inches. There is a white-flowered race, *I. c. alba*, of exquisite beauty when in bloom, but in my experience is not so robust as the blue-flowered kind. There is also a form called Crested Fairy, which is a bicolor with pale lavender standards changing to white, and blue falls. The Crested Dwarf Iris will grow in sun or light shade—if the shade is too heavy, few or no blooms will be produced; in full sun blooming will be heavy, but the growth may be poor and, if a dry spell is experienced, the plants may die unless they are watered. *Iris tectorum*, the Roof Iris, is so-called because it is seen growing on the ridges of thatched roofs in Japan. There is an interesting legend in connection with this. It seems that during a time of famine in Japan the Emperor issued an edict to the effect that nothing should be planted in the ground except that which could be used for food. The ladies of Japan used the ground-up

Crested Iris, *Iris cristata*. BROOKLYN BOTANIC GARDEN

rhizomes of this Iris for face powder and, as they could not possibly do without this aid to beauty, and as the Iris is not a food plant, they set them in the roofs of their houses and thus by-passed the Emperor's ban. (Incidentally, *I. florentina, I. germanica,* and *I. pallida* are grown in the vicinity of Florence, Italy, for their violet-scented rhizomes, which are dug in August, cleaned, dried, and powdered for use as an ingredient of tooth and face powders. In so far as I have been able to learn, this is the only use made of Iris other than that contributed by their beauty.)

The Roof Iris is a favorite of mine. It grows 12 to 15 inches high with rather flat flowers of lavender-blue; the white-flowered form is even more beautiful, but, like the White Dwarf Crested Iris, seems to be less robust. Full sun is necessary in the North; I am inclined to think that dappled shade is preferable in warmer areas. In Nashville, Tennessee, last year about May 1, I saw thriving colonies of the blue and the white forms growing in dappled high shade cast by tall trees in thin woodland. Thorough underdrainage, a loose, porous soil, and ample organic matter, such as flaky leafmold, seem to be conducive to its continued happiness. It is advisable to sow seeds annually in case the old plants die from winter.

VESPER IRIS (*I. dichotoma*). This unique late-blooming Iris (August to September) has a fan of leaves up to a foot or more tall and a branching inflorescence which in rich soil may attain a height of 5 feet. The flowers are small but freely produced; they open in the afternoon and last only a few hours. The ground color is white, spotted and striped with blue-purple, so that the general effect is lavender. It is a short-lived perennial, but readily reproduces from seeds sown as soon as they are ripe in early fall; or under glass in March.

KNIPHOFIA (*Tritoma*), Poker-plant, Torch-lily. These natives of Africa used to be thought of as being of dubious hardiness, but in recent years several hybrids have been produced which, if planted in well-drained soil that is not too rich and if the leaves are left on to protect the crowns over winter, seem to be able to withstand below-zero temperatures without injury. They have broad, grasslike leaves up to 3 feet long, forming a tuft of foliage from which arises stout flower stalks clothed with closely packed flowers near to the tip. The following have survived several winters in my garden in the mid-Hudson Valley: Primrose Beauty, yellow flowers in early summer on 2½-foot stalks; Springtime, upper half of inflorescence coral-red, lower cream-colored, about 3 feet; Vanilla, small pale yellow flowers on 2-foot stalks, May–June. Other reputedly hardy hybrids include: Coral Sea, coral-red flowers in June and July, 2½ feet; Golden Scepter, golden-yellow flowers in June and July, 3 feet. Two of dubious hardiness without added protection are: Crown of Gold, early blooming, with recurrent lemon-yellow flowers all summer; White Fairy, white flowers, 2 feet, with narrow grassy foliage.
. They should always be planted in the spring in preference to the fall; in regions where their hardiness is doubtful they can be protected in place by tying the leaves into a pony-tail in the fall and dumping two pailfuls of coal ashes (preferably those that have been exposed to the weather for six months or so) around the base of the plants. If this is not sufficient, they can be dug up in the fall, stored in slightly moist sand in a cold cellar all winter, and planted out again in the spring.

Lilium, Lily. The true Lilies are the most important of the hardy summer-flowering bulbs because of their beauty, fragrance, and variety in form and coloring. On the basis of form they can be divided into four main groups. The Trumpet Lilies, such as the Regal and the Madonna Lily; those with wide-open flowers known as Ball or Saucer types—Gold-banded Lily and Showy Japanese Lily; cup-shaped lilies with erect, wide-open flowers, including the Candlestick Lily and *L. elegans;* and the Martagon or Turks-cap group, which have nodding flowers with the petals reflexed and includes such kinds as Maxwill and the Coral Lilies.

Until fairly recently most Lilies were considered difficult to grow (some still are), but nowadays, with increasing knowledge of their culture and scientific investigation of the origin of their varied troubles and methods of combating them, together with the fact that commercial growers of Lilies are becoming more keenly cognizant of the importance of selling healthy planting stock than they used to be in the old days, there need be no difficulty in maintaining some of the most beautiful Lilies in a healthy condition. The control measures that can be practiced by the home gardener include: selection of resistant species; segregation of susceptible kinds from those which are moderately susceptible; the avoidance of mosaic diseases by raising plants from seeds and the destruction of insect vectors which are capable of transmitting the virus from infected plants to healthy ones.

The Lilies discussed below are for the most part easily grown kinds resistant to disease and suitable for culture in the perennial garden; additional species and varieties not too difficult will be found in the Tabular List of Perennials in the Appendix. If you want to grow Lilies in still greater variety, I would suggest that you study one or more of the good books dealing solely with Lilies, such as LILIES FOR AMERICAN GARDENS, by George L. Slate, Chas. Scribner's Sons; and GARDEN LILIES, by Allan and Esther MacNeil, Oxford University Press.

Lilium auratum, Gold-banded Lily, is only moderately easy to grow, but it is so beautiful and spectacular in bloom that it is well worth a trial. Success is more likely nowadays because the practice of raising plants from seed enables dealers to supply the customer with disease-free bulbs to start with. The Gold-banded Lily grows

4 to 6 feet tall, with flowers up to a foot across, a dozen or more open at once on each stalk when well-grown and happy. The flowers are white, crimson spotted, with a yellow band down the center of each perianth segment (petal). There are numerous garden forms varying in the color and extent of markings.

L. candidum is the well-known Madonna Lily, with its pure white trumpets displayed in a stately manner on 3- to 5-foot stalks. This species sometimes is bothered by botrytis disease, which involves dusting or spraying with Bordeaux mixture, starting early in the spring and repeating at fortnightly intervals until the flower buds are formed. The Cascade strain is supposed to be easy to grow and more vigorous than the ordinary kind. It has done well with me, but as I did not have any other Madonna Lilies for comparison, I cannot say from my own experience whether or not the claim is justified.

L. dauricum, a Candlestick Lily, and its relatives, *L. elegans* and *L. umbellatum,* will thrive even in a city back yard. There are numerous named garden forms differing in the color of their upward-facing, cup-shaped flowers and in the time of blooming. These Candlestick Lilies, because of their easy culture, are particularly good for the beginner to start with; and the comparatively low growth, seldom in excess of 2½ feet, makes them appropriate for use in the small garden.

L. Davidi is a Turks-cap with orange-red or scarlet, black-spotted flowers, freely produced on stems up to 5 or 6 feet tall. The variety *Willmottiae* needs help because it is so productive of flowers that their weight causes the weak stems to topple over unless they are given support.

L. Hansoni is a Turks-cap of a different color with orange-yellow, brown-flecked flowers more closely clustered at the tips of the stalks than those of the preceding. It is one of the first to grow in the spring, consequently it is subject to injury by late frosts. Have some light protection ready nearby—cheesecloth or newspapers—that can be thrown over the shoots if frost threatens.

L. Henryi is a handsome Lily of amiable disposition—it will grow almost anywhere. Its blooms, carried on stalks 5 to 9 feet tall, in shape are reminiscent of those of *speciosum,* but are smaller and orange-yellow in color. Although it will grow in open exposures, the

Coral Lily hybrid, *Lilium pumilum*. MALCOLM R. KINNEY

flower color is likely to fade in full sun; therefore, it is desirable to plant it in partial shade.

L. pumilum, the Coral Lily, often is listed in catalogues as *L. tenuifolium*. It is a dainty little Lily, usually less than 2 feet tall, with bright scarlet flowers. It is a short-lived perennial, but is easily raised from seeds. The seedlings usually bloom the first or second year after germination. There are several named garden varieties.

L. regale, Regal Lily. This is one of the most popular Lilies today. There are good reasons for this. It is a handsome Lily, its tubular flowers white with a yellow throat, marked with red on the outside; normally it grows 3 to 4 feet high, but I have seen specimens up to 8 feet tall, bearing up to twenty-five blooms per stalk. Then, too, it is tolerant as to soil and seems to grow well almost anywhere. Like *L. Hansoni*, it appears aboveground very early in the spring and the shoots are likely to be injured by late frosts. It might be worth while in regions subject to these conditions to try to delay emergence by mulching the ground heavily in the spring to keep the roots cool.

L. speciosum, Showy Japanese Lily, has long been a favorite in gardens. It has large white flowers with recurved perianth segments, having a pink flush, which usually are spotted with pink and crimson. There is considerable variation in this species and numerous named forms which vary in color and markings and in time of bloom. The one most commonly grown is variety *rubrum*, the petals of which are white, heavily suffused with red, dotted with crimson. It is possible to have speciosums in bloom from August until October by a selection of varieties; the earliest to bloom is *L. speciosum* var. *pumilum*, which starts to flower early in August.

Unlike Tulips, Narcissi, and Hyacinths, Lilies are likely to be injured if the bulbs are removed from their natural element, the soil, for any lengthy period. Those gardeners are fortunate who live near a Lily nursery, so that freshly dug stock can be obtained. Ideally Lily bulbs should be dug up with the roots attached, as soon as they have matured, which is when the leaves begin to wither, and should be replanted immediately without removing the roots. Madonna Lilies should be planted in August so that they have time to develop their basal tufts of leaves before winter sets in; other kinds should be planted as soon as it is possible to get the dealer to send them to you. Some, such as *speciosum* and other late-maturing species, may not reach you until the ground is frozen. This difficulty can be overcome by (1) heavily mulching the planting stations with straw to prevent the soil from freezing; (2) by having a store of soil and 6-inch pots under cover so that the bulbs can be potted upon their arrival. These can be stored over winter in a cold frame or a cold cellar and planted out in the spring when frost has left the ground.

DEPTH OF PLANTING AND DISTANCE APART Lilies are of two kinds—those which produce roots only from the base of the bulbs, known as basal-rooting; and those which in addition to the basal roots produce them also on the stem between the top of the bulb and the soil surface. These are called stem-rooting. The bulbs of the base-rooting kinds—candidum, testaceum—should be covered by no more than 2 or 3 inches of soil; the stem-rooting kinds can be planted between two and three times the height of the bulb—the exact depth depending in part on the size of the bulb and the character of the soil; if the soil is a heavy clay loam, use shallow planting, covering the bulbs with soil equal to twice the height of the bulb; in sandy soil make it three times the height of the bulb. Lilies in the perennial garden usually are planted in groups of from three to a dozen bulbs. The distance apart of the bulbs in the groups depends upon the size of the plants: those of the Coral Lily can be set 6 inches apart in the group; *L. dauricum* and similar varieties can be set 9 inches apart; while the tall growers, Regals, Madonnas, Maxwill, and so on, should have 12 inches between the bulbs to allow for the natural increase in their number.

SOIL Although there are a few Lilies that are found growing wild in swampy or wet situations—*L. superbum* and *L. pardalinum*, for examples—most of them grow best in deep, moist, but well-drained soil. The optimum soil reaction for most Lilies is pH6.0 to pH6.5. Ideally the soil should be a sandy loam richly supplied with organic matter that can be flaky leafmold or peat moss with thoroughly rotted manure dug in well below the bulbs. When Lilies are planted in a bed by themselves, double digging (see Chapter Two) is desirable; in the flower border along with other perennials the best way is to dig a hole large enough to accommodate the bulbs it is to receive and an inch or two deeper than the depth to which they are to be planted. Then put in a layer of rotted manure or leafmold, dig it deeply in the bottom of the hole, make firm by tramping, and cover with an inch or two of unmanured soil before planting the bulbs.

PLACEMENT In general, Lilies are like Clematis in that they like to have their feet in shade and their heads in full sun. These conditions are provided in the flower border by the proximity of other perennials which shade the ground and help give the Lilies the cool root run in which they delight. When grown by themselves in open beds, they should be given a mulch of organic matter, 2 to 3 inches thick, which will serve the same function as the perennials in keeping the soil cool. Many Lily growers have had great success by using a mulch of sawdust (see Chapter Twelve, page 137).

PROPAGATION Lilies are propagated by natural multiplication of the bulbs; by scaling—the removal of some of the outer scales and planting them; by bulbils, developed by some species in the axils of the leaves; and by seeds. For full details of these processes I must refer you to books specializing in Lilies, two of which are mentioned on page 241.

This is not the place to go into the intricacies of the hybrid Lilies—

Group of Bellingham Hybrid Lilies—*Lilium Sargentiae* in foreground.
MALCOLM R. KINNEY

that is a subject for the specialists. Some of them are still scarce and, therefore, expensive. I would, however, suggest that you keep your eye open for the Aurelian group with yellow trumpets; Bellingham hybrids, the *Martagon* x *Hansoni* crosses, which include the Backhouse hybrids, among the best known of which is Brocade and Sceptre; Maxwill (*Maximowiczi* x *Willmottiae*), a very fine Turkscap with thirty or forty orange-red blooms carried on a 6-foot stem; the Preston hybrids (*Willmottiae* x *dauricum*), which includes the "Stenographer Series," among the best known of which are Brenda Watts and Lilian Cummings; and *umbellatum* (*dauricum* x *bulbiferum* and others), including such garden forms as Apricot, Golden-Fleece, and Grandiflorum.

Maxwill Lily, *Lilium Maximowiczi* x. *Willmottiae*.
MALCOLM R. KINNEY

LINUM, Flax. The Flax that is used for making linen and is a source of linseed oil is *L. usitatissimum,* of no ornamental value. There are several perennial species used for garden adornment. These include: *L. flavum* (Golden Flax), which has yellow flowers and stems about 18 inches tall; it is not reliably hardy in the North.

L. narbonnense has flowers about 1½ inches across, sky blue with a white eye; *L. perenne* is similar with smaller pale blue flowers; there is a white-flowered form of this.

The blue-flowered perennial kinds have small blue-green leaves and a light, airy grace that is appealing; they would be of still greater value if they did not drop their fleeting flowers soon after noon.

LUPINUS, Lupine. These are annual or perennial herbs, with a few shrubs and subshrubs. The species most suitable for perennial gardens is *L. polyphyllus* and its garden forms. About twenty years ago the garden world was set agog by the introduction of Russell Lupines. These are amazing in their floriferousness and variety of coloring. They grow from 3 to 5 feet tall, and the upper two thirds of the flower stalks consist of a densely packed spike of pealike blooms of almost every conceivable color—self and bicolors. They were developed by George Russell of Yorkshire, England, after many years of hybridizing and selection. In my experience they have been cantankerous; others succeed with them, and they are well worth the trial by anyone who likes a somewhat overwhelming display of color. The character of the soil does not seem to be important providing it is well drained. If you don't succeed when one- or two-year-old plants are set out, try starting the seeds in pots of sandy soil in spring, soaking them overnight in tepid water prior to planting them. Set the young plants in their flowering positions without disturbing the roots as soon as the roots reach the bottom of the pot.

LYCHNIS, Campion, Catchfly, and Maltese Cross. This comprises a group of annuals, biennials and perennials; some of them rather weedy. Most important for our purposes are the following:

L. chalcedonica, Maltese Cross, which grows 2 to 3 feet, with the stems topped by clusters of vivid scarlet flowers shaped like Maltese crosses in June and July.

L. coronaria is the Mullein-pink or Rose-campion. This is a biennial or perennial with white-woolly leaves and a branching inflorescence, 2 to 2½ feet high with showy cerise flowers which appeal more to men than to the ladies. It is suitable for naturalizing in sun or part shade, as well as for the flower border.

L. Haageana is a hybrid with flowers almost 2 inches across of orange-red, scarlet, or crimson on stalks usually not more than a foot tall. In my experience it is not a long-lived perennial. It seems to do best in partial shade.

Perennial border showing Hemerocallis and Lupines in foreground.
GOTTSCHO-SCHLEISNER

L. viscaria, German Catchfly, is an early-blossoming species with red or purple flowers in interrupted clusters on 1-foot stalks. There is a double-flowered form and one with white blooms.

NEPETA, Catmint. These are aromatic herbs; one, *N. cataria,* has a dubious recommendation from a gardener's viewpoint of being attractive to cats. There are only two species that are commonly grown for ornament: *N. macrantha,* a somewhat sprawly character about 3 feet tall with lavender-blue sage-like flowers in small clusters; and *N. Mussini*, well and favorably known as a gray-leaved plant with lavender-blue flowers over a long period in early summer; much used for edgings and the front row of the border. One named Souv. de André Chaudron (sold in this country as Blue Beauty) probably is a garden form of the preceding. It has blue flowers and is said to produce twenty to thirty spikes of bloom on one plant; suitable for use as a cut flower.

OENOTHERA, Evening-primrose, Sundrop. The only species of Oenothera commonly grown in the East is *O. fruticosa* and its variety *Youngi*. These are free-flowering plants about 2 feet tall producing their flowers—buttercup-yellow in *fruticosa;* lemon-yellow in *Youngi* —during June and July.

In the Midwest states the following are popular and should be grown more extensively in the East: *O. caespitosa,* a dwarf species from the central United States with 3-inch white or pink flowers; *O. missouriensis* has prostrate branches with ascending tips less than 12 inches tall with bright yellow flowers about 4 inches across; and *O. speciosa* (Showy Evening-primrose), with erect stems 1 to 2 feet tall; the white, changing to pink, flowers are almost 3 inches in diameter.

PAEONIA, Peony. About twenty-five species of Paeonia have been recognized, but the many hundreds of garden forms of herbaceous Peonies have been developed largely from two species—*P. albiflora,* the Chinese species, and *P. officinalis,* the European or Common Peony. The widespread use of Peonies in the gardens for a hundred or more years is sufficient evidence of their adaptability to most climates and soils. Best results are obtained when they are planted in deep, well-drained, rather clayey soil well supplied with plant foods; and when exposed to full sunshine. Their performance in regions where a cool temperature prevails at blooming time is more satisfactory than farther south, where the hot weather causes the blooms to fade too quickly. However, they can be grown all over the United States with suitable attention to irrigation in dry districts, except for the coastal region of the Southern states and Florida. In order to get best results fertility of the soil must be maintained by annual applications of rotted manure lightly forked into the ground away from the crowns and by applications of fertilizers such as 5-10-5 at the rate of a half pound per square yard.

Peony Festiva Maxima, first introduced to cultivation 1851.
J. HORACE MCFARLAND COMPANY

Often one hears complaints of failure to bloom of Peonies; this may be caused by one or more factors such as: too deep planting (the buds on the tops of the roots should not be more than 2 inches below the surface); disease (especially the botrytis blight or bud-rot); attacks by root nematodes; lack of plant foods in the soil; and too much shade.

So as to aid in controlling botrytis blight and some other diseases of Peony, the foliage should be cut off just below the soil surface in the fall and destroyed by burning. When the plants are severely infected, it may be necessary to supplement this control measure by spraying them with Bordeaux mixture, starting when the shoots are about 6 inches above the ground; continue at weekly intervals until buds are formed. Plants infested with nematodes, as evidenced by gnarled swellings on the roots, should be dug up with the surrounding soil and burned. Peonies planted in the lawn or in the vicinity of trees may fail to bloom because the grass and tree roots make too many demands on the fertility of the soil.

By making a selection of early, midseason, and late varieties it is possible to have Peony blooms for about 5 weeks, starting with *P. tenuifolia* (Fern-leaved Peony) and the *officinalis* hybrids; followed by early singles and early Japanese; followed in turn by early midseason and late varieties among the doubles. Following is a selection of twelve good varieties of Peonies for a starter. If you are really interested in Peonies, it would be well to obtain catalogues of Peony specialists, some of which are beautifully illustrated in color; and/or join the American Peony Society.

Here are a dozen recommended varieties of Peonies, new and old, mostly moderate in price (figures in parentheses are ratings of the American Peony Society, 10 being the maximum):

FESTIVA MAXIMA: (9.3) an old double variety which has been at the top for years; massive white flowers with red markings; blooms early.

FLOWER GIRL: (9.27) double flesh-white flowers of medium size and height; early blooming; dainty rather than massive.

KRINKLED WHITE: (9.04) single. Crinkled white petals; slender, sturdy stems.

LE CYGNE: (9.9) double. Very large, well-formed white flowers with tinge of green at the center. One of the best when well grown.

MAN O'WAR: (9.3) single. Bright scarlet-red with conspicuous yellow stamens; strong, erect grower.

MONS. JULES ELIE: (9.2) double. Very large, rose-pink with incurved center silvery pink; tall stems; popular for over sixty years.

NIPPON BEAUTY: (9.27) Japanese type. Rich deep red which doesn't fade; strong grower, stiff stems; outstanding; late.

NIPPON GOLD: (9.02) Japanese. Pink with yellow crinkled petaloids; strong grower; good for cutting.

PHILLIPPE RIVOIRE: (9.2) double. Bright rich crimson of beautiful form; decidedly fragrant, medium-size flowers on stiff stems; late midseason.

REINE HORTENSE: (8.7) semi-double. Large, flat flowers of shell pink with crimson-flecked center; very fragrant; tall with strong stems; midseason.

SEA SHELL: recent single. Bright lively pink with center of yellow stamens; attractive in the garden and in flower arrangements; midseason.

WALTER FAXON: (9.3) double. Delicate rose flowers of medium size; blooms midseason; fragrant.

PAPAVER, Poppy. Except for the Iceland and Oriental Poppies very few nurserymen carry any of the other perennial kinds, some of the best of which are listed in the Tabular List in the Appendix.

P. nudicaule, Iceland Poppy, is one of the most delightful plants for the perennial garden, with fragrant 3-inch flowers on slender stalks about a foot high. Flower colors are varied, ranging from white through yellow and orange shades to red; blooming from May to July or even longer in gardens where it thrives. Unfortunately being native to the Arctic Regions, it does not like hot summers, consequently it is difficult to make it happy in the Northeast except in those regions where cool nights are experienced. Another drawback is that it does not stand the kind of travel that involves being cooped up in a packing case for a week or more. For this reason it is advisable to raise them from seeds at home unless they can be bought locally.

P. orientale, Oriental Poppy. Recently I was reading about a man, not a nurseryman, who grew Oriental Poppies by the hundred. While I would not attempt to dictate to anyone as to what he should grow, or should not grow, it does seem to me that hundreds of Oriental Poppies are too much of a good thing especially in a small garden. You see, their flowering period is of short duration, and when the blooms fade the foliage begins to look shabby and gets rattier and rattier until it finally dies early in August. Even so, they make such a striking display when in bloom that they cannot be entirely omitted; other plants such as Babys-breath can be planted nearby to hide the disheveled Poppy foliage.

Nowadays we are no longer restricted to the rather overwhelming orange-red of the old-time Oriental Poppies. There are varieties available now to fit every taste; the color ranges from white through pale pink to deep rose, with orange and crimson-scarlet, plus bicolors such as the gorgeous white and orange Snowflame. In size they vary from the 18 to 24 inches of Little Darling to Curtis Giant Flame with flowers a foot across on 4-foot stems.

Here is a selection of good varieties mostly moderately priced:

BARR'S WHITE: glistening white with purple-black spots; free-blooming habit.

BEAUTY OF LIVERMERE: dark crimson with black blotch.

CAVALIER: scarlet-red with crinkled petals. Free blooming, new.

CURTIS GIANT FLAME: red flowers, 12 inches across on 4-foot stems.

ENCHANTRESS: soft rose; delicate but lovely color, best in light shade.

G. I. JOE: cerise-red with black blotch. Compact and free-flowering; late.

HELEN ELIZABETH: pure pink, heavily crinkled petals without spots.

HENRI CAYEUX IMPROVED: attractive old rose; large flowers which keep color best in light shade.

INDIAN CHIEF: beautiful mahogany; handsome plant; free-blooming habit.

MAY SADLER: salmon-pink with black spots; free-blooming.

SNOWFLAME: unusual blend of white and flame-orange. Striking in bloom.

SPRING MORN: shell-pink; tall yet compact habit; free-flowering.

Oriental Poppies cannot endure wet feet, so be very sure that the soil is properly underdrained. Unless they are planted at the right season, they are sometimes difficult to establish in gardens; on the other hand they are equally difficult to get rid of once they are thoroughly established. Some varieties tend to spread rather freely and unless every particle of root is dug up, they are likely to spring up again from the roots that are left behind. The best time to transplant them is in August, when they are dormant; if spring planting is adopted, obtain, if possible, plants in pots grown from cuttings.

PENSTEMON, Beard-tongue. I have a feeling that there are great possibilities for Penstemons in the perennial garden, especially if plant breeders get around to using *P. digitalis* as a parent. This is native from Maine to South Dakota and Texas; grows in poor soil, where its height is likely to be less than 2 feet, or in rich soil, where it may attain 5 feet. While its white or pinkish flowers are pleasant, they could doubtless be improved by crossing them with some of the large-flowered, showy garden kinds, which in my experience are not reliably hardy. The only species that seems to be at all common in gardens in the Northeast is *P. barbatus,* which normally grows to 3–4 feet though it is capable of attaining 6 feet; it has red flowers on slender stalks which often topple over unless supported; and *P. Torreyi,* a similar species with large scarlet flowers. Pink Beauty, 4 to 5 feet, and Pink Sprite, 1½ feet, probably are developments from these two species.

The so-called, hardy large-flowered Penstemons allied by implication to *P. gloxinioides*—a race derived in all probability from *P. Hartwegi,* Mexico; and *P. cobaea,* Missouri to Texas—have not survived the winters in my garden. Perhaps in a climate no more severe than that of Long Island, N.Y., the following would grow successfully. Garnet, described as producing a succession of Gloxinia-like flowers from June until frost on 12- to 18-inch stalks; and Firebird, said to be "perpetual-blooming," with flowers the size of Foxgloves on stems 18 to 24 inches tall.

Full sun and thoroughly drained soil are necessary.

Summer Phlox, Atlanta. J. HORACE MCFARLAND COMPANY

Yellow Violas, blue and white Balloon Flowers in effective contrast.
GOTTSCHO-SCHLEISNER

PHLOX. Like the preceding, the Phloxes are predominantly North American in origin. By a selection of species and varieties it is possible to have some kind or other of them in bloom from early spring until the fall. By starting with *P. subulata*—the Moss-Phlox and its garden varieties blooming in April and May—the tide of bloom is carried along with *P. divaricata*, Wild Blue Phlox or Wild Sweet William, and *P. Arendsi*, a hybrid Phlox (supposedly a cross between *P. divaricata* and *P. paniculata*), followed closely by an early-flowering strain of *P. carolina* until in July the long-blooming Garden Phloxes come into the picture and remain there until September.

P. Arendsi. The following garden forms are said to grow very well indeed in shady situations and to be almost continually in bloom from late May until frost: Charlotte, white with dark lilac eyes; Emmy, pale lilac; Inga, orchid-lavender; Hilda, white with pink eye. All of them grow between 1½ and 2 feet tall.

P. carolina, early-blooming forms usually listed in catalogues under the name *P. suffruticosa*. Miss Lingard, white, about 2 feet tall, is the only garden Phlox we could rely on to survive year after year in the Brooklyn Botanic Garden. It starts to bloom in June. Miss Verboom is described as a rose-magenta counterpart; Belle Pyramid is a much better color—clear pink.

P. divaricata is well adapted for naturalizing in humusy soil and partial shade. A garden form known as *P. d. Laphami* has larger flowers of bright violet-blue and in my experience stays in bloom over a longer period.

P. nivalis (*setacea*), Trailing Phlox. This has pink or white flowers about 1 inch across; var. *sylvestris* has rosy-red flowers up to 1¼ inches in diameter; the variety Camla, probably the best of the group, is a compact grower with pure pink flowers freely produced.

P. paniculata. This is the Garden or Summer Phlox that is the mainstay of the August garden; available in a great variety of colors. There is a constant influx of new garden names, but I "hae ma doots" whether they are better than the best of the old varieties. Following is a selection of varieties that I list with some misgivings because many gardeners have violent prejudices concerning the colors of Phlox, and it must be admitted that it is difficult to combine them without their warring either among themselves or with other garden flowers in the vicinity. Therefore, I suggest that if you live within reasonable distance of a nursery which grows them, it would be a good plan to visit it in August, pick out the kinds that appeal to you, and either place an order for spring or fall delivery; or, if you have a place ready for them so that they can be planted right away, have them dug up with a ball of earth (see page 80) and take them with you.

The following is a list of good garden varieties:

BLUE BOY: 2½ feet. Dark violet-blue; needs white Phlox for companion.

CHARLES CURTIS: 3 feet. Orange-red, finest of its color; strong plant; all summer bloom.

CHEERFULNESS: 3½ feet. Salmon-red; vigorous growth.

COLUMBIA: 2½ feet. Lovely cameo-pink; continuous bloom.

DAILY SKETCH: 3½ feet. Salmon with red eye; arresting rose in mass.

LEO SCHLAGETER: 3 feet. Lovely glowing red; combines well with yellow, pink, or white.

MARY LOUISE: 2½ feet. Snow-white; very large heads of bloom.

PINKETTE: 2½ feet. Exquisite blush-pink; needs semi-shade; all-summer bloom.

PROGRESS: 2½ feet. Light blue with purple eye; makes for stunning color effects.

SIR JOHN FALSTAFF: 2½–3 feet. Rich salmon-pink; enormous flowers.

SONJA: 2 feet. Unusual combination of pale blue with yellow eye.

WIDAR: 2½ feet. Violet with white eye.

P. subulata, Moss-Phlox. This grows wild in many parts of eastern North America. In the form most commonly seen the flowers are a bright magenta which gives a rather strenuous color effect especially when it is associated with (as is often the case) the brilliant yellow *Alyssum saxatile*. There are many named garden varieties with pleasing colors such as: Blue Hill, pure "blue"; Crimson Beauty; Fairy, pale blue with dark purple eye, compact habit; Snowhite; Vivid, bright pink with dark pink eye. These grow from 4 to 6 inches tall with mosslike foliage and a tendency to spread laterally. Plant in full sun in soil that is not too acid.

Phlox in general need a rich deep moist soil. Except where noted above they will grow in full sun or in dappled shade. Although the garden Phlox is absolutely indispensable in those regions where it will grow, it must be admitted that it is subject to various troubles, most of which can be lessened by good culture. Spider mites are particularly injurious. It is important to get after these pests before they make much headway, so keep a close watch on the plants, and if the foliage has a mottled yellow appearance, look on the undersides of a leaf with a hand lens, and if mites are seen, spray them with a miticide such as Aramite, Dimite, Marvel Spray, etc., right away, or dust the underside of the foliage with dusting sulphur. Sulphur is also a remedy for mildew, which makes a dirty-white felted mass on the leaves. In some gardens root-knot nematodes (eel worms—microscopic worms) cause knots to form on the roots and distort the shoots. The remedy is to dig up infected plants and destroy them by burning; and treat the soil with a larvacide, Formalin, or DD. There is a trouble supposedly physiological in origin that causes the leaves to die progressively from the base of the plant upward. This is said to be controlled by cutting the stems of the Phlox close to the soil either in the fall or in the spring while the plants are still dormant. Fading flower clusters should be cut off for two reasons: (1) to aid in prolonging the season of bloom; and (2) to prevent seed formation. If the seeds fall to the ground, some of them will germinate, grow up, and smother the good variety. Almost invariably the seedling plants revert to the muddy rose-purple of the ancestral form.

PRIMULA, Primrose. Although upwards of three hundred species of Primula have been described, comparatively few are available for our purpose. Some need the protection of a greenhouse, many are better suited for culture in the rock garden, others can thrive only in regions which have a cool summer climate, and some of the Himalayan representatives have never been successfully grown under cultivation. About the only species, varieties, and hybrids that can be grown in most gardens are those listed in the tables in the Appendix; of these, the most valuable are *P. japonica, P. polyantha,* and *P. vulgaris.*

P. japonica, Japanese Primrose, is an excellent plant for swampy ground in full sun or part shade, although it will grow quite well in

Polyanthus Primrose, *Primula polyantha* Hose-in-Hose. STEENSON & BAKER

the flower border if watered during dry spells. The leaves resemble those of Cos Lettuce. From the tufted foliage flower stems rise to a height of about 2 feet with clusters of 1-inch flowers arranged in tiers. The colors of the varieties range from white to rose-red and purple. If you can get a clear crimson variety, I would advise eliminating all others, because they cross freely and self-sown seedlings exhibit a variety of muddy colorings.

P. polyantha. The Polyanthus Primrose is a hybrid race believed to be made up of the Cowslip, *P. veris;* the Oxlip, *P. elatior;* and the Common or English Primrose, *P. vulgaris.* They are characterized by flowers up to 1½ inches across, displayed in umbels on leafless scapes 9 to 12 inches high. They are obtainable in several strains—Munstead, Colossal, Hose-in-Hose, etc.—in various colors.

The flowers of *Primula vulgaris,* the English Primrose of literature, are similar to those of Polyanthus except that they seem to be

English Primrose, *Primula vulgaris*. STEENSON & BAKER

produced on single stems, often nestling among the foliage; and there is perhaps a greater range of color in them including "blues."

Both Polyanthus and English Primrose are valuable for early-spring display, the last-named being the first to bloom. Their cultural requirements also are practically the same. Soil should be deep, moist, and rich with rotted cow manure or compost. Part shade is desirable. For further information concerning their culture see page 163. Seeds sown in early spring will produce flowering plants for the following year; they will be at their best the second year; the third year they will probably need to be divided.

RUDBECKIA, Coneflower. This group contains annuals, biennials, and perennials. It includes such well-known plants as Golden Glow, a perennial; Black-eyed Susan and Brown-eyed Susan, native plants which may behave as annuals or biennials. In catalogues Rudbeckia is likely to be confused with Echinacea (which see), also called Coneflower.

R. laciniata hortensia (*fl. pl.*) is the Golden Glow which can be seen flourishing in sun or part shade alongside barns and houses in country districts in the Northeast. It may attain a height of 9 feet in rich soil, which puts it out of the small-garden class; another disturbing feature is the red lice with which it is almost invariably infested.

R. speciosa, Showy Coneflower, is perhaps the best of all for garden use. It is long-blooming and if you like yellow, it is indispensable. The garden form known as Goldsturm probably belongs here. Ultimately growing to 2 feet or a little more, it may not reach more than a foot in height during the first season. It is covered with yellow daisies 2 or 3 inches across with conspicuous black-purple "cones." *R. subtomentosa*, Sweet Coneflower, does not appeal to me very much. Perhaps it is because there is too much of it in a garden near here. It is a coarse, showy plant up to 6 feet tall with grayish leaves and yellow flowers with a brownish "cone."

SALVIA, Sage. Annuals, biennials, perennials, and shrubs are included in this genus of many species, most of which fall short of being really worth while. The following, however, have merit:

S. farinacea, Mealycup Sage, is a perennial which is not really hardy north of New York City; therefore, in cold regions it is customary to treat it as a half-hardy annual and start it from seeds every year. It grows 2½ to 3 feet with numerous slender racemes of violet-blue flowers emerging from white-woolly calyxes so that the general effect is lavenderish. There is also a white-flowered form. Blooms for about two months in August and September.

S. Pitcheri, often sold as *S. azurea grandiflora*, has one fault—the floppy tendency of its flower stems, which necessitates support of some kind. The flowers are clear azure blue, about 1 inch long on stems which arise 2 to 4 feet high.

THALICTRUM, Meadow-rue. These are plants without petals, their floral effect being dependent in some on the conspicuous stamens and in others on the colored sepals. Their finely divided foliage, sometimes almost fernlike, is attractive. They vary in height from 4 inches to 4 feet. There are numerous species, among the best of which are the following:

T. aquilegifolium. This grows to 3 feet with erect stems; the stamens are pink and purple and the rather inconspicuous sepals are white. May to June.

T. dipterocarpum, Chinese Meadow-rue, is a handsome plant when well grown, but it is rather cantankerous and does not thrive everywhere; perhaps it is not thoroughly winter-hardy. It has panicles of nodding flowers with lilac sepals in July and August. A similar species, *T. Rochebrunianum,* which grows 5 to 6 feet high and is not well known at present, may be of easier culture. The best plants I have seen of this were growing in Burlington, Vermont. Here my one objection to it is its bare legs—the lower foliage is skimpy at flowering time. I am trying to naturalize it in thin woodland.

T. kiusianum is a little gem, no more than 3 to 4 inches tall, with lavender flowers. This, when growing in humus soil and dappled shade, is capable of spreading into a patch a foot or more across, producing its flowers practically all summer long. Neither one of these two last-named species is commonly offered for sale at present and a search through catalogues of specialists in perennials, or the *Plant Buyers Guide,* is necessary to obtain planting stock.

T. glaucum is valuable chiefly for its gray-blue foliage, although its soft yellow, panicled flowers in dense clusters are also attractive. Its 4-foot height makes it a valuable plant for the rear rank of the border.

TROLLIUS, Globe-flower. These, in general, are swamp plants, although they will thrive in the flower border if watered during dry spells. They have large Buttercup-like flowers, useful for cutting. *T. asiaticus* has orange flowers on 2-foot stalks in May and June with scattered blooms to August; *T. europaeus,* lemon-yellow about 1½ feet, May–August; *T. Ledebouri,* with yellow flowers on 1½-foot stems, is a late starter blooming from June to August.

VERBASCUM, Mullein. The Mulleins are used more freely in England than they are here. Perhaps a reason for their lack of popularity with American gardeners is that they are not long-lived—indeed, many of them are biennials. The garden forms may not come true from seeds, but they can easily be propagated by root cuttings (see Chapter Fourteen on Propagating the Plants).

V. Chaixi has white-woolly leaves and spirelike panicles of yellow blooms rising to 3 feet.

V. olympicum, Olympian Mullein, is similar but larger, in general up to 6 feet tall. It is handsome in bloom. I remember the striking appearance of a row almost a hundred yards long of this species used as a background to a border in the Cambridge University Botanic Garden in England. It is doubtful that I should have included this here, because I have the impression that it is definitely a biennial rather than a perennial.

V. phoeniceum, Purple Mullein, has purple or red flowers produced on racemes up to 5 feet tall. The named garden forms, Cotswold Gem, growing to 4 feet, amber flowers with purple centers; and Pink Domino, 3 feet, with rosy pink flowers, probably are derivatives of this species. These have not been too permanent in my garden, tending to peter out the second year. Anyone having a hot, dry situation to contend with, in which the Mulleins thrive, should try them.

V. blattaria, the Moth Mullein, a Eurasian species which ranges in height from 2 to 6 feet with yellow or white flowers, is suitable for naturalizing in sunny meadows.

VERONICA, Speedwell. Flowers of the Speedwells in general are tiny but nonetheless effective because they are carried in freely produced, many-flowered spikes or racemes. Their colors are predominantly blue; there are varieties with pinkish flowers, but in my opinion they are not worth bothering with.

V. incana, Hoary Speedwell, is a good plant for edging or in the front rank of the border. The leaves are so heavily clothed with hair that the green color is obscured and they look almost white. The flowers on hoary stems usually 1 to 1½ feet high are clear blue. When flowering is finished in July, the old stalks should be cut off so that the low, tufted foliage can be seen to best advantage.

V. latifolia (teucrium) is a variable species; some varieties are dwarf, including one densely tufted kind known as *V. rupestris,* and some varieties may attain 2 feet. These taller-growing kinds need to be supported by putting in twigs around the clump before the flower stems flop over.

V. maritima (longifolia) subsessilis is probably the best of all for the perennial garden. Growing to a height of 2½ to 3 feet, it is clothed with racemes of blue flowers during August and September.

V. spicata, Blue Peter, 1½ feet, and Blue Spire, 2 feet, are believed to be better than the species *V. spuria* (*amethystina*); the garden form known as Royal Blue, which blooms in June and July with gentian-blue flowers on 15-inch stems, is perhaps the best.

VIOLA, Violet, Pansy, Tufted-Pansy. The most important groups of this large genus for the perennial garden are the Pansies, probably derived mainly from *Viola tricolor;* the Tufted-Pansies or Violas derived chiefly from *V. cornuta* with possibly a mixture of *V. gracilis;* and the Sweet Violet, *V. odorata*, which, while not showy, can find a place in the front rank of the border. Native Violets are useful for naturalizing.

Viola cornuta, Tufted-Pansy. In gardens where they grow well these are among the most valuable of all the low-growing plants because of their long-flowering habits. Their flowers should be kept picked off, otherwise they will go to seed, and, unless you are meticulous in the use of the hoe, the following year you will have a large array of Violas, growing here and there, most of them inferior to the parent plant. Also they will remain longer in bloom when they are not enfeebled by seed bearing. There are numerous named garden forms, some of which are temperamental in most gardens. For example, Purple Heart is a first-class plant in some gardens, but resolutely fails to grow for me; but Royal Purple thrives like the proverbial green Bay tree. The best advice I can give as to varieties is to obtain several and then propagate from cuttings those which grow the best for you.

Viola odorata. This is a species from which the sweet-scented Violet of the florist is derived. These thrive better in a moderate climate—one that is not too hot in summer, not too cold in winter. Any of a half-dozen or so varieties offered by specialists in perennials could be chosen in these mild regions. But for a severe climate I would suggest trying Rosina, a low-growing, pink-flowered variety; and Royal Robe, a strong-growing variety with violet-colored flowers which, however, is said to be a shy bloomer in some situations.

This concludes our discussion of perennials. I think that just about all of the worth-while kinds are included either here or in the Table and Lists in the Appendix. If any are left out, it is because of an oversight on my part, or because they have too many failings, or because I just don't like their looks.

Appendix

The Tables and Lists which follow are the work of my old and valued friend H. E. Downer, formerly Horticulturist at Vassar College. They have been amplified by me by the inclusion of some of the hardy summer-flowering bulbs.

TABULAR LIST OF PERENNIALS

BOTANICAL NAME	COMMON NAME	FAMILY
Acanthus mollis	Bears-breech	*Acanthaceae*—Acanthus
A. m. latifolius	Broad-leaved Acanthus	*Acanthaceae*—Acanthus
Achillea filipendulina	Fernleaf Yarrow	*Compositae*—Daisy
A. millefolium roseum	Red Milfoil	*Compositae*—Daisy
A. ptarmica Perrys White	Perrys Sneezewort	*Compositae*—Daisy
A. p. Boule de Neige	Double Sneezewort	*Compositae*—Daisy
Aconitum autumnale	Autumn Monkshood	*Ranunculaceae*—Buttercup
A. Fischeri	Fischers M.	*Ranunculaceae*—Buttercup
A. F. Wilsoni	Wilsons M.	*Ranunculaceae*—Buttercup
A. napellus	Monkshood	*Ranunculaceae*—Buttercup
A. n. album	White M.	*Ranunculaceae*—Buttercup
A. n. Sparksi	Sparks M.	*Ranunculaceae*—Buttercup
Actaea alba	White Baneberry	*Ranunculaceae*—Buttercup
A. rubra	Red B.	*Ranunculaceae*—Buttercup
Adenophora confusa (*A. Farreri*)	Farrers Lilybell	*Campanulaceae*—Bellflower
A. lilifolia	Gland Bellflower	*Campanulaceae*—Bellflower
A. Potanini	Ladybell	*Campanulaceae*—Bellflower
Adonis vernalis	Spring Adonis	*Ranunculaceae*—Buttercup
Aethionema grandiflorum	Persian Stone-cress	*Cruciferae*—Mustard
Ajuga Brockbanki	Brockbanks Bugle	*Labiatae*—Mint
A. genevensis	Alpine B.	*Labiatae*—Mint
A. reptans	Carpet B., Common B.	*Labiatae*—Mint
A. r. alba	White B.	*Labiatae*—Mint
A. r. rubra	Red-leaved B.	*Labiatae*—Mint
Alchemilla vulgaris	Ladys-mantle	*Rosaceae*—Rose
Alstroemeria aurantiaca	Golden Peruvian-lily	*Amaryllidaceae*—Amaryllis
Alyssum saxatile	Golden-tuft	*Cruciferae*—Mustard
A. s. compactum	Dwarf G.-t.	*Cruciferae*—Mustard
A. s. luteum	Pale G.-t.	*Cruciferae*—Mustard
Amsonia tabernaemontana	Amsonia	*Apocynaceae*—Dogbane
Anaphalis margaritacea	Pearl Everlasting	*Compositae*—Daisy
Anchusa azurea (*italica*)	Italian Alkanet	*Boraginaceae*—Borage
A. a. Dropmore	Dropmore A.	*Boraginaceae*—Borage
A. a. Pride of Dover	Dover A.	*Boraginaceae*—Borage
A. Barrelieri	Barreliers A.	*Boraginaceae*—Borage
A. caespitosa	Tufted A. (Blue Stars)	*Boraginaceae*—Borage

ORIGIN	SEASON	COLOR	HEIGHT
S. Europe	July–Aug.	whitish rose	2 –2½ ft.
Garden	July–Aug.	rosy purple	2½–3 ft.
Orient	June–Sept.	yellow	3 –5 ft.
Garden	June–Sept.	rose	2 –3 ft.
Garden	June–Sept.	white	1½–2 ft.
Garden	June–Sept.	white	2 –2½ ft.
N. China	Aug.–Sept.	deep blue	4 –5 ft.
Asia	Aug.–Sept.	pale blue	4 –5 ft.
Asia	Sept.–Oct.	violet-blue	5 –6 ft.
Europe	June–July	blue	3 –4 ft.
Garden	June–July	white	3 –4 ft.
Garden	July–Aug.	violet-blue	4 –5 ft.
N. America	May–Sept.	white fls. & frt.	1½–2 ft.
N. America	May–Sept.	white fls. & red frt.	1½–2 ft.
China	July–Aug.	deep blue	2 –3 ft.
Europe–Asia	July–Aug.	blue	2 –3 ft.
W. China	July–Aug.	blue	3 –4 ft.
Europe	April	yellow	1 –1½ ft.
Persia	May–June	rosy pink	1 –1½ ft.
Garden	May–June	deep blue	3 –5 in.
Europe	May–June	bright blue	6 –9 in.
Europe	May–June	blue	3 –6 in.
Garden	May–June	white	3 –6 in.
Garden	May–June	dark purple lvs.	3 –6 in.
Europe	May–June	greenish	1 –1½ ft.
Chile	July–Aug.	orange	2½–3 ft.
Europe	April–May	yellow	9 –12 in.
Garden	April–May	yellow	6 –9 in.
Garden	April–May	pale yellow	6 –9 in.
Europe	May–June	pale blue	2½–3 ft.
N. America	July–Aug.	white	1 –3 ft.
Medit. region	May–June	deep blue	3 –5 ft.
Garden	May–June	deep blue	3 –5 ft.
Garden	May–June	light blue	3 –5 ft.
Eu.–Asia Min.	May–June	dark blue	2 ft.
?	May–July	dark blue	1 –1½ ft.

BOTANICAL NAME	COMMON NAME	FAMILY
A. myosotidiflora (see Brunnera)		
Anemone hupehensis	Dwarf Japanese Anemone	Ranunculaceae—Buttercup
A. japonica	Japanese A.	Ranunculaceae—Buttercup
A. j. alba	Japanese A.	Ranunculaceae—Buttercup
A. j. Queen Charlotte	Japanese A.	Ranunculaceae—Buttercup
A. j. Whirlwind	Japanese A.	Ranunculaceae—Buttercup
A. pulsatilla	Pasque Flower	Ranunculaceae—Buttercup
A. p. alba	White P. F.	Ranunculaceae—Buttercup
A. sylvestris	Snowdrop Anemone	Ranunculaceae—Buttercup
Anthemis Sancti-Johannis	St. Johns Daisy	Compositae—Daisy
A. tinctoria	Golden Marguerite	Compositae—Daisy
A. t. Kelwayi	Kelways G. M.	Compositae—Daisy
A. t. Moonlight	Pale M.	Compositae—Daisy
A. t. Perry's var.	Perrys M.	Compositae—Daisy
Antirrhinum majus vars.	Snapdragon	Scrophulariaceae—Figwort
Aquilegia caerulea	Colorado Columbine	Ranunculaceae—Buttercup
A. c. hybrids	Hybrid C. C.	Ranunculaceae—Buttercup
A. canadensis	Common American C.	Ranunculaceae—Buttercup
A. chrysantha	Golden C.	Ranunculaceae—Buttercup
A. clematiflora	Clematis-fld. C.	Ranunculaceae—Buttercup
A. flabellata	Fan C.	Ranunculaceae—Buttercup
A. f. nana	Dwarf Fan C.	Ranunculaceae—Buttercup
A. hybrida	Long-spurred C.	Ranunculaceae—Buttercup
A. glandulosa	Altaian C.	Ranunculaceae—Buttercup
A. longissima	Long-spurred C.	Ranunculaceae—Buttercup
A. Skinneri	Mexican C.	Ranunculaceae—Buttercup
A. vulgaris	European C.	Ranunculaceae—Buttercup
A. v. hybrids	Short-spurred C.	Ranunculaceae—Buttercup
Arabis albida	Wall Rock-cress	Cruciferae—Mustard
A. a. fl. pl.	Double R.-c.	Cruciferae—Mustard
A. a. variegata	Variegated R.-c.	Cruciferae—Mustard
Armeria maritima	Thrift	Plumbaginaceae—Leadwort
A. m. Laucheana	Lauches Thrift	Plumbaginaceae—Leadwort
A. hybrids	Hybrid T.	Plumbaginaceae—Leadwort
Artemisia albula Silver King	Silver King	Compositae—Daisy
A. lactiflora	White Mugwort	Compositae—Daisy

ORIGIN	SEASON	COLOR	HEIGHT
China	Aug.–Sept.	rosy mauve	1 –1½ ft.
Asia	Sept.–Oct.	rosy purple	3 –5 ft.
Garden	Sept.–Oct.	white	3 –5 ft.
Garden	Sept.–Oct.	pink, semi-dbl.	3 –5 ft.
Garden	Sept.–Oct.	white, semi-dbl.	3 –5 ft.
Europe	April	bluish purple	6 –15 in.
Garden	April	white	6 –15 in.
Europe–Asia	May–June	white	12 –18 in.
Europe	May–Sept.	orange-yellow	2 –3 ft.
Europe–Asia	May–Sept.	yellow	2 –3 ft.
Garden	May–Sept.	yellow	2 –3 ft.
Garden	May–Sept.	pale yellow	2 –3 ft.
Garden	May–Sept.	golden yellow	2 –3 ft.
Garden	June–Sept.	various	½–2½ ft.
N. America	May–June	blue and white	1½–2 ft.
Garden	May–June	various	2 –2½ ft.
N. America	May–June	scarlet & yellow	1 –2 ft.
N. America	May–July	yellow	2½–3 ft.
Garden	May–June	various	1½–2 ft.
Japan	May–June	lilac-white	1 –1½ ft.
Garden	May–June	white	8 –12 in.
Garden	May–June	various	1½–3 ft.
Siberia	May–June	blue & white	1 –1¼ ft.
Mex.–s.w. Texas	May–July	pale yellow	2 –3 ft.
Mexico	May–July	red & yellow	2 –3 ft.
Europe	May–July	purple & white	1½–2½ ft.
Garden	May–July	various	1½–2½ ft.
Caucasus	April–May	white	6 –10 in.
Garden	April–May	white	6 –10 in.
Garden	all season	lvs. grn. & yellow	6 –10 in.
Europe	May–June	rose-pink	6 –9 in.
Garden	May–June	crimson	9 –12 in.
Garden	May–Aug.	pink & red shades	1 –2 ft.
N. America	May–Oct.	silver leaves	3 –3½ ft.
China	Aug.–Sept.	creamy white	4 –5 ft.

BOTANICAL NAME	COMMON NAME	FAMILY
A. *Schmidtiana*	Satiny Wormwood	*Compositae*—Daisy
A. *S. nana*		
Silver Mound	Silver-mound Artemisia	*Compositae*—Daisy
A. *Stelleriana*	Old Woman, Beech Wormwood	*Compositae*—Daisy
Aruncus sylvester	Goats-beard	*Rosaceae*—Rose
Asclepias tuberosa	Butterfly-weed	*Asclepiadaceae*—Milkweed
Asperula odorata	Sweet Woodruff	*Rubiaceae*—Madder
Asphodeline lutea	Jacobs-rod	*Liliaceae*—Lily
Aster alpinus	Alpine Aster	*Compositae*—Daisy
A. *amellus*	Italian A.	*Compositae*—Daisy
A. *a.* King George	It. A. var.	*Compositae*—Daisy
A. *a.* Mrs. R. Wood	It. A. var.	*Compositae*—Daisy
A. *Frikarti*	Wonder of Staffa	*Compositae*—Daisy
A. *hybridus nanus*	Dwarf A.	*Compositae*—Daisy
A. *novae-angliae*	New England A.	*Compositae*—Daisy
A. *n.-a.* vars.	Michaelmas Daisies	*Compositae*—Daisy
A. *novi-belgi*	New York A.	*Compositae*—Daisy
A. *n.-b.* vars.	Michaelmas Daisies	*Compositae*—Daisy
A. *tataricus*	Tartarian Daisy	*Compositae*—Daisy
Astilbe Arendsi	Hybrid Astilbe	*Saxifragaceae*—Saxifrage
A. *biternata*	False Goats-beard	*Saxifragaceae*—Saxifrage
A. *japonica*	Florists' Spirea	*Saxifragaceae*—Saxifrage
A. *j. rubens*	Spirea	*Saxifragaceae*—Saxifrage
A. *rosea* Peach Blossom	Spirea	*Saxifragaceae*—Saxifrage
A. *r.* Queen Alexandra	Spirea	*Saxifragaceae*—Saxifrage
Astrantia major	Masterwort	*Umbelliferae*—Carrot
Aubrieta deltoidea	Purple Rock-cress	*Cruciferae*—Mustard
A. *d.* vars.	Purple R.-c.	*Cruciferae*—Mustard
Baptisia australis	False Indigo	*Leguminoseae*—Pea
Begonia Evansiana	Evans Begonia	*Begoniaceae*—Begonia
Belamcanda chinensis	Blackberry-lily	*Iridaceae*—Iris
Bergenia crassifolia	Leather Saxifrage	*Saxifragaceae*—Saxifrage
Bocconia cordata	Plume-poppy	*Papaveraceae*—Poppy
Boltonia asteroides	Aster-like Bol.	*Compositae*—Daisy
B. *latisquama*	Broad-scaled B.	*Compositae*—Daisy
Brunnera macrophylla	Dwarf Anchusa	*Boraginaceae*—Borage
Buphthalmum speciosum	Showy-Oxeye	*Compositae*—Daisy

ORIGIN	SEASON	COLOR	HEIGHT
Japan	all season	silver leaves	1½–2 ft.
Japan	all season	silver leaves	1 ft.
Asia–N. America	all season	yellow, silvery lvs.	2 –2½ ft.
N. America	June–July	white	5 –7 ft.
N. America	July	orange	2½–3 ft.
Europe	May–June	white	6 –8 in.
Medit. region	June–July	yellow	3 –4 ft.
Eur.–N. America	May–June	violet	8 –10 in.
Europe	July–Aug.	purple	1½–2 ft.
Garden	July–Aug.	violet-blue	1½–2 ft.
Garden	July–Aug.	rose	1½–2 ft.
Garden	July–Nov.	blue	1½–2 ft.
Garden	Aug.–Sept.	various	6 –12 in.
N. America	Sept.–Oct.	purple	4 –5 ft.
Garden	Sept.–Oct.	pink & purple	3 –5 ft.
N. America	Sept.–Oct.	violet-blue	3 –5 ft.
Garden	Sept.–Oct.	various	3 –5 ft.
Siberia	Oct.	purple	5 –7 ft.
Garden	June–July	various	2 –3 ft.
N. America	June–July	creamy white	5 –6 ft.
Japan	June–July	white	1½–3 ft.
Garden	June–July	rosy crimson	1½–3 ft.
Garden	July	light pink	2½–3 ft.
Garden	July	deep pink	2½–3 ft.
Europe	May	silvery pink	2 –3 ft.
Medit. region	April–May	purple	3 –6 in.
Garden	April–May	purple shades	3 –6 in.
N. America	May–June	blue	4 –4½ ft.
Asia	July–Sept.	flesh-pink	2 ft.
China–Japan	July–Aug.	orange	3 –4 ft.
Siberia	April–May	rosy purple	1 –1½ ft.
China–Japan	July–Aug.	creamy	6 –8 ft.
N. America	Aug.–Sept.	white	5 –8 ft.
N. America	Aug.–Sept.	pinkish	4 –5 ft.
Siberia	April–May	blue	9 –15 in.
Europe–Asia	June–July	yellow	3 –4 ft.

BOTANICAL NAME	COMMON NAME	FAMILY
Calimeris incisa	Cut-leaved Calimeris	*Compositae*—Daisy
Callirhoe involucrata	Poppy-mallow	*Malvaceae*—Mallow
Caltha palustris	Marsh-marigold	*Ranunculaceae*—Buttercup
Camassia Cusicki	Cusicks Camass	*Liliaceae*—Lily
C. esculenta	Midland C.	*Liliaceae*—Lily
C. Leichtlini	Leichtlins C.	*Liliaceae*—Lily
Campanula alliariaefolia	Bellflower	*Campanulaceae*—Bellflower
C. bononiensis	Russian Bellflower	*Campanulaceae*—Bellflower
C. carpatica	Carpathian Harebell	*Campanulaceae*—Bellflower
C. c. alba	Carpathian H.	*Campanulaceae*—Bellflower
C. glomerata	Clustered Bellflower	*Campanulaceae*—Bellflower
C. g. superba	Clustered B.	*Campanulaceae*—Bellflower
C. lactiflora	Milk-white B.	*Campanulaceae*—Bellflower
C. l. caerulea	Skim-milk B.	*Campanulaceae*—Bellflower
C. latifolia	Great B.	*Campanulaceae*—Bellflower
C. l. alba	White Grt. B.	*Campanulaceae*—Bellflower
C. l. macrantha	Royal B.	*Campanulaceae*—Bellflower
C. persicifolia	Peach-lvd. B.	*Campanulaceae*—Bellflower
C. p. alba	Peach-lvd. B.	*Campanulaceae*—Bellflower
C. p. Moerheimi	Moerheims B.	*Campanulaceae*—Bellflower
C. p. Telham Beauty	Giant Pch.-lvd. B.	*Campanulaceae*—Bellflower
C. rotundifolia	Scotch Bluebell	*Campanulaceae*—Bellflower
Cassia marilandica	Wild Senna	*Leguminosae*—Pea
Catananche caerulea	Cupids-dart	*Compositae*—Daisy
Centaurea babylonica	Babylonian Centaury	*Compositae*—Daisy
C. dealbata	Whitened Knapweed	*Compositae*—Daisy
C. macrocephala	Showy Centaury	*Compositae*—Daisy
C. montana	Mountain Bluet	*Compositae*—Daisy
C. ruthenica	Russian Knapweed	*Compositae*—Daisy
Centranthus ruber	Red Valerian	*Valerianaceae*—Valerian
Cephalaria alpina	Alpine Cephalaria	*Dipsaceae*—Teasel
C. tatarica	Tatarian C.	*Dipsaceae*—Teasel
Cerastium tomentosum	Snow-in-summer	*Caryophyllaceae*—Pink
Ceratostigma plumbaginoides	Blue Leadwort	*Plumbaginaceae*—Leadwort
Chelone glabra	White Turtle-head	*Scrophulariaceae*—Figwort
C. Lyoni	Pink T.-h.	*Scrophulariaceae*—Figwort
Chrysanthemum arcticum	Arctic Daisy	*Compositae*—Daisy
C. a. hybrids	A. D. hybrids	*Compositae*—Daisy

ORIGIN	SEASON	COLOR	HEIGHT
Siberia	July–Aug.	light purple	1½–2 ft.
Mexico	June–Sept.	red-purple	9 –12 in.
N. America	April–May	yellow	12 –18 in.
Oregon	May–June	pale blue	2½–3 ft.
Pa. to Ga. & Texas	May–June	light blue	2 ft.
Brit. Col. to Cal.	May–June	dark blue to cream	2 ft.
Asia Minor	June–July	white	2 –3 ft.
E. Eur.–W. Asia	June	purple	2 –3 ft.
Europe	July–Sept.	blue	9 –15 in.
Garden	July–Sept.	white	9 –15 in.
S. Europe	June–July	purple	1½–2 ft.
Garden	June–July	violet	1½–2 ft.
Caucasus	July–Aug.	milk white	4 –5 ft.
Garden	July–Aug.	pale blue	4 –5 ft.
Europe–Asia	May–June	purplish blue	3 –4 ft.
Garden	May–June	white	3 –4 ft.
Garden	May–June	royal blue	3 –4 ft.
Europe	June–July	blue	2 –3 ft.
Garden	June–July	white	2 –3 ft.
Garden	June–July	semi-double white	2 –3 ft.
Garden	June–July	china blue	2 –3 ft.
Eur.–N. America	June–Sept.	blue	1 –1½ ft.
N. America	July–Aug.	yellow	3 –5 ft.
S. Europe	June–Aug.	blue	1½–2 ft.
Asia Minor	July	yellow	6 –12 ft.
Asia Minor	June–Aug.	rosy red	1½–2 ft.
Armenia	July–Aug.	yellow	3 –4 ft.
Europe	June–Sept.	blue	1½–2 ft.
Eur.–W. Asia	July	pale yellow	3 –4 ft.
Eur.–S.W. Asia	June–July	crimson	2½–3 ft.
S. Europe	June–July	pale yellow	5 –6 ft.
Russia	July–Sept.	cream-white	5 –6 ft.
Europe	June	white	6 in.
China	Aug.–Oct.	blue	12 in.
N. America	July–Sept.	pinkish white	2½–3 ft.
N. America	Aug.–Sept.	deep rose	3 –3½ ft.
Arctic region	Sept.–Oct.	white	6 –12 in.
Garden	Sept.–Oct.	various	1½–2½ ft.

BOTANICAL NAME	COMMON NAME	FAMILY
C. balsamita	Costmary	*Compositae*–Daisy
C. coccineum	Pyrethrum, Painted Daisy	*Compositae*–Daisy
C. c. vars.	Hybrid Pyrethrum	*Compositae*–Daisy
C. coreanum	Korean Daisy	*Compositae*–Daisy
C. maximum	White-weed	*Compositae*–Daisy
C. m. vars.	Shasta Daisy	*Compositae*–Daisy
C. morifolium vars.	Garden Chrysanthemum	*Compositae*–Daisy
C. nipponicum	Nippon Daisy	*Compositae*–Daisy
C. uliginosum	Giant D.	*Compositae*–Daisy
Chrysogonum virginianum	Golden-star	*Compositae*–Daisy
Cimicifuga racemosa	Black-Snake-root, Fairy-candle	*Ranunculaceae*–Buttercup
C. simplex	Bugbane	*Ranunculaceae*–Buttercup
Clematis heracleaefolia	Bush Clematis	*Ranunculaceae*–Buttercup
C. h. Davidiana	Bush Clematis	*Ranunculaceae*–Buttercup
C. integrifolia	Bush Clematis	*Ranunculaceae*–Buttercup
C. recta	Bush Clematis	*Ranunculaceae*–Buttercup
C. stans	Bush Clematis	*Ranunculaceae*–Buttercup
Codonopsis clematidea		*Campanulaceae*–Bellflower
Convallaria majalis	Lily-of-the-valley	*Liliaceae*–Lily
C. m. Fortunei	Giant L.-v.	*Liliaceae*–Lily
Coreopsis grandiflora	Tickseed	*Compositae*–Daisy
C. lanceolata	Lance-leaved T.	*Compositae*–Daisy
C. l. fl. pl.	Double T.	*Compositae*–Daisy
C. rosea	Pink T.	*Compositae*–Daisy
C. verticillata	Thread-leaved T.	*Compositae*–Daisy
Coronilla varia	Crown Vetch	*Leguminosae*–Pea
Corydalis cheilanthifolia	Fern-leaved Fumitory	*Fumariaceae*–Fumitory
C. lutea	Yellow F.	*Fumariaceae*–Fumitory
C. nobilis	Noble F.	*Fumariaceae*–Fumitory
Delphinium cardinale	Scarlet Larkspur	*Ranunculaceae*–Buttercup
D. cheilanthum	Garland L.	*Ranunculaceae*–Buttercup
D. c. formosum	Garland L.	*Ranunculaceae*–Buttercup
D. c. Belladonna	Belladonna L.	*Ranunculaceae*–Buttercup
D. c. Bellamosum		*Ranunculaceae*–Buttercup
D. elatum	Candle Larkspur	*Ranunculaceae*–Buttercup
D. grandiflorum	Chinese L.	*Ranunculaceae*–Buttercup
Delphinium g. album	White C. L.	*Ranunculaceae*–Buttercup

ORIGIN	SEASON	COLOR	HEIGHT
W. Asia	Aug.–Sept.	yellow	2 –3 ft.
Persia	June–July	red	1 –2 ft.
Garden	June–July	var. sing. & dbl.	1 –2 ft.
Asia	Sept.–Oct.	white	1½–2½ ft.
Europe	June–July	white	2 –3 ft.
Garden	June–July	white, sing. & dbl.	2 –3 ft.
China	July–Nov.	various	1 –4 ft.
Japan	Sept.–Oct.	white	2 –4 ft.
Europe	Aug.–Sept.	white	5 –7 ft.
N. America	April–June	yellow	9 –12 in.
N. America	July–Aug.	white	5 –8 ft.
Kamchatka	Sept.–Oct.	white	2½–3 ft.
China	Aug.–Sept.	blue	3 –4 ft.
Asia	Aug.–Sept.	deep blue	3 –4 ft.
Eur.–Asia	June–July	blue	2 –2½ ft.
S. Europe	June	white	4 –5 ft.
Japan	Sept.–Oct.	blue	4 –5 ft.
Cent. Asia	June	pale blue	2 –3 ft.
Eur., Asia, N. America	May	white	6 –9 in.
Garden	May	white	8 –10 in.
N. America	June–Oct.	yellow	2 –2½ ft.
N. America	June–Oct.	yellow	2 ft.
Garden	June–Oct.	yellow	2½–3 ft.
N. America	June–Oct.	rose	1½–2 ft.
N. America	June–Oct.	yellow	2 –2½ ft.
Europe	June–Sept.	pinkish white	1 –2 ft.
China	May–June	pale yellow	1 –1½ ft.
S. Europe	May–Nov.	yellow	12 –15 in.
Siberia	May–June	white & yellow	12 –15 in.
S. California	June–July	scarlet	2 –3 ft.
Siberia–China	June–July	blue	3 –4 ft.
Garden	June–July	indigo blue	4 –5 ft.
Garden	June–July	pale blue	3 –4 ft.
Garden	June–July	dark blue	4 –5 ft.
Europe	June–July	blue	5 –8 ft.
China	June–Sept.	blue	2 –3 ft.
Garden	June–Sept.	white	2 –3 ft.

BOTANICAL NAME	COMMON NAME	FAMILY
D. nudicaule	Red L.	*Ranunculaceae*—Buttercup
D. tatsienense	Tatsien L.	*Ranunculaceae*—Buttercup
Dianthus Allwoodi	Allwoods Pink	*Caryophyllaceae*—Pink
D. barbatus	Sweet William	*Caryophyllaceae*—Pink
D. b. vars.	Giant S. W.	*Caryophyllaceae*—Pink
D. caryophyllus	Carnation	*Caryophyllaceae*—Pink
D. c. Grenadin	Grenadin C.	*Caryophyllaceae*—Pink
D. c. Marguerite	Marguerite C.	*Caryophyllaceae*—Pink
D. chinensis Heddewigi	Rainbow or Chinese Pink	*Caryophyllaceae*—Pink
D. Knappi	Knapps P.	*Caryophyllaceae*—Pink
D. latifolius	Button or Broad-leaved P.	*Caryophyllaceae*—Pink
D. plumarius	Cottage P.	*Caryophyllaceae*—Pink
D. p. semperflorens	Long-season P.	*Caryophyllaceae*—Pink
D. p. hybrids	Garden P.	*Caryophyllaceae*—Pink
Dicentra eximia	Plumy or Fringed Bleeding-heart	*Fumariaceae*—Fumitory
D. formosa	California B.-h.	*Fumariaceae*—Fumitory
D. f. Sweetheart	White Calif. B.-h.	*Fumariaceae*—Fumitory
D. spectabilis	Bleeding-heart	*Fumariaceae*—Fumitory
D. s. alba	White B.-h.	*Fumariaceae*—Fumitory
Dictamnus albus	Gas-plant, Dittany	*Rutaceae*—Rue
D. a. caucasicus	Giant F.	*Rutaceae*—Rue
D. a. rubra	Fraxinella	*Rutaceae*—Rue
Digitalis ambigua	Yellow Foxglove	*Scrophulariaceae*—Figwort
D. lanata	Woolly F.	*Scrophulariaceae*—Figwort
D. Lutzi	Hybrid F.	*Scrophulariaceae*—Figwort
D. purpurea	Common F.	*Scrophulariaceae*—Figwort
D. p. alba	White F.	*Scrophulariaceae*—Figwort
D. p. gloxiniaeflora	Giant F.	*Scrophulariaceae*—Figwort
Dodecatheon meadia	Shooting-star	*Primulaceae*—Primrose
Doronicum caucasicum	Leopards-bane	*Compositae*—Daisy
D. plantagineum	Leopards-bane	*Compositae*—Daisy
Dracocephalum grandiflorum	Dragonhead	*Labiateae*—Mint
D. Ruyschiana	Ruyschs D.	*Labiateae*—Mint
Echinacea purpurea	Purple Coneflower	*Compositae*—Daisy
Echinops ritro	Globe-thistle	*Compositae*—Daisy
E. sphaerocephalus	Globe-thistle	*Compositae*—Daisy

ORIGIN	SEASON	COLOR	HEIGHT
N. Cal.	June–July	red	1½–2 ft.
W. China	June–July	violet-blue	2 –3 ft.
Garden	June–July	various	9 –12 in.
Eur.–Asia	June–July	red, purple	1 –2 ft.
Garden	June–July	various, sing. & dbl.	1 –2 ft.
S. Eur.–India	June–Sept.	pale rose	1 –2 ft.
Garden	June–Sept.	various	1 –2 ft.
Garden	June–Sept.	various	1 –2 ft.
Garden	June–Sept.	various	1 –1½ ft.
S.E. Europe	June–Sept.	yellow	1 –1½ ft.
Garden	June–Sept.	various	10 –15 in.
Europe	June–July	rose	10 –15 in.
Garden	June–Sept.	various	10 –15 in.
Garden	June–July	various	10 –15 in.
E. N. America	April–Oct.	rose-pink	1½–2 ft.
Brit. Col.–Cal.	May–July	rosy purple	1 –1½ ft.
Garden	May–Oct.	white	12 –15 in.
Japan	May–June	rosy red	2 –3 ft.
Garden	May–June	white	1½–2 ft.
S. Eur.–N. China	May–June	white	2 –3 ft.
Garden	May–June	reddish	2 –3 ft.
Garden	May–June	rosy purple	2 –3 ft.
Eur.–W. Asia	June–July	yellow	2 –3 ft.
S.E. Europe	June–July	creamy white	2 –3 ft.
Garden	June–July	salmon shades	3 –4 ft.
W. Europe	June–July	purple	3 –4 ft.
Garden	June–July	white	3 –4 ft.
Garden	June–July	various	3 –4 ft.
N. America	May–June	rose	1 –1½ ft.
S. Eur.–Asia Minor	April–May	yellow	1½–2 ft.
Europe	April–May	yellow	3 –4 ft.
Siberia	June–July	blue	1 ft.
Siberia	June–July	blue	1½–2 ft.
N. America	July–Aug.	red-purple	3 –5 ft.
Eur.–Asia Minor	July–Aug.	steel blue	2 –3 ft.
Eur.–N. Africa	July–Aug.	pale blue	5 –7 ft.

BOTANICAL NAME	COMMON NAME	FAMILY
Epilobium angustifolium	Fire-weed	*Onagraceae*—Evening-primrose
E. a. alba	White Willow-herb	*Onagraceae*—Evening-primrose
Epimedium grandiflorum	Barrenwort	*Berberidaceae*—Barberry
E. g. niveum	White B.	*Berberidaceae*—Barberry
E. pinnatum	Persian B.	*Berberidaceae*—Barberry
Eremurus himalaicus	Foxtail-lily, Desert-candle	*Liliaceae*—Lily
E. robustus	Giant F.-l.	*Liliaceae*—Lily
E. Shelford	Hybrid F.-l.	*Liliaceae*—Lily
Erigeron speciosus	Showy Fleabane	*Compositae*—Daisy
E. s. vars.	Showy Fleabane	*Compositae*—Daisy
Eryngium alpinum	Eryngo	*Umbelliferae*—Carrot
E. maritimum	Sea-holly	*Umbelliferae*—Carrot
E. Oliverianum	Olivers E.	*Umbelliferae*—Carrot
E. planum	Flat-leaved E.	*Umbelliferae*—Carrot
Erysimum asperum	Siberian Wallflower	*Cruciferae*—Mustard
E. ochroleucum	Alpine W.	*Cruciferae*—Mustard
Eupatorium coelestinum	Mist-flower	*Compositae*—Daisy
E. purpureum	Joe-Pye Weed	*Compositae*—Daisy
E. rugosum	White Snakeroot	*Compositae*—Daisy
Euphorbia corollata	Flowering Spurge	*Euphorbiaceae*—Spurge
E. epithymoides	Yellow S.	*Euphorbiaceae*—Spurge
Filipendula hexapetala	Dropwort	*Rosaceae*—Rose
F. palmata	Palmate Meadow-sweet	*Rosaceae*—Rose
F. rubra	Queen-of-the-prairie	*Rosaceae*—Rose
F. ulmaria	Queen-of-the-meadow	*Rosaceae*—Rose
Fritillaria imperialis	Crown Imperial	*Liliaceae*—Lily
Gaillardia aristata	Blanket-flower	*Compositae*—Daisy
G. a. vars.	Blanket-flower	*Compositae*—Daisy
Galega officinalis	Goats-rue	*Leguminosae*—Pea
G. o. alba	White G.-r.	*Leguminosae*—Pea
G. o. Hartlandi	Hartlands G.-r.	*Leguminosae*—Pea
Galium mollugo	White Bedstraw	*Rubiaceae*—Madder
Galtonia candicans	Summer-hyacinth	*Liliaceae*—Lily
Gaura Lindheimeri	White Gaura	*Onagraceae* —Evening-primrose
Gentiana Andrewsi	Closed Gentian	*Gentianaceae*—Gentian
G. septemfida		*Gentianaceae*—Gentian
Geranium Endressi	Endres Cranesbill	*Geraniaceae*—Geranium

ORIGIN	SEASON	COLOR	HEIGHT
Eur.–Asia–N. America	August	rosy purple	5 –7 ft.
Garden	August	white	4 –5 ft.
Japan	April–May	red & white	1 ft.
Garden	April–May	white	1 ft.
Persia	April–May	yellow	1 ft.
Himalayas	May	white	4 –6 ft.
Cent. Asia	May–June	pink	5 –8 ft.
Garden	May–June	peach shades	5 –8 ft.
N. America	June–July	violet-purple	1½–2 ft.
Garden	June–July	various, sing. & dbl.	1½–2 ft.
Europe	July–Aug.	blue	1½–2 ft.
Europe	July–Aug.	pale blue	1 –1½ ft.
Garden	July–Aug.	blue	2½–3 ft.
Eur.–Asia	July–Aug.	blue	2½–3 ft.
Asia–N. America	May	orange-yellow	1 –2 ft.
Europe	May	yellow	1 ft.
N. America	Sept.–Oct.	blue	2 –3 ft.
N. America	Aug.–Sept.	pink-purple	5 –8 ft.
N. America	Aug.–Sept.	white	3 –4 ft.
N. America	July–Aug.	white	2 –3 ft.
Europe	May–June	yellow	12 –15 in.
Eur.–Asia	June–July	white	2½–3 ft.
Siberia	June–July	pale pink	2½–3 ft.
N. America	June–July	pink	5 –6 ft.
Eur.–Asia–N. America	June–July	white	5 –6 ft.
Persia	May	red or yellow	3 –4 ft.
N. America	June–Oct.	yellow & crimson	2 –2½ ft.
Garden	June–Oct.	red & yellow vars.	2 –3 ft.
Eur., W. Asia	June–Aug.	lilac-purple	2 –3 ft.
Europe	June–Aug.	white	2 –3 ft.
Garden	June–Aug.	lilac	2 –3 ft.
Europe	June–Aug.	white	2½–3 ft.
S. Africa	summer	white	3 –4 ft.
N. America	July–Sept.	white	3 –4 ft.
N. America	Aug.–Sept.	deep blue	2 ft.
Asia	July–Aug.	azure-blue	1 –1½ ft.
Europe	June–July	rose	1 –1½ ft.

BOTANICAL NAME	COMMON NAME	FAMILY
G. grandiflorum	Cranesbill	*Geraniaceae*—Geranium
G. ibericum	Iberian C.	*Geraniaceae*—Geranium
G. i. album	White I. C.	*Geraniaceae*—Geranium
G. sanguineum	Blood-red C.	*Geraniaceae*—Geranium
G. sylvaticum	Forest-loving Cranesbill	*Geraniaceae*—Geranium
Geum Borisi	Boris Avens	*Rosaceae*—Rose
G. chiloense	Chilian A.	*Rosaceae*—Rose
G. c. Fire Opal		*Rosaceae*—Rose
G. c. Mrs. Bradshaw		*Rosaceae*—Rose
G. c. Princess Juliana		*Rosaceae*—Rose
G. c. Red Wings		*Rosaceae*—Rose
Gillenia trifoliata	Bowmans Root	*Rosaceae*—Rose
Gypsophila acutifolia	Chalk-plant	*Caryophyllaceae*—Pink
G. Oldhamiana	Babys-breath	*Caryophyllaceae*—Pink
G. paniculata	Babys-breath	*Caryophyllaceae*—Pink
G. p. Bristol Fairy	Double B.-b.	*Caryophyllaceae*—Pink
G. repens Bodgeri	Bodgers Gypsophila	*Caryophyllaceae*—Pink
Helenium autumnale	Sneezeweed	*Compositae*—Daisy
H. a. pumilum magnificum	Dwarf S.	*Compositae*—Daisy
H. a. Riverton Beauty		*Compositae*—Daisy
H. a. Riverton Gem		*Compositae*—Daisy
H. a. rubrum		*Compositae*—Daisy
H. Hoopesi	Hoopes S.	*Compositae*—Daisy
Helianthus angustifolius	Swamp Sunflower	*Compositae*—Daisy
H. decapetalus	Thin-leaved S.	*Compositae*—Daisy
H. d. fl. pl.	Double S.	*Compositae*—Daisy
H. laetiflorus	Showy S.	*Compositae*—Daisy
H. Maximiliani	Maximilians S.	*Compositae*—Daisy
H. mollis	Ashy S.	*Compositae*—Daisy
H. rigidus	Stiff S.	*Compositae*—Daisy
Helianthus rigidus "Miss Mellish"		*Compositae*—Daisy
H. salicifolius	Willow-leaved S.	*Compositae*—Daisy
Heliopsis helianthoides	Oxeye, Orange Sunflower	*Compositae*—Daisy
H. h. Pitcheriana	Pitchers O.	*Compositae*—Daisy
H. scabra	Rough O.	*Compositae*—Daisy
H. s. incomparabilis	Golden Sunflower	*Compositae*—Daisy

ORIGIN	SEASON	COLOR	HEIGHT
N. Asia	June–July	lilac	12 –15 in.
S.W. Asia	June–Sept.	purple	12 –15 in.
Garden	June–Sept.	white	12 –15 in.
Eur., W. Asia	June–Sept.	red-purple	1½–2 ft.
Eur., W. Asia	June–Sept.	violet	2 –2½ ft.
Garden	May–Aug.	orange	12 –15 in.
Chile	June–Aug.	scarlet	1½–2 ft.
Garden	June–Aug.	orange-scarlet	1½–2 ft.
Garden	June–Aug.	scarlet, dbl.	1 –1½ ft.
Garden	June–Aug.	orange	1 –1½ ft.
Garden	June–Aug.	scarlet	1 –1½ ft.
N. America	June–July	white	3 –4 ft.
Caucasus	July–Aug.	white	3 –3½ ft.
Japan	Aug.–Oct.	pink	2 –3 ft.
Europe	June–July	white	2½–3 ft.
Garden	July–Sept.	white, dbl.	3 ft.
Garden	July–Sept.	pale pink, dbl.	1 –1½ ft.
N. America	Aug.–Sept.	yellow	3 –5 ft.
Garden	July–Sept.	yellow	1½–2 ft.
Garden	Aug.–Sept.	lemon	3 –4 ft.
Garden	Aug.–Sept.	gold & red	4 –5 ft.
Garden	Aug.–Sept.	brick-red	4 –5 ft.
N. America	June–July	yellow	2 –3 ft.
N. America	Aug.–Sept.	yellow	5 –7 ft.
N. America	Aug.–Sept.	yellow	4 –5 ft.
Garden	Aug.–Sept.	yellow	4 –5 ft.
N. America	Aug.–Sept.	yellow	6 –8 ft.
N. America	Sept.–Oct.	yellow	10 –12 ft.
N. America	July–Sept.	yellow	4 –5 ft.
N. America	Aug.–Sept.	yellow	6 –8 ft.
Garden	Aug.–Sept.	yellow	6 –8 ft.
N. America	Sept.–Oct.	yellow	8 –10 ft.
N. America	July–Sept.	yellow	4 –5 ft.
Garden	July–Sept.	orange	3 –4 ft.
N. America	July–Sept.	yellow	3 –4 ft.
Garden	July–Sept.	orange	3 –4 ft.

BOTANICAL NAME	COMMON NAME	FAMILY
Helleborus niger	Christmas-rose	*Ranunculaceae*—Buttercup
H. n. altifolius	Large C.-r.	*Ranunculaceae*—Buttercup
H. orientalis	Eastern Hellebore	*Ranunculaceae*—Buttercup
H. o. atrorubens	Dark-red E. H.	*Ranunculaceae*—Buttercup
H. viridis	Green H.	*Ranunculaceae*—Buttercup
Hemerocallis aurantiaca	Orange Daylily	*Liliaceae*—Lily
H. Dumortieri	Dumortiers D.	*Liliaceae*—Lily
H. flava	Lemon D.	*Liliaceae*—Lily
H. fulva	Tawny D.	*Liliaceae*—Lily
H. f. Kwanso	Double T. D.	*Liliaceae*—Lily
H. Middendorffi	Middendorffs D.	*Liliaceae*—Lily
H. minor	Lesser D.	*Liliaceae*—Lily
H. Thunbergi	Thunbergs D.	*Liliaceae*—Lily
H. hybrids	Hybrid D.	*Liliaceae*—Lily
Hesperis matronalis	Dames-rocket	*Cruciferae*—Mustard
H. m. alba	White D.-r.	*Cruciferae*—Mustard
Heuchera brizoides	Pink Alum-root	*Saxifragaceae*—Saxifrage
H. sanguinea	Coral-bells	*Saxifragaceae*—Saxifrage
H. s. Perrys White	White C.-b.	*Saxifragaceae*—Saxifrage
H. s. vars.	Coral-bells	*Saxifragaceae*—Saxifrage
Hibiscus moscheutos	Rose-mallow	*Malvaceae*—Mallow
H. m. Mallow Marvels	Mallow Marvels	*Malvaceae*—Mallow
Hosta coerulea	Blue Plantain-lily	*Liliaceae*—Lily
H. Fortunei	Fortunes P.	*Liliaceae*—Lily
H. F. variegata	Variegated F. P.	*Liliaceae*—Lily
H. lancifolia	Narrow-leaved P.	*Liliaceae*—Lily
H. l. albo-marginata	Variegated N.-l. P.	*Liliaceae*—Lily
H. Plantaginea	Fragrant P.	*Liliaceae*—Lily
H. Sieboldiana	Short-cluster P.	*Liliaceae*—Lily
H. undulata	Wavy-leaved P.	*Liliaceae*—Lily
Hypericum ascyron	Great St. Johns Wort	*Hypericaceae* —St. Johns Wort
Hyssopus officinalis	Hyssop	*Labiatae*—Mint
Iberis gibraltarica	Gibraltar Candytuft	*Cruciferae*—Mustard
I. sempervirens	Perennial C.	*Cruciferae*—Mustard
I. s. Snowflake	Large-flowered P. C.	*Cruciferae*—Mustard
Incarvillea Delavayi		*Bignoniaceae*—Bignonia
Inula glandulosa superba	Superb Elecampane	*Compositae*—Daisy

ORIGIN	SEASON	COLOR	HEIGHT
Europe	Nov.–Feb.	white	12 –15 in.
Garden	Nov.–Feb.	white	12 –18 in.
Asia Minor	Mar.–April	white-purple	12 –18 in.
Hungary	Mar.–April	red-purple	12 –18 in.
Europe	Mar.–April	yellowish green	12 –15 in.
Japan	July–Aug.	orange	2½–3 ft.
Japan	May–June	orange	1½–2 ft.
Europe	May–June	yellow	2½–3 ft.
Eur.–Asia	July–Aug.	orange-red	4 –5 ft.
Garden	July–Aug.	orange-red, dbl.	4 –5 ft.
Siberia	June–July	orange	1 –2 ft.
Japan	June–July	yellow	1½–2 ft.
Japan	July–Aug.	lemon	3 –4 ft.
Garden	June–Aug.	various	2½–5 ft.
Europe	June–July	purple	2 –3 ft.
Garden	June–July	white	2 –3 ft.
Garden	June–July	pink	1 –1½ ft.
N. America	June–July	red	1½–2 ft.
Garden	June–July	white	1 –1½ ft.
Garden	June–July	red shades	1 –2 ft.
N. America	Aug.–Sept.	rose-pink	5 –8 ft.
Garden	Aug.–Sept.	various	5 –6 ft.
Asia	July–Aug.	lavender-blue	1½–2 ft.
Japan	July–Aug.	pale lilac	2 –3 ft.
Garden	July–Aug.	pale lilac	2 –3 ft.
Japan	July–Sept.	lilac	1½–2 ft.
Garden	July–Sept.	lilac	1½–2 ft.
Japan	Aug.	white	2 –2½ ft.
Japan	June–July	pale lilac	2 –3 ft.
Undetermined	Aug.–Sept.	lavender-blue	1 –2 ft.
N. America	July–Aug.	yellow	4 –6 ft.
. Europe	June–Aug.	purple-blue	1½–2 ft.
Spain	May–June	pale lilac	9 –12 in.
. Europe	May–June	white	9 –12 in.
Garden	June	white	9 –12 in.
China	June–July	rose-purple	1 –2 ft.
Garden	July–Sept.	yellow	2½–3 ft.

BOTANICAL NAME	COMMON NAME	FAMILY
I. helenium	Elecampane	*Compositae*—Daisy
I. Royleana	Himalayan E.	*Compositae*—Daisy
Iris chrysographes	Goldvein Iris	*Iridaceae*—Iris
I. cristata	Crested Dwarf I.	*Iridaceae*—Iris
I. c. alba	White C. D. I.	*Iridaceae*—Iris
I. Delavayi	Delavays I.	*Iridaceae*—Iris
I. dichotoma	Vesper I.	*Iridaceae*—Iris
I. foliosa	Leafy Blue Flag	*Iridaceae*—Iris
I. fulva	Copper-flower Iris	*Iridaceae*—Iris
I. germanica vars.	Tall Bearded Iris	*Iridaceae*—Iris
I. g. florentina	Orris Root	*Iridaceae*—Iris
I. halophila		*Iridaceae*—Iris
I. Hoogiana		*Iridaceae*—Iris
I. Kaempferi vars.	Japanese Iris	*Iridaceae*—Iris
I. ochroleuca	Yellow-banded Flag	*Iridaceae*—Iris
I. orientalis	Oriental Iris	*Iridaceae*—Iris
I. pallida dalmatica	Sweet I.	*Iridaceae*—Iris
I. pseudacorus	Yellow Flag	*Iridaceae*—Iris
I. pumila vars.	Dwarf Bearded Iris	*Iridaceae*—Iris
I. sibirica	Siberian I.	*Iridaceae*—Iris
I. s. vars.	Siberian I.	*Iridaceae*—Iris
I. spuria	Spurious I.	*Iridaceae*—Iris
I. s. vars.		*Iridaceae*—Iris
I. susiana	Mourning I.	*Iridaceae*—Iris
I. tectorum	Roof I.	*Iridaceae*—Iris
I. t. alba	Roof I.	*Iridaceae*—Iris
I. Wilsoni	Wilsons I.	*Iridaceae*—Iris
Jasione perennis	Shepherds Scabious	*Campanulaceae*—Bellflow
Jeffersonia diphylla	Twin-leaf	*Berberidaceae*—Barberry
Kirengeshoma palmata		*Saxifragaceae*—Saxifrage
Kniphofia hybrida	Torch-lily	*Liliaceae*—Lily
K. uvaria	Poker-plant	*Liliaceae*—Lily
K. u. vars.	Poker-plant	*Liliaceae*—Lily
Lactuca perennis	Blue Lettuce	*Compositae*—Daisy
Lamium album	White Dead-nettle	*Labiatae*—Mint
Lamium maculatum	Purple D.-n.	*Labiatae*—Mint
Lathyrus latifolius	Everlasting Pea	*Leguminosae*—Pea
L. l. albus	White E. P.	*Leguminosae*—Pea

ORIGIN	SEASON	COLOR	HEIGHT
Eur.–N. Asia	July–Sept.	yellow	4 –6 ft.
Himalayas	July–Sept.	orange	1½–2 ft.
W. China	May–June	violet-purple	2 –2½ ft.
N. America	May–June	lavender-blue	6 in.
Garden	May–June	white	6 in.
S.W. China	June–July	red-violet	3 –4 ft.
Siberia to W. China	Aug.–Sept.	lavender	3 –5 ft.
N. America	June–July	bluish purple	2 –3 ft.
N. America	June–July	coppery red	2 –3 ft.
Garden	May–June	various	2 –4 ft.
S. Europe	May–June	white, tinted blue	1½–2 ft.
N.W. India	June–July	white-yellow	2 –2½ ft.
Turkestan	May–June	blue	1 –1½ ft.
Asia	June–July	various	3 –3½ ft.
Asia Minor	July	white-yellow	3 –4 ft.
Asia	May–June	blue-purple	1½–2 ft.
S.E. Europe	May–June	lavender-blue	3 –4 ft.
Eur.–Asia	June	yellow	3 –4 ft.
Garden	April–May	various	4 –9 in.
Cent. Europe	May–June	purplish blue	3 ft.
Garden	May–June	blue & white	3 ft.
S. Europe	June–July	lilac-purple	1½–2 ft.
Garden	June–July	various	2 –3 ft.
Asia Minor	July–Aug.	gray-purple	12 in.
China	June–July	blue-purple	12 –15 in.
Garden	June–July	white	12 –15 in.
China	June–July	yellow	2½–3 ft.
S. Europe	June–July	blue	1 ft.
N. America	May	white	12 –15 in.
Japan	Aug.–Sept.	yellow	3 –4 ft.
Garden	July–Sept.	red & yellow	2 –4 ft.
. Africa	Aug.–Sept.	scarlet-yellow	3 –4 ft.
Garden	Aug.–Sept.	scarlet-yellow	4 –6 ft.
. Europe	June	blue	2 ft.
Europe	May–Sept.	white	8 –12 in.
Eur.–Asia	May–Sept.	red-purple	8 –12 in.
Europe	July–Sept.	deep rose	6 –8 ft.
Garden	July–Sept.	white	6 –8 ft.

BOTANICAL NAME	COMMON NAME	FAMILY
L. vernus	Spring Vetchling	*Leguminosae*—Pea
Leucojum aestivum	Summer Snowflake	*Amaryllidaceae*—Narcissu
L. vernum	Spring S.	*Amaryllidaceae*—Narcissu
Liatris pycnostachya	Blazing Star	*Compositae*—Daisy
L. scariosa September Glory	Gay-feather	*Compositae*—Daisy
L. s. alba		*Compositae*—Daisy
Ligularia clivorum	Groundsel	*Compositae*—Daisy
L. Wilsoniana	Giant G.	*Compositae*—Daisy
Lilium amabile		*Liliaceae*—Lily
L. a. luteum		*Liliaceae*—Lily
L. auratum	Gold-banded Lily	*Liliaceae*—Lily
L. callosum		*Liliaceae*—Lily
L. canadense	Meadow L.	*Liliaceae*—Lily
L. candidum	Madonna L.	*Liliaceae*—Lily
L. dauricum	Candlestick L.	*Liliaceae*—Lily
L. Davidi	Davids L.	*Liliaceae*—Lily
L. Davmottiae		*Liliaceae*—Lily
L. elegans		*Liliaceae*—Lily
L. formosanum	Formosa L.	*Liliaceae*—Lily
L. Hansoni	Hansons L.	*Liliaceae*—Lily
L. Henryi	Henrys L.	*Liliaceae*—Lily
L. Leichtlini Maximowiczi		*Liliaceae*—Lily
L. L. Wadai		*Liliaceae*—Lily
L. leucanthum chloroaster (*centifolium*)		*Liliaceae*—Lily
L. pardalinum	Leopard Lily	*Liliaceae*—Lily
L. pumilum (*tenuifolium*)	Coral L.	*Liliaceae*—Lily
L. regale	Regal L.	*Liliaceae*—Lily
L. Sargentiae		*Liliaceae*—Lily
L. speciosum	Showy Japanese L.	*Liliaceae*—Lily
L. superbum	American Turks-cap L.	*Liliaceae*—Lily
L. testaceum	Nankeen L.	*Liliaceae*—Lily
L. tigrinum	Tiger L.	*Liliaceae*—Lily
Limonium latifolium	Sea lavender	*Plumbaginaceae*—Leadwort
Linum flavum	Golden Flax	*Linaceae*—Flax
L. narbonnense	Blue F.	*Linaceae*—Flax
L. n. album	White F.	*Linaceae*—Flax

ORIGIN	SEASON	COLOR	HEIGHT
Europe	April–May	purplish blue	1 –1½ ft.
Europe	May	white	1 –1½ ft.
Europe	Mar.–April	white	9 –12 in.
N. America	Aug.–Sept.	purple	4 –5 ft.
Garden	Aug.–Sept.	purple	5 –6 ft.
Garden	Aug.–Sept.	white	4 –5 ft.
Asia	July–Aug.	yellow	3 –4 ft.
China	July–Aug.	yellow	4 –5 ft.
Korea	June	red	2½–3 ft.
Garden?	June	yellow	2½–3 ft.
Japan	August	white & gold	4 –6 ft.
Japan	July	brick-red	2 –3 ft.
E. N. America	August	or., yellow, red	4 –6 ft.
Asia Minor	June–July	white	3 –5 ft.
N.E. Asia	June	apricot	1½–3 ft.
China	June–July	orange-red	4 –6 ft.
Garden	June–July	cinnabar-red	4 –6 ft.
Garden	June–July	orange-red	1½–2 ft.
Formosa	Aug.–Sept.	white	5 –7 ft.
Japan	June–July	orange-yellow	3 –4 ft.
China	June–July	orange-yellow	5 –9 ft.
Japan	July–Aug.	salmon-red	4 –6 ft.
Garden?	July–Aug.	orange-red	4 –6 ft.
China	July	white	5 –8 ft.
Oregon to California	July	light orange-red	5 –7 ft.
N.E. Asia	June	scarlet	1½–2 ft.
China	June–July	white	4 –7 ft.
W. China	July–Aug.	white	4 –6 ft.
Japan	Aug.–Sept.	white & pink	3 –5 ft.
E. N. America to Mo.	August	or.-scarlet to yellow	5 –8 ft.
Garden	June–July	apricot	5 –7 ft.
China, Japan	July–Aug.	or.-red, spotted	5 –7 ft.
Eur.–Asia	July–Aug.	purplish blue	1½–2 ft.
Europe	June–July	yellow	1½–2 ft.
S. Europe	June–July	blue	1½–2 ft.
Garden	June–July	white	1½–2 ft.

BOTANICAL NAME	COMMON NAME	FAMILY
L. perenne	Perennial F.	*Linaceae*—Flax
Liriope muscari	Lily-turf	*Liliaceae*—Lily
Lobelia cardinalis	Cardinal Flower	*Lobeliaceae*—Lobelia
L. syphilitica	Great Blue Lobelia	*Lobeliaceae*—Lobelia
L. s. alba	G. White L.	*Lobeliaceae*—Lobelia
Lupinus polyphyllus	Perennial Lupine	*Leguminosae*—Pea
L. p. vars.	Garden Lupines	*Leguminosae*—Pea
L. Russell hybrids	Russell L.	*Leguminosae*—Pea
Lychnis Arkwrighti	Hybrid Campion	*Caryophyllaceae*—Pink
L. chalcedonica	Maltese Cross	*Caryophyllaceae*—Pink
L. coronaria	Mullein-pink	*Caryophyllaceae*—Pink
L. flos-Jovis	Flower-of-Jove	*Caryophyllaceae*—Pink
L. Haageana	Haages Campion	*Caryophyllaceae*—Pink
L. viscaria	German Catchfly	*Caryophyllaceae*—Pink
L. v. vars.		*Caryophyllaceae*—Pink
Lysimachia clethroides	Japanese Loosestrife	*Primulaceae*—Primrose
Lythrum salicaria	Purple Loosestrife	*Lythraceae*—Loosestrife
L. s. superbum		*Lythraceae*—Loosestrife
L. s. Red Beacon		*Lythraceae*—Loosestrife
Malva alcea	Alcea Mallow	*Malvaceae*—Mallow
M. moschata	Musk M.	*Malvaceae*—Mallow
M. m. alba	White M. M.	*Malvaceae*—Mallow
Mertensia virginica	Virginia-bluebells	*Boraginaceae*—Borage
Monarda didyma	Bee-balm	*Labiatae*—Mint
M. d. Cambridge Scarlet	Bee-balm	*Labiatae*—Mint
M. d. vars.	Bee-balm	*Labiatae*—Mint
Nepata macrantha	Large-flowered Catmint	*Labiatae*—Mint
N. Mussini	Border C.	*Labiatae*—Mint
N. Souv. de André Chaudron		*Labiatae*—Mint
Oenothera fruticosa	Sundrop	*Onagraceae* —Evening-primrose
O. f. Youngi	Sundrop	*Onagraceae* —Evening-primrose
O. missouriensis	Missouri Evening-primrose	*Onagraceae* —Evening-primrose
O. speciosa	Showy E.-p.	*Onagraceae* —Evening-primrose
Paeonia albiflora	Chinese Peony	*Ranunculaceae*—Buttercup

ORIGIN	SEASON	COLOR	HEIGHT
Europe	May–July	blue	1½–2 ft.
Asia	July–Aug.	lilac-purple	9 –12 in.
N. America	Aug.–Sept.	bright red	2 –4 ft.
N. America	Aug.–Sept.	blue	2 –4 ft.
Garden	Aug.–Sept.	white	2 –4 ft.
N. America	May–June	blue	3 –5 ft.
Garden	May–June	various	3 –5 ft.
Garden	May–June	various	3 –5 ft.
Garden	June–July	scarlet	1½–2 ft.
Siberia	June–July	scarlet	2½–3 ft.
S. Europe	June–July	crimson	2½–3 ft.
S. Europe	June–July	pink	1½ ft.
Garden	June–July	red shades	1 ft.
Eur.–N. Asia	May–June	red-purple	1 ft.
Garden	May–June	various	1 ft.
Asia	July–Aug.	white	2½–3 ft.
Old World	July–Sept.	purple	3 –4 ft.
Garden	July–Sept.	rose-purple	3 –4 ft.
Garden	July–Sept.	cerise	3 –4 ft.
Europe	June–Aug.	rosy purple	2 –3 ft.
Europe	June–Aug.	rose	2 ft.
Garden	June–Aug.	white	2 ft.
N. America	April–May	blue	1 –2 ft.
N. America	July–Aug.	red	3 –4 ft.
Garden	July–Aug.	scarlet	.3 ft.
Garden	July–Aug.	various	3 –4 ft.
Siberia	June–Aug.	lavender-blue	3 ft.
Caucasus	June–Aug.	lavender	1 –1½ ft.
Garden	June–Aug.	blue	1 –1½ ft.
N. America	June–July	yellow	2 –3 ft.
Garden	June–July	lemon	2 –2½ ft.
S.W. United States	July–Aug.	yellow	10 –12 in.
S.W. United States	July–Aug.	white	1 –2 ft.
Asia	May–June	white	2 –3 ft.

BOTANICAL NAME	COMMON NAME	FAMILY
P. a. vars.	Garden P.	Ranunculaceae—Buttercup
P. Mlokosewitschi		Ranunculaceae—Buttercup
P. officinalis	Common P.	Ranunculaceae—Buttercup
P. o. vars.	Garden P.	Ranunculaceae—Buttercup
P. tenuifolia	Fern-leaved P.	Ranunculaceae—Buttercup
Papaver bracteatum	Bracteate Poppy	Papaveraceae—Poppy
P. lateritium		Papaveraceae—Poppy
P. nudicaule	Iceland P.	Papaveraceae—Poppy
P. n. vars.	Iceland P.	Papaveraceae—Poppy
P. orientale	Oriental P.	Papaveraceae—Poppy
P. o. vars.	Oriental P.	Papaveraceae—Poppy
P. pilosum	Olympic P.	Papaveraceae—Poppy
P. rupifragum	Iberian P.	Papaveraceae—Poppy
P. thibeticum	Tibet P.	Papaveraceae—Poppy
Paradisea liliastrum	St. Bruno-lily	Liliaceae—Lily
Peltiphyllum peltatum	Umbrella Saxifrage	Saxifragaceae—Saxifrage
Penstemon barbatus	Beard-tongue	Scrophulariaceae—Figwort
P. b. Pink Beauty	Beard-tongue	Scrophulariaceae—Figwort
P. cyananthus	Smooth Penstemon	Scrophulariaceae—Figwort
P. digitalis	Foxglove P.	Scrophulariaceae—Figwort
P. grandiflorus	Large-flowered P.	Scrophulariaceae—Figwort
P. hirsutus	Hairy P.	Scrophulariaceae—Figwort
P. ovatus	Oval-leaved P.	Scrophulariaceae—Figwort
P. spectabilis	Showy P.	Scrophulariaceae—Figwort
P. Torreyi	Torreys P.	Scrophulariaceae—Figwort
Phlox Arendsi	Hybrid Phlox	Polemoniaceae—Phlox
P. carolina	Thick-leaf P.	Polemoniaceae—Phlox
P. divaricata	Wild Sweet William	Polemoniaceae—Phlox
P. d. Laphami	Laphams Phlox	Polemoniaceae—Phlox
P. glaberrima	Smooth P.	Polemoniaceae—Phlox
P. nivalis	Trailing P.	Polemoniaceae—Phlox
P. paniculata vars.	Summer P.	Polemoniaceae—Phlox
P. stolonifera	Creeping P.	Polemoniaceae—Phlox
P. subulata	Moss-P.	Polemoniaceae—Phlox
P. s. vars.	Moss-P.	Polemoniaceae—Phlox
Physostegia virginiana	False Dragonhead	Labiatae—Mint
P. v. Summer Glow		Labiatae—Mint
P. v. Vivid	Dwarf F. D.	Labiatae—Mint

ORIGIN	SEASON	COLOR	HEIGHT
Garden	May–June	various	2 –4 ft.
Caucasus	May–June	yellow	2 –2½ ft.
S. Europe	May–June	crimson	2 –3 ft.
Garden	May–June	various	2 –4 ft.
S.E. Europe	May–June	crimson	1 –1½ ft.
Persia	May–June	blood red	2 –3 ft.
Armenia	June–Aug.	brick-red	2 ft.
Arctic regions	May–July	white & yellow	1 –2 ft.
Garden	May–July	various	1 –2 ft.
Asia Minor	June	scarlet	2 –4 ft.
Garden	June	various	2 –4 ft.
Greece	June	brick-red	2 –3 ft.
Spain	June	pale red	1 –1½ ft.
Tibet	May–July	yellow & orange	1 –2 ft.
Europe	May–June	white	1 –2 ft.
W. N. America	May–June	pale rose	2 –4 ft.
Utah–Mexico	June–July	red	3 –5 ft.
Garden	June–July	pink	4 –5 ft.
W. N. America	May–June	blue	2 –3 ft.
N. America	June–July	white	3 –4 ft.
W. N. America	June–July	lavender	3 –5 ft.
N. America	June–July	purple	2 –3 ft.
W. N. America	May–June	purple	2 –3 ft.
W. N. America	June–July	rosy lilac	4 –5 ft.
Col.–Mex.	June–July	scarlet	4 –5 ft.
Garden	May–June	lavender	1 –2 ft.
N. America	June–Sept.	various	3 –4 ft.
N. America	May–June	lavender	1 –1½ ft.
Garden	May–June	violet-blue	1 –1½ ft.
N. America	July	rosy purple	2 –3 ft.
N. America	May–June	pink or white	6 –8 in.
Garden	July–Sept.	various	3 –4 ft.
N. America	May	lilac	9 –12 in.
N. America	April–May	magenta	6 in.
Garden	April–May	various	6 in.
N. America	Aug.–Sept.	rose-white	3 –4 ft.
Garden	Aug.–Sept.	rosy crimson	3 –4 ft.
Garden	Aug.–Oct.	bright pink	1 –1½ ft.

BOTANICAL NAME	COMMON NAME	FAMILY
Platycodon grandiflorum	Balloon Flower	*Campanulaceae*—Bellflower
P. g. Mariesi	Japanese Bellflower	*Campanulaceae*—Bellflower
Polemonium caeruleum	Jacobs Ladder	*Polemoniaceae*—Phlox
P. reptans	Greek Valerian	*Polemoniaceae*—Phlox
P. Richardsoni	Dwarf Jacobs Ladder	*Polemoniaceae*—Phlox
Polygonatum multiflorum	Solomons Seal	*Liliaceae*—Lily
Polygonum bistorta	Snakeweed	*Polygonaceae*—Buckwheat
Potentilla nepalensis	Nepal Cinquefoil	*Rosaceae*—Rose
P. n. Miss Willmott	Miss Willmotts C.	*Rosaceae*—Rose
P. pyrenaica	Pyrenean C.	*Rosaceae*—Rose
Primula Beesiana	Bees Primrose	*Primulaceae*—Primrose
P. Bullesiana		*Primulaceae*—Primrose
P. Bulleyana	Bulleys P.	*Primulaceae*—Primrose
P. elatior	Oxlip	*Primulaceae*—Primrose
P. Florindae	Florindas Primrose	*Primulaceae*—Primrose
P. japonica	Japanese P.	*Primulaceae*—Primrose
P. j. vars.	Japanese P.	*Primulaceae*—Primrose
P. Littoniana	Littons P.	*Primulaceae*—Primrose
P. polyantha	Polyanthus	*Primulaceae*—Primrose
P. Sieboldi	Siebolds P.	*Primulaceae*—Primrose
P. veris	Cowslip	*Primulaceae*—Primrose
P. vulgaris	English Primrose	*Primulaceae*—Primrose
Pulmonaria angustifolia	Lungwort	*Boraginaceae*—Borage
P. saccharata	Bethlehem Sage	*Boraginaceae*—Borage
Ranunculus acris fl. pl.	Double Buttercup	*Ranunculaceae*—Buttercup
Rudbeckia laciniata hortensia	Golden Glow	*Compositae*—Daisy
R. maxima	Large Coneflower	*Compositae*—Daisy
R. speciosa	Showy C.	*Compositae*—Daisy
R. subtomentosa	Sweet C.	*Compositae*—Daisy
Salvia azurea	Blue Sage	*Labiatae*—Mint
S. farinacea	Mealycup S.	*Labiatae*—Mint
S. Pitcheri	Pitchers S.	*Labiatae*—Mint
S. pratensis	Meadow S.	*Labiatae*—Mint
S. p. rubicunda	Red M. S.	*Labiatae*—Mint
Scabiosa caucasica	Pincushion Flower	*Dipsaceae*—Teasel
S. c. vars.	Hybrid Scabious	*Dipsaceae*—Teasel
S. columbaria	Small-flowered S.	*Dipsaceae*—Teasel

ORIGIN	SEASON	COLOR	HEIGHT
E. Asia	June–Aug.	blue-white	2 –3 ft.
Japan	June–Aug.	blue-white	1 –1½ ft.
Europe	May–June	blue-white	2 –3 ft.
N. America	May–June	blue	6 –9 in.
Arctic regions	May–June	light blue	9 –12 in.
Europe	May–June	white	2 –3 ft.
Eur. & Asia	Aug.–Sept.	pink	1 –2 ft.
Himalayas	May–June	red	2 ft.
Garden	May–June	salmon-pink	1 ft.
Pyrenees	May–Aug.	yellow	1 –1½ ft.
China	May	rosy lilac	1 –1½ ft.
Garden	May	various	1 –2 ft.
China	May	deep yellow	1 –2 ft.
Eur.–Persia	April–May	yellow	6 –8 in.
Tibet	June	sulphur-yellow	2 –4 ft.
Japan	May–June	carmine	1 –2 ft.
Garden	May–June	various	1 –2 ft.
China	June	violet-blue	1 –2 ft.
Garden	April–May	various	9 –12 in.
Japan	May	rose to white	8 –10 in.
Europe	April–May	yellow	8 –10 in.
Europe	April–May	various	4 –6 in.
Europe	April–May	blue	1 ft.
Europe	April–May	reddish violet	1 –1½ ft.
Europe	May–June	yellow	2 –3 ft.
N. America	Aug.–Sept.	yellow	5 –9 ft.
N. America	Aug.–Sept.	yellow	5 –9 ft.
N. America	June–Sept.	yellow	2 –3 ft.
N. America	Aug.–Sept.	yellow	5 –6 ft.
N. America	Aug.–Sept.	blue	3 –4 ft.
Texas	Aug.–Sept.	violet-blue	2½–3 ft.
N. America	Aug.–Sept.	deep blue	3 –4 ft.
Europe	May–June	violet-blue	2 –3 ft.
Garden	May–June	rosy red	2 –3 ft.
Caucasus	June–Sept.	light blue	1½–2 ft.
Garden	June–Sept.	blue shades	1½–2½ ft.
Eur.–Asia–Africa	June–Sept.	purplish blue	1½–2 ft.

BOTANICAL NAME	COMMON NAME	FAMILY
S. japonica	Japanese S.	*Dipsaceae*—Teasel
Scutellaria serrata	Showy Skullcap	*Labiateae*—Mint
Sedum spectabile	Showy Sedum	*Crassulaceae*—Orpine
S. s. Brilliant	Showiest S.	*Crassulaceae*—Orpine
Senecio pulcher	Showy Groundsel	*Compositae*—Daisy
Sidalcea candida	White Sidalcea	*Malvaceae*—Mallow
S. malvaeflora Rose Queen	Showy S.	*Malvaceae*—Mallow
Silphium perfoliatum	Indian Cup	*Compositae*—Daisy
Sisyrinchium angustifolium	Blue-eyed Grass	*Iridiceae*—Iris
Smilacina racemosa	False Solomons Seal	*Liliaceae*—Lily
Solidago canadensis	Goldenrod	*Compositae*—Daisy
S. rigida	Stiff G.	*Compositae*—Daisy
S. Shorti	Shorts G.	*Compositae*—Daisy
Solidaster luteus	Hybrid G.	*Compositae*—Daisy
Stachys grandiflora	Woundwort	*Labiatae*—Mint
S. lanata	Lambs-ears	*Labiatae*—Mint
Stokesia laevis	Stokes Aster	*Compositae*—Daisy
Stylophorum diphyllum	Celandine-poppy	*Papaveraceae*—Poppy
Thalictrum aquilegifolium	Meadow-rue	*Ranunculaceae*—Buttercup
T. dipterocarpum	Chinese M.-r.	*Ranunculaceae*—Buttercup
T. glaucum	Glaucous M.-r.	*Ranunculaceae*—Buttercup
Thermopsis caroliniana	Carolina Thermopsis	*Leguminosae*—Pea
Tiarella cordifolia	Foam Flower	*Saxifragaceae*—Saxifrage
Tradescantia virginiana	Spiderwort	*Commelinaceae*—Spiderwort
T. v. vars.	Spiderwort	*Commelinaceae*—Spiderwort
Trillium grandiflorum	Wake-robin	*Liliaceae*—Lily
Trollius asiaticus	Orange Globe-flower	*Ranunculaceae*—Buttercup
T. europaeus	Globe-flower	*Ranunculaceae*—Buttercup
T. Ledebouri	Siberian G.-f.	*Ranunculaceae*—Buttercup
Tunica saxifraga fl. pl.	Double Tunic-flower	*Caryophyllaceae*—Pink
Uvularia grandiflora	Bellwort	*Liliaceae*—Lily
Valeriana officinalis	Garden-heliotrope	*Valerianaceae*—Valerian
Verbascum Chaixi	Nettle-leaved Mullein	*Scrophulariaceae*—Figwort
V. olympicum	Olympian M.	*Scrophulariaceae*—Figwort
V. phoeniceum	Purple M.	*Scrophulariaceae*—Figwort
Verbena canadensis	Clump Verbena	*Verbenaceae*—Vervain
Vernonia noveboracensis	Ironweed	*Compositae*—Daisy
Veronica austriaca	Austrian Speedwell	*Scrophulariaceae*—Figwort

ORIGIN	SEASON	COLOR	HEIGHT
Japan	July–Sept.	violet-blue	1½–2 ft.
N. America	June–Aug.	blue	1 –2 ft.
Asia	Aug.–Sept.	pink	1 –1½ ft.
Garden	Aug.–Sept.	crimson	1 –1½ ft.
S. America	June–Aug.	rosy purple	2 –3 ft.
N. America	June	white	2 –3 ft.
Garden	June–Aug.	rose-pink	3 –4 ft.
N. America	July–Sept.	yellow	6 –8 ft.
N. America	May–June	violet-blue	1 –2 ft.
N. America	May–June	creamy white	2 –3 ft.
N. America	Aug.–Sept.	yellow	4 –5 ft.
N. America	Aug.–Sept.	yellow	4 –5 ft.
N. America	Aug.–Sept.	yellow	3 –4 ft.
Garden	July–Aug.	yellow	2 –2½ ft.
Europe	June–Aug.	rosy purple	2 –3 ft.
Caucasus	June–Aug.	magenta	1 –1½ ft.
N. America	Aug.–Sept.	various	1 ft.
N. America	April–May	yellow	1 –1½ ft.
Eur.–Asia	May–June	purple	3 ft.
W. China	July–Aug.	lilac	3 –4 ft.
S. Europe	June–July	yellow	3 –5 ft.
N. America	June–July	yellow	4 –5 ft.
N. America	May	white	1 ft.
N. America	May–Sept.	violet-purple	2 –3 ft.
Garden	May–Sept.	various	2 –3 ft.
N. America	May	white	1 ft.
Siberia	May–Aug.	orange	2 ft.
Europe	May–Aug.	lemon	1 –1½ ft.
Siberia	June–Aug.	yellow	1 –1½ ft.
Garden	June–Sept.	pink	6 –10 in.
N. America	May–June	lemon	1 –1½ ft.
Eur.–Asia	June–July	whitish	4 –5 ft.
S. Europe	June–July	yellow	2½–3 ft.
Greece	July–Aug.	yellow	5 –6 ft.
S. Europe	June–July	reddish purple	3 –5 ft.
N. America	June–Sept.	reddish purple	1 –1½ ft.
N. America	Aug.–Sept.	purple	5 –8 ft.
Europe	June–July	blue	1½–2 ft.

BOTANICAL NAME	COMMON NAME	FAMILY
V. *incana*	Hoary S.	*Scrophulariaceae*—Figwort
V. *latifolia*	Hungarian S.	*Scrophulariaceae*—Figwort
V. *maritima subsessilis*	Long-leaved S.	*Scrophulariaceae*—Figwort
V. *m. alba*	White L.-l. S.	*Scrophulariaceae*—Figwort
V. *spicata*	Spiked S.	*Scrophulariaceae*—Figwort
V. *s.* vars.		*Scrophulariaceae*—Figwort
V. *spuria* Royal Blue		*Scrophulariaceae*—Figwort
Veronicastrum virginicum	Culvers-root	*Scrophulariaceae*—Figwort
Viola cornuta	Horned Violet, Tufted Pansy	*Violaceae*—Violet
V. *odorata*	Sweet Violet	*Violaceae*—Violet
V. *tricolor hortensis*	Pansy	*Violaceae*—Violet

ORIGIN	SEASON	COLOR	HEIGHT
Europe	June–July	blue	1 –1½ ft.
Europe	May–June	blue	1 –1½ ft.
Europe	Aug.–Sept.	deep blue	2½–3 ft.
Asia	Aug.–Sept.	white	2½–3 ft.
Garden	June–Aug.	blue	1½–2 ft.
Eur.–Asia	June–Aug.	various	1½–2 ft.
Garden	June–July	blue	12 –15 in.
Vermont to Texas	Aug.–Sept.	whitish	5 –7 ft.
Pyrenees	May–Sept.	blue to white	6 –9 in.
Garden	May–Sept.	various	6 –9 in.
Garden	Apr.–June	various	6 –12 in.

BACKGROUND PERENNIALS—TALL

NAME	HEIGHT	SPREAD	REMARKS
Aruncus sylvester	5–7′	2½–3′	large panicles, small white flowers
Bocconia cordata	6–8′	4–6′	handsome leaves, feathery panicles
Boltonia asteroides	5–8′	2–2½′	white Aster-like flowers
Centaurea babylonica	6–12′	2½–3′	silvery leaves, yellow flowers
Chrysanthemum uliginosum	5–7′	3–3½′	large single white flowers, late
Cimicifuga racemosa	5–8′	3–3½′	long racemes, small white flowers
Delphinium elatum vars.	5–6′	3–3½′	erect spikes, mostly blue shades
Echinops sphaerocephalus	5–7′	3–3½′	Thistle-like pale blue flowers
Epilobium angustifolium	5–7′	2–2½′	Willow-like leaves, rosy purple flowers
Eupatorium purpureum	5–8′	3–4′	handsome plant, pinkish purple flowers
Filipendula rubra	5–6′	3–3½′	large panicles, pink flowers
Helenium autumnale vars.	5–6′	2–2½′	yellow and bronze shades
Helianthus salicifolius	8–10′	2½–3′	long drooping leaves, yellow flowers
Hibiscus moscheutos vars.	5–8′	3–4′	stout plants, large, showy flowers
Liatris scariosa vars.	5–6′	2–2½′	showy spikes, purple or white flowers
Rudbeckia subtomentosa	5–6′	2½–3′	grayish leaves, yellow flowers
Silphium perfoliatum	6–8′	3–3½′	coarse growth, yellow flowers
Verbascum olympicum	5–6′	2–2½′	silvery leaves, yellow flowers

NAME	HEIGHT	SPREAD	REMARKS
Vernonia noveboracensis	5–8′	2–2½′	showy clusters, purple flowers, late
Veronicastrum virginicum	5–7′	1½–2′	slender habit, spikes, whitish flowers

BACKGROUND PERENNIALS—MEDIUM

NAME	HEIGHT	SPREAD	REMARKS
Aconitum napellus v. *Sparksi*	4–5′	2–2½′	branching stems, deep blue flowers
Anchusa italica vars.	3–5′	2½–3′	robust plants, blue flowers
Anemone japonica vars.	3–5′	1½–2′	erect flowers, white to pinkish, late
Artemisia lactiflora	4–5′	1½–2′	good accent plant, creamy-white flowers
Aster novae-angliae vars.	4–5′	1½–2′	need support, purple and pink shades
A. novi-belgi vars.	4–5′	1½–2′	need support, white, pink, and blue shades
Baptisia australis	4–4½′	2½–3′	compact, good foliage, blue flowers
Boltonia latisquama	4–5′	1½–2′	pinkish, Aster-like flowers
Chelone Lyoni	3–3½′	2–2½′	good clumps, rose-pink flowers
Clematis recta	4–5′	2½–3′	needs support, white flowers, June
C. stans	4–5′	3–3½′	clusters of blue flowers, late
Delphinium cheilanthum vars.	4–5′	2–2½′	spikes of blue shades
Echinacea purpurea	3–5′	1½–2′	stiff habit, reddish-purple flowers
Helianthus mollis	4–5′	2–2½′	rough grayish leaves, yellow flowers
Lythrum salicaria vars.	3–4′	1½–2′	good in moist soil, rosy-purple flowers

NAME	HEIGHT	SPREAD	REMARKS
Monarda didyma vars.	3–4′	2–2½′	good in semi-shade, red and pinkish shades
Phlox paniculata vars.	3–4′	1½–2′	needs rich soil, large panicles
Thermopsis caroliniana	4–5′	1½–2′	good accent plant, yellow flowers

LOW-GROWING PERENNIALS
–HEIGHT 1 FOOT AND UNDER

Ajuga Brockbanki
A. genevensis
A. reptans & vars.
Alyssum saxatile & vars.
Aquilegia flabellata nana
Arabis albida & vars.
Armeria maritima
Asperula odorata
Aster alpinus
A. hybridus nana
Aubrieta deltoidea & vars.
Callirhoe involucrata
Cerastium tomentosum
Ceratostigma plumbaginoides
Chrysanthemum arcticum
Chrysogonum virginianum
Convallaria majalis
Dianthus Allwoodi
Dracocephalum grandiflorum
Epimedium grandiflorum & vars.
E. pinnatum
Erysimum ochroleucum
Hypericum calycinum
Iberis gibraltarica
I. sempervirens & vars.

Iris cristata & vars.
I. pumila & vars.
I. susiana
Jasione perennis
Lamium album
L. maculatum
Liriope muscari
Lychnis Haageana
L. viscaria & vars.
Oenothera missouriensis
Phlox stolonifera
P. subulata & vars.
Polemonium reptans
P. Richardsoni
Primula elatior
P. polyantha
P. Sieboldi & vars.
P. veris & vars.
P. vulgaris
Pulmonaria angustifolia
Stokesia laevis
Trillium grandiflorum
Tunica saxifraga fl. pl.
Viola cornuta
V. odorata & vars.

LISTS OF PERENNIALS
BY HEIGHT 1-2 FEET

Achillea Perry's White
Actaea alba
A. rubra
Adonis vernalis
Aethionema grandiflorum
Alchemilla vulgaris
Anchusa Barrelieri
A. caespitosa
Anemone hupehensis
A. pulsatilla & vars.
A. sylvestris
Aquilegia caerulea
A. canadensis
A. clematiflora
A. flabellata
A. glandulosa
A. vulgaris & vars.
Armeria maritima & vars.
Aster amellus & vars.
A. Frikarti
Astilbe japonica & vars.
Begonia Evansiana
Bergenia crassifolia
Brunnera macrophylla
Calimeris incisa
Caltha palustris
Campanula carpatica & vars.
C. glomerata & vars.
C. rotundifolia
Catananche caerulea
Centaurea dealbata
C. montana
Chrysanthemum arcticum vars.
C. coccineum & vars.
Coreopsis rosea

Coronilla varia
Corydalis cheilanthifolia
C. lutea
C. nobilis
Delphinium nudicaule
Dianthus barbatus & vars.
D. caryophyllus & vars.
D. Knappi
D. latifolius
D. plumarius & vars.
Dicentra eximia
D. formosa & vars.
D. spectabilis alba
Dodecatheon meadia
Doronicum caucasicum
Dracocephalum Ruyschiana
Erigeron speciosus & vars.
Eryngium alpinum
E. maritimum
Euphorbia epithymoides
Gentiana Andrewsi
G. septemfida
Geranium Endressi
Geranium grandiflorum
G. ibericum & vars.
G. sanguineum
Geum Borisi
G. chiloense & vars.
Gypsophila repens Bodgeri
Helenium autumnale pumilum
Helleborus niger & vars.
H. orientalis & vars.
H. viridis
Hemerocallis Dumortieri
H. Middendorffi

HEIGHT 1–2 FEET, CONT.

H. minor
Heuchera brizoides
H. sanguinea & vars.
Hosta coerulea
H. lancifolia & vars.
H. undulata
Hyssopus officinalis
Incarvillea Delavayi
Inula Royleana
Iris Hoogiana
I. orientalis
I. spuria
I. tectorum & vars.
Jeffersonia diphylla
Lactuca perennis
Lathyrus vernus
Limonium latifolium
Linum flavum
L. narbonnense & vars.
L. perenne
Lychnis Arkwrighti
L. flos-Jovis
Mertensia virginica
Nepeta Mussini
N. Souv. de André Chaudron
Oenothera speciosa
Paeonia tenuifolia
Papaver lateritium
P. nudicaule & vars.
P. rupifragum
P. thibeticum
Paradisea liliastrum

Phlox Arendsi
P. divaricata & vars.
Physostegia Vivid
Platycodon Mariesi
Polygonum bistorta
Potentilla nepalensis & vars.
P. pyrenaica
Primula Beesiana
P. Bullesiana
P. Bulleyana
P. japonica & vars.
P. Littoniana
Pulmonaria saccharata
Scabiosa caucasica
S. columbaria
S. japonica
Scutellaria serrata
Sedum spectabile & vars.
Sisyrinchium angustifolium
Stachys lanata
Stylophorum diphyllum
Trollius asiaticus
T. europaeus
T. Ledebouri
Uvularia grandiflora
Verbena canadensis
Veronica austriaca
V. incana
V. latifolia
V. spicata & vars.
V. spuria & vars.

HEIGHT 2–3 FEET

Acanthus mollis & vars.
Achillea millefolium & vars.
A. Boule de Neige

Adenophora confusa
A. lilifolia
Alstroemeria aurantiaca

Amsonia tabernaemontana

Anthemis Sancti-Johannis

A. tinctoria & vars.

Aquilegia chrysantha

A. longissima

A. Skinneri

Artemisia Stelleriana

Asclepias tuberosa

Astilbe Arendsi

A. rosea vars.

Astrantia major

Campanula alliariaefolia

C. bononiensis

C. persicifolia

Centranthus ruber

Chelone glabra

Chrysanthemum balsamita

C. coreanum

C. maximum & vars.

C. nipponicum

Cimicifuga simplex

Clematis integrifolia

Codonopsis clematidea

Coreopsis grandiflora

C. lanceolata & vars.

C. verticillata

Delphinium cardinale

D. grandiflorum & vars.

D. tatsienense

Dicentra spectabilis

Dictamnus albus & vars.

Digitalis ambigua

D. lanata

Echinops ritro

Eryngium Oliverianum

E. planum

Eupatorium coelestinum

Euphorbia corollata

Filipendula hexapetala

F. palmata

Gaillardia aristata & vars.

Galega officinalis & vars.

Galium mollugo

Geranium sylvaticum

Gypsophila Oldhamiana

G. paniculata & vars.

Helenium Hoopesi

Hemerocallis aurantiaca

H. flava

Hesperis matronalis & vars.

Hosta Fortunei & vars.

H. plantaginea

H. Sieboldiana

Inula glandulosa superba

Iris chrysographes

I. foliosa

I. fulva

I. germanica & vars.

I. halophila

I. Kaempferi vars.

I. sibirica & vars.

I. spuria vars.

I. Wilsoni

Kniphofia hybrida

Lobelia cardinalis

L. syphilitica & vars.

Lychnis chalcedonica

L. coronaria

Lysimachia clethroides

Malva alcea

Nepeta macrantha

Paeonia albiflora & vars.

P. Mlokosewitschi

P. officinalis & vars.

HEIGHT 2–3 FEET, CONT.

Papaver bracteatum
P. pilosum
Pentstemon cyananthus
P. hirsutus
P. ovatus
Phlox glaberrima
Platycodon grandiflorum
Polemonium caeruleum
Polygonatum multiflorum
Primula Florindae
Ranunculus acris fl. pl.

Rudbeckia speciosa
Salvia pratensis & vars.
Senecio pulcher
Sidalcea candida
Smilacina racemosa
Solidaster luteus
Stachys grandiflora
Tradescantia virginiana & vars.
Verbascum Chaixi
Veronica maritima subsessilis &
    vars.

HEIGHT 3–5 FEET

Achillea flilipendulina
Aconitum autumnale
A. Fischeri
A. napellus & vars.
Adenophora Potanini
Anchusa azurea & vars.
Anemone japonica & vars.
Artemisia Silver King
A. lactiflora
Aster novae-angliae & vars.
A. novi-belgi & vars.
Baptisia australis
Belamcanda chinensis
Boltonia latisquama
Campanula lactiflora & vars.
C. latifolia & vars.
Cassia marilandica
Centaurea macrocephala
C. ruthenica
Chelone Lyoni
Clematis heracleaefolia & vars.
C. recta
C. stans

Delphinium cheilanthum & vars.
Digitalis Lutzi
D. purpurea & vars.
Doronicum plantagineum
Echinacea purpurea
Eupatorium rugosum
Gaura Lindheimeri
Gillenia trifoliata
Gypsophila acutifolia
Helenium autumnale & vars.
Helianthus decapetalus & vars.
H. mollis
Heliopsis helianthoides & vars.
H. scabra & vars.
Hemerocallis fulva & vars.
H. Thunbergi
H. hybrids
Hypericum ascyron
Inula helenium
Iris Delavayi
I. ochroleuca
I. pallida dalmatica
I. pseudacorus

HEIGHT 3–5 FEET, CONT.

Kniphofia uvaria & vars.
Liatris pycnostachya
L. scariosa & vars.
Ligularia clivorum
L. Wilsoniana
Lupinus polyphyllus & vars.
Lythrum salicaria & vars.
Monarda didyma & vars.
Papaver orientale & vars.
Peltiphyllum peltatum
Penstemon barbatus & vars.
P. digitalis
P. grandiflorus
P. spectabilis

Phlox paniculata vars.
Physostegia virginiana & vars.
Salvia azurea
S. Pitcheri
Sidalcea Rose Queen
Solidago canadensis
S. rigida
S. Shorti
Thalictrum aquilegifolium
T. dipterocarpum
T. glaucum
Thermopsis caroliniana
Valeriana officinalis
Verbascum phoeniceum

HEIGHT 5–6 FEET

Aconitum Wilsoni
Astilbe biternata
Cephalaria alpina
C. tatarica
Delphinium elatum
D. hybridum
Eremurus himalaicus

Filipendula rubra
F. ulmaria
Helenium autumnale
Hibiscus Mallow Marvels
Liatris September Glory
Rudbeckia subtomentosa
Verbascum olympicum

HEIGHT 6 FEET OR MORE

Aruncus sylvester
Aster tataricus
Bocconia cordata
Boltonia asteroides
Centaurea babylonica
Chrysanthemum uliginosum
Cimicifuga racemosa
Echinops sphaerocephalus
Epilobium angustifolium
Eremurus robustus
E. Shelford
Eupatorium purpureum

Helianthus angustifolius
H. laetiflorus
H. Maximiliani
H. rigidus & vars.
H. salicifolius
Hibiscus moscheutos
Lathyrus latifolius & vars.
Rudbeckia laciniata & vars.
R. maxima
Silphium perfoliatum
Vernonia noveboracensis
Veronicastrum virginicum

SOME GOOD FOLIAGE PERENNIALS

NAME	HEIGHT	SPREAD	REMARKS
Acanthus mollis	2–2½′	2–2½′	large, handsome, cut leaves
Amsonia tabernaemontana	2½–3′	2½–3′	shapely plant, smooth, ovate leaves
Arabis albida variegata	6–10″	1–1½′	spreading, green and yellow foliage
Artemisia albula Silver King	3–3½′	2–2½′	silvery leaves, distinctive effect
Baptisia australis	4–4½′	2½–3′	roundish clump, bluish leaves
Bocconia cordata	6–8′	4–6′	large-lobed blue-green leaves
Cerastium tomentosum	6–8′	2–3′	silvery leaves, spreading plant
Chrysanthemum nipponicum	2–4′	2–3′	shapely form, thick, glossy leaves
Dianthus plumarius vars.	10–15″	1½–2′	effective clumps of gray
Dicentra eximia	1½–2′	1–1½′	graceful fernlike foliage
Dictamnus albus	2–3′	1½–2′	erect clumps, glossy foliage
Echinops ritro	2–3′	1½–2′	silvery-blue, cut leaves, spiny
Epimedium grandiflorum	1′	1½–2′	clumpy, leaves bronzy when young
Euphorbia epithymoides	12–15″	1½–2′	rounded clumps, dark green
Hosta plantaginea	2–2½′	2–2½′	large glossy leaves, deeply ribbed
H. Sieboldiana	2–3′	2–2½′	large leaves of bluish gray
H. undulata	1–2′	1–2′	wavy leaves, splashed creamy white

NAME	HEIGHT	SPREAD	REMARKS
Iberis sempervirens	9–12″	1½–2′	close clump, dark, glossy foliage
Lamium maculatum	8–12″	1½–2′	sprawly, leaves blotched white
Paeonia officinalis vars.	2–3′	2–3′	handsome green divided foliage
Sedum spectabile	1–1½′	1–1½′	rounded form, glaucous leaves
Stachys lanata	1–1½′	1–1½′	tufts of silvery, woolly foliage
Verbascum olympicum	5–6′	1½–2′	large leaves, dense covering, white down
Veronica incana	1–1½′	1–1½′	silvery leaves, effective all season

PERENNIALS FOR HEDGES

NAME	HEIGHT	SPREAD	SPACING
Amsonia tabernaemontana	2½–3′	2½–3′	1–1½′
Artemisia Stelleriana	2–2½′	1–1½′	1′
Baptisia australis	4–4½′	2½–3′	1–1½′
Chelone Lyoni	3–3½′	2½–3′	1–1½′
Chrysanthemum coreanum	1½–2½′	1–1½′	1′
Cushion vars.	1–1½′	1–2′	1′
Dictamnus albus	2–3′	1½–2′	1–1½′
Galega officinalis	2–3′	1½–2′	1′
Helenium autumnale pumilum	1½–2′	1–1½′	1′
Helianthus mollis	4–5′	2–2½′	1–1½′
H. rigidus	6–8′	2½–3′	1–1½′
Hibiscus moscheutos vars.	5–6′	2½–3′	1½–2′
Oenothera fruticosa vars.	2–3′	1½′	1′
Paeonia officinalis vars.	2–4′	2–4′	1½–2′
Rudbeckia subtomentosa	4–6′	2–2½′	1–1½′
Veronica maritima subsessilis	2½–3′	1½–2′	1′
Veronicastrum virginicum	5–7′	1½–2′	1–1½′

PERENNIALS FOR EDGINGS

NAME	HEIGHT IN BLOOM	CHARACTER	REMARKS
Ajuga in variety	3–6″	spreading	forms dense mat
Alyssum saxatile vars.	6–12″	spreading	vars. more compact
Arabis albida vars.	6–10″	spreading	trim after flowering
Armeria maritima	6–9″	compact	neat tufted effect
Asperula odorata	6–8″	spreading	prefers partial shade
Aster hybridus nana vars.	6–12″	spreading	free-flowering, late
Aubrieta deltoidea vars.	3–6″	spreads slowly	needs porous soil
Brunnera macrophylla	9–15″	compact	coarse foliage after flowering
Campanula carpatica	9–15″	compact	prefers partial shade
Cerastium tomentosum	6″	spreading	needs restriction
Ceratostigma plumbaginoides	9–12″	spreading	needs good drainage
Chrysanthemum arcticum	6–12″	spreading	loose habit, late
Dianthus latifolius vars.	10–15″	compact	tufted flower heads
Dianthus plumarius vars.	10–15″	spreading	gray foliage effective
Heuchera sanguinea vars.	1–1½′	compact	needs good drainage
Iberis sempervirens	9–12″	compact	shear after flowering
Iris pumila vars.	4–9″	spreading	foliage may not be lasting
Lychnis viscaria vars.	9–12″	compact	grassy foliage
Nepeta Mussini	1–1½′	spreading	loose effect
Phlox divaricata	1–1½′	spreading	trim after flowering
P. stolonifera	9–12″	spreading	neat appearance

NAME	HEIGHT IN BLOOM	CHARACTER	REMARKS
P. subulata vars.	6″	spreading	forms dense mat
Polemonium reptans	6–9″	spreading	prefers half shade
Primula polyantha	9–12″	compact	divide after flowering
Sedum spurium vars.	3–9″	spreading	close mat, restrict
Stachys lanata	1–1½′	tufted	best when non-flowering
Verbena canadensis	1–1½′	spreading	loose habit, robust
Veronica incana	1–1½′	spreading	neat clump, grayish foliage
Viola cornuta	6–9″	compact	good foliage all season

NARROW PERENNIALS FOR ACCENT

NAME	HEIGHT	TIME OF BLOOM	COLOR
Aconitum Wilsoni	5–6′	Sept.–Oct.	violet-blue
Artemisia lactiflora	4–5′	Aug.–Sept.	creamy white
Boltonia latisquama	4–5′	Aug.–Sept.	pinkish lavender
Centaurea babylonica	6–12′	July	yellow
Echinops sphaerocephalus	5–7′	July–Aug.	pale blue
Epilobium angustifolium	5–7′	Aug.	rosy purple
Helianthus salicifolius	8–10′	Sept.–Oct.	yellow
Liatris scariosa vars.	4–6′	Aug.–Sept.	purple or white
Lythrum salicaria vars.	3–4′	July–Sept.	rosy purple
Rudbeckia maxima	5–9′	Aug.–Sept.	yellow
Verbascum olympicum	5–6′	July–Aug.	yellow
Vernonia noveboracensis	5–8′	Aug.–Sept.	purple
Veronicastrum virginicum	5–7′	Aug.–Sept.	whitish

PERENNIALS FOR CUT FLOWERS

Anemone	Echinops	Kniphofia
Anthemis	Gaillardia	Liatris
Aquilegia	Geum	Lilium
Artemisia	Gypsophila	Lupinus
Aster	Helenium	Nepeta
Centaurea	Heliopsis	Paeonia
Chrysanthemum	Helleborus	Papaver
Coreopsis	Heuchera	Rudbeckia
Delphinium	Hosta	Scabiosa
Dianthus	Iris	Viola

Poppies (Papaver) should be cut early in the morning, choosing flowers that are just about to open. Char the end of the stems in a gas flame or over an electric range and immediately place them in water.

PERENNIALS WITH FRAGRANT FLOWERS

Adenophora lilifolia	*H. Thunbergi*
Aquilegia chrysantha	*Hesperis matronalis*
A. caerulea	*Hosta plantaginea*
Arabis albida	*Iris germanica* vars.
Artemisia lactiflora	*Malva moschata*
Campanula lactiflora	*Oenothera speciosa*
Centranthus ruber	*Paeonia officinalis* vars.
Chrysanthemum vars.	*P. tenuifolia*
Clematis heracleaefolia	*Phlox divaricata*
C. h. Davidiana	*P. paniculata* vars.
C. recta	*P. stolonifera*
Convallaria majalis	*Primula elatior*
Dianthus caryophyllus vars.	*P. Florindae*
D. plumarius vars.	*P. polyantha*
Dictamnus albus & vars.	*P. veris*
Filipendula ulmaria	*P. vulgaris*
Hemerocallis Dumortieri	*Valeriana officinalis*
H. flava	*Viola cornuta*
H. minor	*V. odorata*

PERENNIALS WITH FRAGRANT FOLIAGE

Achillea millefolium
Anthemis tinctoria
Artemisia Stelleriana
Asperula odorata
Chrysanthemum balsamita

Dictamnus albus
Hyssopus officinalis
Malva moschata
Monarda didyma
Nepeta Mussini

PERENNIALS WITH "EVERLASTING" FLOWERS

Anaphalis margaritacea
Catananche coerulea
Echinops ritro
E. sphaerocephalus
Eryngium alpinum
E. maritimum

E. Oliverianum
E. planum
Gypsophila acutifolia
G. paniculata vars.
G. repens Bodgeri
Limonium latifolium

PERENNIALS BY COLOR—WHITE

Achillea millefolium
A. ptarmica & vars.
Aconitum napellus album
Actaea alba
A. rubra
Ajuga reptans alba
Anemone japonica alba
A. j. Whirlwind
A. pulsatilla alba
A. sylvestris
Aquilegia flabellata nana
Arabis albida & vars.
Artemisia lactiflora
Aruncus sylvester
Asperula odorata
Aster Mt. Everest
A. Niobe, dwarf

Astilbe Arendsi Gladstone
A. japonica
Boltonia asteroides
Campanula alliariaefolia
C. carpatica alba
C. lactiflora
C. latifolia alba
C. persicifolia alba
C. p. Moerheimi
Cephalaria tatarica
Cerastium tomentosum
Chrysanthemum arcticum
C. coreanum
C. maximum & vars.
C. nipponicum
C. uliginosum
Cimicifuga racemosa

WHITE, CONT.

C. simplex
Clematis recta
Convallaria majalis
Delphinium grandiflorum album
Dianthus Her Majesty
Dicentra Sweetheart
D. spectabilis alba
Dictamnus albus
Epilobium angustifolium alba
Epimedium grandiflorum niveum
Eremurus himalaicus
Eupatorium rugosum
Euphorbia corollata
Filipendula hexapetala
F. ulmaria
Francoa ramosa
Galega officinalis alba
Galium mollugo
Gaura Lindheimeri
Geranium ibericum album
Gillenia trifoliata
Gypsophila acutifolia
G. paniculata & vars.
Helleborus niger
H. n. altifolius
Hesperis matronalis alba
Heuchera sanguinea alba
Hosta plantaginea
Iberis sempervirens & vars.

Iris cristata alba
I. Kaempferi vars.
Iris sibirica alba
I. tectorum alba
Lamium album
Lathyrus latifolius albus
Liatris scariosa alba
Linum narbonnense album
Lobelia syphilitica alba
Lysimachia clethroides
Malva moschata alba
Paeonia albiflora vars.
P. officinalis vars.
Papaver orientale vars.
Paradisea liliastrum
Penstemon digitalis
Phlox paniculata vars.
P. subulata vars.
P. Miss Lingard
Platycodon grandiflorum album
Polygonatum multiflorum
Primula Sieboldi alba
Sidalcea candida
Smilacina racemosa
Stokesia laevis alba
Tradescantia virginiana alba
Trillium grandiflorum
Veronica spicata alba
Viola cornuta alba

YELLOW

Achillea filipendulina
Adonis vernalis
Alyssum saxatile & vars.
Anthemis tinctoria vars.
Aquilegia chrysantha

A. longissima
Asphodeline lutea
Buphthalmum speciosum
Caltha palustris
Cassia marilandica

YELLOW, CONT.

Centaurea babylonica
C. macrocephala
Cephalaria alpina
Chrysogonum virginianum
Coreopsis grandiflora
C. lanceolata vars.
C. verticillata
Corydalis cheilanthifolia
C. lutea
C. nobilis
Dianthus Knappi
Digitalis ambigua
Doronicum caucasicum
D. plantagineum
Euphorbia epithymoides
Gaillardia aristata
Helenium autumnale & vars.
H. Hoopesi
Helianthus angustifolius
H. sp. & vars.
Heliopsis helianthoides
H. scabra
Hemerocallis flava
H. minor
H. Thunbergi
H. many vars.
Hypericum ascyron
Inula glandulosa superba
I. helenium
Iris pseudacorus
I. Wilsoni

Kirengeshoma palmata
Kniphofia vars.
Ligularia Wilsoniana
Linum flavum
Oenothera fruticosa & vars.
O. missouriensis
Paeonia Mlokosewitschi
Potentilla pyrenaica
Primula Bulleyana
P. elatior
P. Florindae
Primula veris
Ranunculus acris fl. pl.
Rudbeckia laciniata & vars.
R. maxima
R. speciosa
R. subtomentosa
Silphium perfoliatum
Solidago canadensis
S. rigida
S. Shorti
Solidaster luteus
Stylophorum diphyllum
Thalictrum glaucum
Thermopsis caroliniana
Trollius europaeus
T. Ledebouri
Uvularia grandiflora
Verbascum Chaixi
V. olympicum

ORANGE

Alstroemeria aurantiaca
Anthemis Sancti-Johannis
Asclepias tuberosa
Belamcanda chinensis
Gaillardia aristata
Geum Borisi
G. Princess Juliana
Heliopsis helianthoides Pitcheriana
H. scabra incomparabilis

Hemerocallis aurantiaca
H. Dumortieri
H. fulva
H. Middendorffi
H. many vars.
Inula Royleana
Ligularia clivorum
Trollius asiaticus

BLUE

Aconitum autumnale
A. Fischeri
A. F. Wilsoni
A. napellus
A. n. Sparksi
Adenophora confusa
A. lilifolia
A. Potanini
Ajuga Brockbanki
A. genevensis
A. reptans
A. r. rubra
Amsonia tabernaemontana
Anchusa italica & vars.
Aquilegia caerulea
A. glandulosa
Aster Frikarti
Aster novi-belgi vars.
Baptisia australis
Brunnera macrophylla
Campanula carpatica
C. lactiflora caerulea
C. persicifolia

C. p. Telham Beauty
Centaurea montana
Ceratostigma plumbaginoides
Clematis heracleaefolia & vars.
C. stans
Codonopsis clematidea
Delphinium cheilanthum & vars.
D. elatum
D. grandiflorum
D. hybrida, many
Dracocephalum grandiflorum
D. Ruyschiana
Echinops ritro
E. sphaerocephalus
Eryngium alpinum
E. maritimum
E. Oliverianum
E. planum
Eupatorium coelestinum
Gentiana Andrewsi
G. septemfida
Hosta coerulea
H. Fortunei

BLUE, CONT.

H. lancifolia
H. Sieboldiana
H. undulata
Iris cristata
I. germanica vars.
I. Hoogiana
I. pallida dalmatica
I. tectorum
Jasione perennis
Lactuca perennis
Linum narbonnense
L. perenne
Lobelia syphilitica
Lupinus polyphyllus
Mertensia virginica
Nepeta macrantha
N. Mussini
N. Souv. de André Chaudron
Penstemon cyananthus
P. grandiflorus
Phlox Arendsi
P. divaricata

Platycodon grandiflorum
P. g. Mariesi
Polemonium caeruleum
P. reptans
P. Richardsoni
Pulmonaria angustifolia
Salvia azurea
S. Pitcheri
S. pratensis
Scabiosa caucasica
S. c. vars.
Scutellaria serrata
Stokesia laevis
Tradescantia virginiana vars.
Veronica austriaca
V. incana
V. latifolia
V. maritima subsessilis
V. spicata & vars.
V. spuria Royal Blue
Viola cornuta

VIOLET

Aster alpinus
A. amellus King George
A. novi-belgi
Campanula glomerata superba
Delphinium tatsienense
Geranium sylvaticum
Iris chrysographes

I. Delavayi
I. Kaempferi vars.
Phlox divaricata Laphami
Scabiosa japonica
Sisyrinchium angustifolium
Tradescantia virginiana

BLUISH-PURPLE SHADES

Anemone pulsatilla
Aquilegia vulgaris
Aster amellus
A. tataricus
Aubrieta deltoidea
Calimeris incisa
Campanula bononiensis
C. glomerata
C. latifolia
Erigeron speciosus & vars.
Galega officinalis
Geranium ibericum
Hesperis matronalis
Iris germanica vars.
I. Kaempferi vars.

I. orientalis
I. sibirica
I. spuria
Lathyrus vernus
Liatris pycnostachya
L. September Glory
Limonium latifolium
Liriope muscari
Penstemon hirsutus
P. ovatus
Scabiosa columbaria
Thalictrum aquilegifolium
T. dipterocarpum
Tradescantia virginiana vars.
Vernonia noveboracensis

REDDISH-PURPLE SHADES

Anemone hupehensis
A. japonica
A. novae-angliae & vars.
Aubrieta deltoidea vars.
Callirhoe involucrata
Dicentra formosa
Dictamnus albus rubra
D. a. caucasicus
Digitalis purpurea
Echinacea purpurea
Epilobium angustifolium
Eupatorium purpureum
Geranium sanguineum
Incarvillea Delavayi
Iris Kaempferi vars.

Lamium maculatum
Lychnis viscaria
Lythrum salicaria & vars.
Malva alcea
Penstemon spectabilis
Phlox glaberrima
P. subulata
Primula Beesiana
P. japonica
Pulmonaria saccharata
Senecio pulcher
Stachys grandiflora
Verbascum phoeniceum
Verbena canadensis

RED SHADES

Aquilegia canadensis
A. Skinneri
Aster vars.
Centranthus ruber
Chrysanthemum coccineum
Delphinium cardinale
D. nudicaule
Dianthus barbatus vars.
Epimedium grandiflorum
Gaillardia Burgundy
Geum chiloense
G. c. Fire Opal
G. c. Mrs. Bradshaw
Helenium autumnale rubrum
Heuchera sanguinea & vars.
Hibiscus moscheutos hybrids
Iris fulva

Kniphofia uvaria vars.
Lobelia cardinalis
Lychnis Arkwrighti
L. chalcedonica
L. coronaria
L. Haageana
Monarda didyma & vars.
Paeonia officinalis
P. tenuifolia
Papaver bracteatum
P. orientale
P. pilosum
Penstemon barbatus
P. Torreyi
Potentilla nepalensis
Sedum spectabile Brilliant

PINK AND ROSE SHADES

Achillea millefolium roseum
Aethionema grandiflorum
Armeria maritima & vars.
Aster vars.
Astilbe rosea vars.
Astrantia major
Bergenia crassifolia
Boltonia latisquama
Centaurea dealbata
Chelone Lyoni
Coreopsis rosea
Dianthus plumarius & vars.
Dicentra eximia
D. spectabilis

Dodecatheon meadia
Eremurus robustus
E. Shelford
Filipendula palmata
F. rubra
Geranium Endressi
Gypsophila Oldhamiana
G. repens Bodgeri
Hibiscus moscheutos
H. m. hybrids
Heuchera brizoides
Lathyrus latifolius
Lupinus polyphyllus vars.
Lychnis flos-Jovis

PINK AND ROSE SHADES, CONT.

Malva moschata
Paeonia vars.
Peltiphyllum peltatum
Penstemon Pink Beauty
Phlox paniculata vars.
Physostegia virginiana & vars.
Polygonum bistorta

Potentilla Miss Willmott
Primula Sieboldi
Salvia pratensis rubicunda
Sedum spectabile
Sidalcea Rose Queen
Tunica saxifraga fl. pl.

BLOOMING CALENDAR

Opening in April

Adonis vernalis
Alyssum saxatile & vars.
Anemone pulsatilla & vars.
Arabis albida & vars.
Aubrieta deltoidea & vars.
Bergenia crassifolia
Brunnera macrophylla
Caltha palustris
Chrysogonum virginianum
Dicentra eximia
Doronicum caucasicum
Epimedium grandiflorum & vars.
E. pinnatum

Helleborus orientalis & vars.
H. viridis
Lathyrus vernus
Mertensia virginica
Phlox subulata vars.
Primula elatior
P. polyantha
P. veris
P. vulgaris
Pulmonaria angustifolia
P. saccharata
Stylophorum diphyllum

Opening in May

Actaea alba
A. rubra
Aethionema grandiflorum
Ajuga, all kinds
Alchemilla vulgaris
Amsonia tabernaemontana
Anchusa azurea & vars.
A. Barrelieri

A. caespitosa
Anemone sylvestris
Anthemis Sancti-Johannis
A. tinctoria & vars.
Aquilegia, all kinds
Armeria maritima & vars.
Asperula odorata
Aster alpinus

OPENING IN MAY, CONT.

Astrantia major
Baptisia australis
Campanula latifolia & vars.
Convallaria majalis
Corydalis cheilanthifolia
C. lutea
C. nobilis
Dicentra formosa & vars.
D. spectabilis & vars.
Dictamnus albus & vars.
Dodecatheon meadia
Erysimum ochroleucum
Euphorbia epithymoides
Geum Borisi
Hemerocallis Dumortieri
H. flava
Iberis gibraltarica
I. sempervirens & vars.
Iris chrysographes
I. cristata & vars.
I. germanica vars.
I. Hoogiana
I. orientalis
I. pallida dalmatica
I. pumila & vars.
Jeffersonia diphylla
Lamium album
L. maculatum
Linum perenne
Lupinus polyphyllus & vars.
Lychnis viscaria & vars.
Paeonia albiflora vars.
P. Mlokosewitschi
P. officinalis & vars.
P. tenuifolia

Papaver bracteatum
P. nudicaule & vars.
P. thibeticum
Paradisea liliastrum
Peltiphyllum peltatum
Penstemon cyananthus
P. ovatus
Phlox Arendsi
P. divaricata & vars.
P. stolonifera
Polemonium caeruleum
P. reptans
P. Richardsoni
Polygonatum multiflorum
Potentilla nepalensis & vars.
P. pyrenaica
Primula Beesiana
P. Bullesiana
P. Bulleyana
P. japonica & vars.
P. Sieboldi & vars.
Ranunculus acris fl. pl.
Salvia pratensis & vars.
Sisyrinchium angustifolium
Smilacina racemosa
Thalictrum aquilegifolium
Tradescantia virginiana & vars.
Trillium grandiflorum
Trollius asiaticus
T. europaeus
Uvularia grandiflora
Veronica latifolia
Viola cornuta
V. odorata vars.

Opening in June

Achillea filipendulina
A. millefolium & vars.
A. ptarmica vars.
Aconitum napellus & vars.
Aruncus sylvester
Asphodeline lutea
Astilbe Arendsi
A. biternata
A. japonica & vars.
A. rosea & vars.
Buphthalmum speciosum
Callirhoe involucrata
Campanula alliariaefolia
C. bononiensis
C. carpatica & vars.
C. glomerata & vars.
C. persicifolia & vars.
C. rotundifolia
Catananche caerulea
Centaurea dealbata
C. montana
Centranthus ruber
Cephalaria alpina
Cerastium tomentosum
Chrysanthemum coccineum & vars.
C. maximum & vars.
Clematis integrifolia
C. recta
Codonopsis clematidea
Coreopsis grandiflora
C. lanceolata & vars.
C. rosea
C. verticillata
Coronilla varia
Delphinium, all kinds
Dianthus, all kinds
Digitalis, all kinds

Dracocephalum grandiflorum
D. Ruyschiana
Eremurus himalaicus
E. robustus
E. Shelford
Erigeron speciosus & vars.
Filipendula hexapetala
F. palmata
F. rubra
F. ulmaria
Gaillardia aristata & vars.
Galega officinalis & vars.
Galium mollugo
Geranium Endressi
G. grandiflorum
G. ibericum & vars.
G. sanguineum
G. sylvaticum
Geum chiloense & vars.
Gillenia trifoliata
Helenium Hoopesi
Hemerocallis Middendorffi
H. minor
H. hybrids
Hesperis matronalis & vars.
Heuchera brizoides
H. sanguinea & vars.
Hosta Sieboldiana
Hyssopus officinalis
Incarvillea Delavayi
Iris Delavayi
I. foliosa
I. fulva
I. halophila
I. Kaempferi & vars.
I. pseudacorus
I. spuria & vars.

I. tectorum & vars.
I. Wilsoni
Jasione perennis
Lactuca perennis
Linum flavum
L. narbonnense & vars.
Lychnis Arkwrighti
L. chalcedonica
L. coronaria
L. flos-Jovis
Malva alcea
M. moschata & vars.
Nepeta macrantha
N. Mussini
N. Souv. de André Chaudron
Oenothera fruticosa & vars.
Papaver lateritium
P. orientale & vars.
P. pilosum
P. rupifragum
Penstemon barbatus & vars.
P. digitalis
P. grandiflorus
P. spectabilis

P. Torreyi
Phlox carolina
Platycodon grandiflorum & vars.
Primula Florindae
P. Littoniana
Rudbeckia speciosa
Scabiosa caucasica & vars.
S. columbaria
Scutellaria serrata
Senecio pulcher
Sidalcea candida
S. Rose Queen
Stachys grandiflora
Thalictrum glaucum
Trollius Ledebouri
Tunica saxifraga fl. pl.
Valeriana officinalis
Verbascum Chaixi
V. phoeniceum
Verbena canadensis
Veronica austriaca
V. incana
V. spicata & vars.
V. spuria Royal Blue

Opening in July

Acanthus mollis & vars.
Aconitum Sparksi
Adenophora confusa
A. lilifolia
A. Potanini
Alstroemeria aurantiaca
Anaphalis margaritaceae
Asclepias tuberosa
Aster amellus & vars.

A. Frikarti
Astilbe rosea vars.
Begonia Evansiana
Belamcanda chinensis
Calimeris incisa
Campanula lactiflora & vars.
Cassia marilandica
Centaurea babylonica
C. macrocephala

OPENING IN JULY, CONT.

C. ruthenica
Cephalaria tatarica
Chelone glabra
Chrysanthemum Cushion vars.
Cimicifuga racemosa
Echinacea purpurea
Echinops ritro
E. sphaerocephalus
Eryngium alpinum
E. maritimum
E. Oliverianum
E. planum
Euphorbia corollata
Gaura Lindheimeri
Gentiana septemfida
Gypsophila acutifolia
G. paniculata & vars.
G. Bodgeri
Helianthus mollis
Heliopsis helianthoides & vars.
H. scabra & vars.
Hemerocallis aurantiaca
H. fulva & vars.
H. Thunbergi
H. hybrids
Hosta coerulea

H. Fortunei & vars.
H. lancifolia & vars.
Hypericum ascyron
Inula glandulosa superba
I. helenium
I. Royleana
Iris ochroleuca
I. susiana
Kniphofia hybrids
Lathyrus latifolia & vars.
Ligularia clivorum
L. Wilsoniana
Limonium latifolium
Liriope muscari
Lythrum salicaria & vars.
Monarda didyma & vars.
Oenothera missouriensis
O. speciosa
Phlox glaberrima
P. paniculata vars.
Physostegia virginiana
Scabiosa japonica
Silphium perfoliatum
Solidaster luteus
Thalictrum dipterocarpum
Verbascum olympicum

Opening in August

Aconitum autumnale
A. Fischeri
Anemone hupehensis
Artemisia lactiflora
Boltonia asteroides
B. latisquama
Ceratostigma plumbaginoides

Chelone Lyoni
Chrysanthemum balsamita
C. uliginosum
Clematis heracleaefolia
Epilobium angustifolium & vars.
Eupatorium purpureum
E. rugosum

OPENING IN AUGUST, CONT.

Gentiana Andrewsi
Gypsophila Oldhamiana
Helenium autumnale & vars.
Helianthus angustifolius
H. decapetalus & vars.
H. laetiflorus
H. rigidus & vars.
Hibiscus moscheutos & vars.
Hosta plantaginea
H. undulata
Kirengeshoma palmata
Kniphofia uvaria & vars.
Liatris pyconostachya
L. scariosa & vars.
Lobelia cardinalis
L. syphilitica & vars.

Physostegia Summer Glow & Vivid
Polygonum bistorta
Rudbeckia laciniata & vars.
R. maxima
R. subtomentosa
Salvia azurea
S. Pitcheri
Sedum spectabile & vars.
Solidago canadensis
S. rigida
S. Shorti
Stokesia laevis
Vernonia noveboracensis
Veronica maritima subsessilis
   & vars.
Veronicastrum virginicum

Opening in September

Aconitum Wilsoni
Anemone japonica & vars.
Aster novae-angliae & vars.
A. novi-belgi & vars.
Chrysanthemum arcticum
C. a. hybrids
C. coreanum

C. morifolium vars.
C. nipponicum
Cimicifuga simplex
Clematis stans
Eupatorium coelestinum
Helianthus Maximiliani
H. salicifolius

Opening in October

Aster tataricus

Opening in November

Helleborus niger & vars.

SELECTED PERENNIALS FLOWERING
OVER FAIRLY LONG SEASON

Achillea Boule de Neige
Anthemis Sancti-Johannis
A. tinctoria vars.
Aquilegia chrysantha
Armeria maritima vars.
Aster Frikarti
Callirhoe involucrata
Campanula rotundifolia
Centaurea montana
Chrysanthemum maximum vars.
Chrysanthemum Cushion vars.
Coreopsis grandiflora
Coronilla varia
Delphinium grandiflorum
Dianthus caryophyllus
D. latifolius vars.
D. plumarius vars.
Dicentra eximia
Gaillardia aristata vars.
Galega officinalis vars.
Galium mollugo
Gaura Lindheimeri
Geranium ibericum & vars.
G. sanguineum
G. sylvaticum
Gerberia Jamesoni hybrids
Geum Borisi
G. chiloense & vars.
Gypsophila paniculata Bristol Fairy
G. Bodgeri

Heliopsis scabra vars.
Heuchera sanguinea vars.
Lamium album
L. maculatum
Linum perenne
Lythrum salicaria vars.
Malva moschata
Monarda didyma vars.
Nepeta macrantha
N. Mussini
Oenothera fruticosa & vars.
O. missouriensis
Papaver lateritium
P. nudicaule vars.
Phlox paniculata vars.
Physostegia Vivid
Platycodon grandiflorum vars.
Potentilla pyrenaica
Rudbeckia speciosa
Salvia Pitcheri
Scabiosa caucasica vars.
Scutellaria serrata
Sidalcea Rose Queen
Tradescantia virginiana vars.
Trollius asiaticus
Tunica saxifraga fl. pl.
Verbena canadensis
Veronica maritima subsessilis
V. spicata vars.
Viola cornuta

PERENNIALS FOR SHADE

NAME	DEEP OR LIGHT	REMARKS
Aconitum in variety	light	rich soil
Actaea	deep	rich soil
Ajuga in variety	light	not particular
Anemone hupehensis	light	rich, well-drained soil
A. japonica & vars.	light	rich, well-drained soil
A. sylvestris	light	not particular
Aquilegia in variety	light	well-drained soil
Aruncus sylvester	light	rich, moist soil
Asperula odorata	deep	not particular
Astilbe in variety	light	rich, moist soil
Brunnera macrophylla	light	not particular
Campanula in variety	light	well-drained soil
Chelone glabra	light	moist soil
C. Lyoni	light	moist soil
Cimicifuga racemosa	deep	rich, moist soil
C. simplex	deep	rich, moist soil
Convallaria majalis	deep	sandy soil, plenty humus
Corydalis in variety	light	well-drained soil
Dicentra in variety	light	well-drained soil
Digitalis in variety	light	sandy soil, plenty humus
Dodecatheon meadia	light	moist loam
Doronicum in variety	light	moist loam
Dracocephalum in variety	light	sandy soil, plenty humus
Epilobium angustifolium	light	moist loam
Epimedium in variety	deep	rich, moist soil
Eupatorium coelestinum	light	not particular
E. rugosum	deep	not particular
Filipendula palmata	light	moist loam
F. rubra	light	moist loam
F. ulmaria	light	moist loam
Galium mollugo	light	not particular
Geranium ibericum	light	well-drained soil
Hemerocallis in variety	deep	good soil, dry or moist
Heuchera in variety	light	well-drained soil
Hosta in variety	deep	good soil, dry or moist

NAME	DEEP OR LIGHT	REMARKS
Lobelia cardinalis	deep	rich, moist soil
L. syphilitica	deep	rich, moist soil
Mertensia virginica	deep	rich, moist soil
Monarda didyma & vars.	light	not particular
Phlox divaricata	light	rich, moist soil
P. paniculata vars.	light	good soil, plenty humus
P. stolonifera	light	prefers limy soil
Platycodon grandiflorum	light	well-drained, loamy soil
Polemonium in variety	light	rich, moist soil
Polygonatum multiflorum	deep	rich, moist soil
Primula in variety	light	rich, moist soil
Pulmonaria in variety	deep	porous soil, not too dry
Smilacina racemosa	deep	rich, moist soil
Thalictrum in variety	deep	rich, well-drained soil
Tradescantia virginiana vars.	light	not particular
Trillium grandiflorum	deep	rich, moist soil
Trollius in variety	light	sandy loam, plenty humus
Uvularia grandiflora	deep	light, rich soil
Viola cornuta	light	loamy soil with humus

DROUGHT RESISTERS
—TOLERANT OF POOR SOIL IN SUN

Achillea millefolium

Alyssum saxatile

Anaphalis margaritacea

Anchusa caespitosa

Anthemis tinctoria & vars.

Arabis albida

Artemisia albula

A. Stelleriana

Asclepias tuberosa

Baptisia australis

Callirhoe involucrata

Cassia marilandica

Centaurea macrocephala

Cerastium tomentosum

Coreopsis grandiflora

Coronilla varia

Dianthus plumarius vars.

Euphorbia corollata

Gaillardia aristata

Gaura Lindheimeri

Geranium sanguineum

Hemerocallis fulva

Iberis sempervirens

Iris germanica vars.

Linum perenne

Oenothera fruticosa

DROUGHT RESISTERS, CONT.

Phlox subulata
Rudbeckia speciosa
Salvia Pitcheri
S. pratensis

Thermopsis caroliniana
Tunica saxifraga fl. pl.
Verbascum olympicum

TOLERANT OF WET SOIL

Aruncus sylvester
Astilbe biternata
A. japonica
A. rosea
Astrantia major
Caltha palustris
Chelone glabra
C. Lyoni
Chrysanthemum uliginosum
Cimicifuga racemosa
Epilobium angustifolium
Eupatorium purpureum
Filipendula palmata
Gentiana Andrewsi
Hemerocallis in var.
Hibiscus moscheutos

Hosta in var.
Iris Kaempferi
I. pseudacorus
I. sibirica
Ligularia clivorum
L. Wilsoniana
Lobelia cardinalis
L. syphilitica
Lysimachia clethroides
Lythrum salicaria
Monarda didyma
Peltiphyllum peltatum
Ranunculus acris fl. pl.
Trollius asiaticus
T. europaeus
Veronia noveboracensis

PREFERRING ACID SOIL

Actaea alba
Chelone glabra
C. Lyoni
Cimicifuga racemosa

Dicentra eximia
Digitalis purpurea
Mertensia virginica
Trillium grandiflorum

PREFERRING ALKALINE, LIMY SOIL

Clematis species
Delphinium in var.
Dictamnus in var.
Echinops species

Eryngium species
Gypsophila in var.
Heliopsis scabra

PERENNIALS WHICH DO NOT NEED FREQUENT REPLANTING—THOSE STARRED RESENT IT

Acanthus
Aconitum
Actaea
Adenophora
°Alstroemeria
Amsonia
°Anchusa
Anemone
Armeria
°Asclepias
Baptisia
Bergenia
°Callirhoe
Caltha
Cassia
Cimicifuga
Clematis
Convallaria
Dicentra
°Dictamnus
Echinops
°Eryngium
Euphorbia
Galega
Gaura

Gentian
Geranium
°Gypsophila
°Helleborus
Hemerocallis
Hosta
°Incarvillea
Kirengeshoma
Kniphofia
°Lathyrus
Liatris
°Limonium
°Lupinus
Lythrum
°Mertensia
Oenothera
Paeonia
°Papaver
°Platycodon
Scabiosa
Sedum
Sidalcea
Thalictrum
Thermopsis
Trollius

PERENNIALS WHICH REQUIRE REPLANTING EVERY FEW YEARS—THOSE STARRED PERHAPS ANNUALLY

Achillea ptarmica vars.
Anthemis
Arabis
°*Aster hybridus nana*
°*A. novae-angliae* vars.
°*A. novi-belgi* vars.

Astilbe
Boltonia
Campanula
Centaurea
Cerastium
Chelone

Chrysanthemum maximum vars.
°C. morifolium vars.
C. uliginosum
Doronicum
Erigeron
°*Eupatorium coelestinum*
°*E. rugosum*
Gaillardia
Geum
Helenium
Helianthus
Heliopsis
Heuchera
Lysimachia

Monarda
Penstemon
Phlox
Physostegia
Polemonium
Primula polyantha vars.
Pulmonaria
Rudbeckia laciniata fl. pl.
R. subtomentosa
Solidago
Stokesia
Tradescantia
Veronica

PERENNIALS USUALLY INVASIVE

Achillea The Pearl
Ajuga reptans vars.
Artemisia Stelleriana
Bocconia cordata
Boltonia asteroides
Cerastium tomentosum
Convallaria majalis
Coronilla varia
Epilobium angustifolium
Eupatorium coelestinum

Eupatorium rugosum
Helianthus sp. & vars.
Hemerocallis fulva
Lysimachia clethroides
Monarda didyma vars.
Papaver orientale, some vars.
Phlox subulata
Physostegia virginiana
Solidago canadensis
Valeriana officinalis

PERENNIALS LATE STARTING IN SPRING

Alstroemeria aurantiaca
Anemone japonica
Ceratostigma plumbaginoides
Eupatorium coelestinum

Hibiscus moscheutos vars.
Hosta sp.
Incarvillea Delavayi

ALPHABETICAL LIST OF COMMON PLANT NAMES WITH THEIR BOTANICAL EQUIVALENT NAMES

Alkanet—Anchusa
Alpine Strawberry—*Fragaria vesca*
Alpine Wallflower—*Erysimum ochroleucum*
Alum-root—Heuchera
Anchusa, Dwarf—*Brunnera macrophylla*
Andromeda—Pieris
Anemone, Japanese—*Anemone japonica*
Arctic Daisy—*Chrysanthemum arcticum*
Aster, New England—*Aster novae-angliae*
Aster, New York—*Aster novi-belgi*
Aster, Stokes—*Stokesia laevis*
Avens—Geum

Babylonian Centaury—*Centaurea babylonica*
Babys-breath—Gypsophila
Bachelor Button—Centaurea
Balloon Flower—Platycodon
Baneberry—Actaea
Barberry—Berberis
Barrenwort—Epimedium
Basket-of-Gold—*Alyssum saxatile*
Beard-tongue—Penstemon
Bears-breech—Acanthus
Beauty-bush—*Kolkwitzia amabilis*
Bedstraw, White—*Galium mollugo*
Bee-balm—Monarda
Bellflower—Campanula
Bellwort—Uvularia
Bethlehem Sage—*Pulmonaria saccharata*
Black Snake-root—*Cimicifuga racemosa*
Blackberry-lily—Belamcanda
Blanket-flower—Gaillardia
Blazing Star—*Liatris pycnostachya*
Bleeding-heart—Dicentra
Bloodroot—*Sanguinaria canadensis*
Blue Flag—*Iris foliosa*
Blue Leadwort—*Ceratostigma plumbaginoides*
Blue Lettuce—*Lactuca perennis*
Blue-beard—*Caryopteris incana*
Blue-eyed Grass—Sisyrinchium
Bluebell, English—*Scilla nonscripta*
Bluebell, Scotch—*Campanula rotundifolia*
Bluebell, Spanish—*Scilla campanulata*

Bluebell, Virginia- —*Mertensia virginica*
Bowmans Root—*Gillenia trifoliata*
Box Barberry—*Berberis Thunbergi minor*
Boxwood—Buxus
Bridal Wreath—*Spiraea prunifolia plena*
Bristol Fairy—*Gypsophila paniculata*
Bugbane—*Cimicifuga simplex*
Bugle—Ajuga
Bugloss—*Anchusa azurea*
Burning-bush—Dictamnus
Buttercup—Ranunculus
Butterfly-bush—Buddleia
Butterfly-weed—*Asclepias tuberosa*
Button Pink—*Dianthus latifolius*

Camass—Camassia
Camomile—*Anthemis nobilis*
Campion—Lychnis
Candle Larkspur—*Delphinium elatum*
Candytuft—Iberis
Canterbury Bells—*Campanula medium*
Cardinal Flower—Lobelia
Carnation—*Dianthus caryophyllus*
Carpathian Harebell—*Campanula carpatica*
Catchfly—Lychnis
Catmint—Nepeta
Celandine-poppy—*Stylophorum diphyllum*
Centaury, Babylonian—*Centaurea babylonica*
Chalk-plant—Gypsophila
Chaste-tree—Vitex
China Fleece-vine—*Polygonum Auberti*
Chinese Wallflower—*Erysimum asperum*
Christmas-rose—Helleborus
Cinquefoil—Potentilla
Columbine—Aquilegia
Coneflower—Rudbeckia
Coneflower, Purple—*Echinacea purpurea*
Coral-bells—Heuchera
Cornflower—Centaurea
Costmary—*Chrysanthemum balsamita*
Cottage Pink—*Dianthus plumarius*
Cowslip—*Primula veris*
Crab-apple—Malus
Cranesbill—Geranium
Creeping Charley—*Lysimachia nummularia*
Crown Imperial—*Fritillaria imperialis*

Crown Vetch—*Coronilla varia*
Cupids-dart—Catananche

Daisy, Arctic—*Chrysanthemum arcticum*
Daisy, Giant—*Chrysanthemum uliginosum*
Daisy, Korean—*Chrysanthemum coreanum*
Daisy, Nippon—*Chrysanthemum nipponicum*
Daisy, Painted—*Chrysanthemum coccineum*
Daisy, St. Johns—*Anthemis Sancti-Johannis*
Daisy, Shasta—*Chrysanthemum maximum*
Daisy, Tartarian—*Aster tartaricus*
Dames-rocket—*Hesperis matronallis*
Daylily—Hemerocallis
Dead-nettle—Lamium
Desert-candle—Eremurus
Dittany—Dictamnus
Dragonhead—Dracocephalum
Dropwort—*Filipendula hexapetala*
Dutchmans-breeches—*Dicentra cucullaria*
Dwarf Alberta Spruce—*Picea glauca conica*
Dwarf Anchusa—*Brunnera macrophylla*
Dwarf Japanese Quince—*Chaenomeles japonica*

Elecampane—Inula
English Daisy—*Bellis perennis*
English Primrose—*Primula vulgaris*
Eryngo—Eryngium
Eurasian Wood Forget-me-not—*Myosotis sylvatica*
Evening-primrose—Oenothera
Everlasting, Pearl—Anaphalis
Everlasting Pea—*Lathyrus latifolius*

Fairy-candle—*Cimicifuga racemosa*
False Dragonhead—*Physostegia virginiana*
False Goats-beard—*Astilbe biternata*
False Indigo—Baptisia
False Solomons Seal—Smilacina
Fern-leaved Fumitory—*Corydalis cheilanthifolia*
Fire-weed—*Epilobium angustifolium*
Flag—Iris
Flame Azalea—*Rhododendron calendulaceum*
Flax—Linum
Fleabane—Erigeron
Fleur-de-lis—Iris
Floating-heart—Nymphoides

Florists' Spirea—*Astilbe japonica*
Flower-of-Jove—*Lychnis flos-Jovis*
Flowering Quince—Chaenomeles
Foam Flower—*Tiarella cordifolia*
Forget-me-not—Myosotis
Foxglove—Digitalis
Foxtail-lily—Eremurus
Fraxinella—Dictamnus
Fumitory, Fern-leaved—*Corydalis cheilanthifolia*
Fumitory, Noble—*Corydalis nobilis*
Fumitory, Yellow—*Corydalis lutea*

Garden-heliotrope—*Valeriana officinalis*
Garland-flower—*Daphne cneorum*
Gas-plant—*Dictamnus*
Gay-feather—*Liatris scariosa*
Gentian—Gentiana
Geranium, Wood—*Geranium maculatum*
German Catchfly—*Lychnis viscaria*
Germander—*Teucrium chamaedrys*
Giant Daisy—*Chrysanthemum uliginosum*
Gland Bellflower—*Adenophora lilifolia*
Globe-flower—Trollius
Globe-thistle—Echinops
Goats-beard—*Aruncus sylvester*
Goats-beard, False—*Astilbe biternata*
Goats-rue—Galega
Golden Glow—*Rudbeckia laciniata hortensia*
Golden Marguerite—*Anthemis tinctoria*
Golden-star—*Chrysogonum virginianum*
Golden-tuft—*Alyssum saxatile*
Goldenrod—Solidago
Grass, Blue-eyed—Sisyrinchium
Grass Pink—*Dianthus plumarius*
Greek Valerian—*Polemonium reptans*
Groundsel—*Lignlaria clivorum*
Groundsel, Showy—*Senecio pulcher*

Harebell—Campanula
Heliotrope, Garden- —*Valeriana officinalis*
Hellebore—*Helleborus*
Hills-of-Snow—*Hydrangea arborescens grandiflora*
Hinoki Cypress—*Chamaecyparis obstrusa*
Holly—Ilex
Hollyhock—*Althaea rosea*
Hyssop—Hyssopus

Iceland Poppy—*Papaver nudicaule*
Indian Cup—*Silphium perfoliatum*
Indigo, False—Baptisia
Ironweed—Vernonia
Ivy, English—*Hedera helix*

Jacobs Ladder—*Polemonium caeruleum*
Jacobs-rod—Asphodeline
Japanese Anemone—*Anemone japonica*
Japanese Flowering Cherry—*Primus amanogawa*
Japanese Loosestrife—*Lysimachia clethroides*
Japanese Spurge—*Pachysandra terminalis*
Joe-Pye Weed—*Eupatorium purpureum*

Knapweed—Centaurea
Korean Daisy—*Chrysanthemum coreanum*

Ladybell—*Adenophora Potanini*
Ladys-mantle—Alchemilla
Lambs-ears—*Stachys lanata*
Larkspur—Delphinium
Larpent Plumbago—*Ceratostigma plumbaginoides*
Lavender—*Lavandula officinalis*
Lavender, Sea- —Limonium
Lavender-cotton—*Santolina chamaecyparissus*
Leadwort, Blue—*Ceratostigma plumbaginoides*
Leather Saxifrage—Bergenia
Leopards-bane—Doronicum
Lilac—Syringa
Lily—Lilium
Lily, Blackberry- —Belamcanda
Lily, Foxtail- —Eremurus
Lily, Madonna—*Lilium candidum*
Lily, Meadow- —*Lilium canadense*
Lily, Plantain- —Hosta
Lily, Torch- —Kniphofia
Lily-of-the-valley—Convallaria
Lily-turf—Liriope
Lilybell—Adenophora
Loosestrife, Japanese—*Lysimachia clethroides*
Loosestrife, Purple—*Lythrum salicaria*
Lungwort—*Pulmonaria angustifolia*
Lupine—Lupinus

Madonna Lily—*Lilium candidum*
Madwort—Alyssum

Mallow—Malva
Maltese Cross—*Lychnis chalcedonica*
Marguerite, Golden—*Anthemis tinctoria*
Marsh-marigold—*Caltha palustris*
Masterwort—Astrantia
Meadow-lily—*Lilium canadense*
Meadow-rue—Thalictrum
Meadow-sweet—*Filipendula palmata*
Michaelmas Daisy—Aster
Milfoil—*Achillea millefolium*
Mist-flower—*Eupatorium coelestinum*
Monkshood—Aconitum
Moss-Phlox—*Phlox subulata*
Mountain Bluet—*Centaurea montana*
Mugwort—Artemisia
Mullein—Verbascum
Mullein-pink—*Lychnis coronaria*
Musk Mallow—*Malva moschata*

New England Aster—*Aster novae-angliae*
New York Aster—*Aster novi-belgi*
Nippon Daisy—*Chrysanthemum nipponicum*
Noble Fumitory—*Corydalis nobilis*

Old Woman—Artemisia
Orange Sunflower—Heliopsis
Oriental Poppy—*Papaver orientale*
Orris Root—*Iris germanica florentina*
Oxeye—Heliopsis
Oxlip—*Primula elatior*

Pachysandra—*Pachysandra terminalis*
Painted Daisy—*Chrysanthemum coccineum*
Pansy—*Viola tricolor*
Pasque Flower—*Anemone pulsatilla*
Pea, Everlasting—*Lathyrus latifolius*
Pearl Everlasting—Anaphalis
Peony—Paeonia
Persian Lilac—*Syringa persica*
Peruvian-lily—*Alstroemeria*
Pincushion Flower—Scabiosa
Pink—Dianthus
Plantain-lily—Hosta
Plume-poppy—*Bocconia cordata*
Poker-plant—Kniphofia
Polyanthus—*Primula polyantha*

Poppy—Papaver
Poppy-mallow—Callirhoe
Primrose—Primula
Primrose, English—*Primula vulgaris*
Privet—*Ligustrum obtusifolium*
Purple Coneflower—*Echinacea purpurea*
Purple Loosestrife—*Lythrum salicaria*
Purple Rock-cress—Aubrieta
Pyrethrum—*Chrysanthemum coccineum*

Queen-of-the-meadow—*Filipendula ulmaria*
Queen-of-the-prairie—*Filipendula rubra*
Quince, Dwarf Japanese—*Chaenomeles japonica*
Quince, Flowering—Chaenomeles

Red Valerian—*Centranthus ruber*
Rock-cress, Purple—Aubrieta
Rock-cress, White—Arabis
Rose-campion—*Lychnis coronaria*
Rose-mallow—*Hibiscus moscheutos*

Sage—Salvia
Sage, Bethlehem—*Pulmonaria saccharata*
St. Bruno-lily—*Paradisea liliastrum*
St. Johns Daisy—*Anthemis Sancti-Johannis*
St. Johns Wort—Hypericum
Saxifrage, Leather—Bergenia
Saxifrage, Umbrella—*Peltiphyllum peltatum*
Scabious—Scabiosa
Scotch Bluebell—*Campanula rotundifolia*
Scotch Pink—*Dianthus plumarius*
Sea-holly—*Eryngium maritimum*
Sea-lavender—Limonium
Sea-pink—*Armeria maritima*
Senna, Wild—Cassia
Shasta Daisy—*Chrysanthemum maximum*
Shepherds Scabious—Jasione
Shooting-star—Dodecatheon
Showy Groundsel—*Senecio pulcher*
Showy-Oxeye—Buphthalmum
Siberian Iris—*Iris sibirica*
Siberian Squill—*Scilla sibirica*
Skullcap—Scutellaria
Smoke-tree—*Cotinus coggygria*
Snake-root, Black—*Cimicifuga racemosa*
Snake-root, White—*Eupatorium rugosum*

Snakeweed—*Polygonum bistorta*
Snapdragon—Antirrhinum
Sneezeweed—Helenium
Sneezewort—*Achillea ptarmica*
Snow-in-summer—*Cerastium tomentosum*
Snowflake—Leucojum
Solomons Seal—Polygonatum
Solomons Seal, False—Smilacina
Somerset—*Daphne Burkwoodi*
Speedwell—Veronica
Spiderwort—Tradescantia
Spirea, Florists'—*Astilbe japonica*
Spitfire—Chaenomeles
Spring Adonis—Adonis
Spring Vetchling—*Lathyrus vernus*
Spurge—Euphorbia
Spurge, Japanese—*Pachysandra terminalis*
Squill—Scilla
Squirrel-corn—Dicentra
Star Magnolia—*Magnolia stellata*
Starwort—Aster
Stokes Aster—*Stokesia laevis*
Stone-cress—Aethionema
Stonecrop—Sedum
Summer-hyacinth—Galtonia
Sundrop—*Oenothera fruticosa*
Sunflower—Helianthus
Sunflower, Orange—Heliopsis
Sweet William—*Dianthus barbatus*
Sweet Woodruff—Asperula

Tartarian Daisy—*Aster tataricus*
Thrift—Armeria
Thyme, Common—*Thymus vulgaris*
Tickseed—Coreopsis
Torch-lily—Kniphofia
Trailing Periwinkle—*Vinca minor*
Tufted-Pansy—*Viola cornuta*
Tunic-flower—Tunica
Turtle-head—Chelone
Twin-leaf—Jeffersonia

Umbrella Saxifrage—*Peltiphyllum peltatum*

Valerian Red—Centranthus
Vanhouttes Spirea—*Spiraea Vanhouttei*

Violet—Viola
Virginia-bluebells—*Mertensia virginica*

Wake-robin—Trillium
Wall Rock-cress—*Arabis albida*
Wallflower, Alpine—*Erysimum ochroleucum*
Wallflower, Chinese—*Erysimum asperum*
White Bedstraw—*Galium mollugo*
White Snake-root—*Eupatorium rugosum*
Whitened Knapweed—*Centaurea dealbata*
Wild Senna—Cassia
Wild Sweet William—*Phlox divaricata*
Willow-herb—*Epilobium angustifolium*
Wind-flower—Anemone
Wintercreeper—*Euonymus Fortunei*
Wood Geranium—*Geranium maculatum*
Woodruff, Sweet—Asperula
Wormwood—Artemisia
Woundwort—Stachys

Yarrow—Achillea
Yellow Flag—*Iris pseudacorus*
Yellow Fumitory—*Corydalis lutea*
Yew—Taxus

Index

Common names of plants have generally been listed after generic names, e.g. *Aconitum* (Aconite, Monkshood). See also the Appendix, pages 267–340, for alphabetical and classified lists of perennials. Numbers in boldface indicate pages with illustrations.